Chicken Soup for the Soul®

Merry Christmas!

*Chicken Soup for the Soul: Merry Christmas!*
*101 Joyous Holiday Stories*
Amy Newmark. Foreword by Santa Claus.

Published by Chicken Soup for the Soul Publishing, LLC www.chickensoup.com
Copyright © 2015 by Chicken Soup for the Soul Publishing, LLC. All Rights Reserved.

The publisher gratefully acknowledges the many publishers and individuals who granted Chicken Soup for the Soul permission to reprint the cited material.

Front cover artwork courtesy of iStockphoto.com/Shaiith (©Shaiith).
Interior artwork of Santa hat courtesy of iStockphoto.com/ZaharovEvgeniy (©ZaharovEvgeniy).
Interior artwork of santa claus sleigh courtesy of iStockphoto.com/gyener (©gyener).
Back cover artwork of Santa courtesy of iStockphoto.com/LindsayMichelet (©LindsayMichelet).
Photo of Amy Newmark courtesy of Susan Morrow at SwickPix.

*Cover and Interior by Daniel Zaccari*

Distributed to the booktrade by Simon & Schuster. SAN: 200-2442

**Publisher's Cataloging-In-Publication Data**
*(Prepared by The Donohue Group, Inc.)*

Chicken soup for the soul : Merry Christmas! : 101 joyous holiday stories
/ [compiled by] Amy Newmark ; foreword by Santa Claus.

   pages ; cm

   ISBN: 978-1-61159-953-4

   1. Christmas--Literary collections. 2. Christmas--Anecdotes. 3. Hanukkah--Literary collections. 4. Hanukkah--Anecdotes. 5. Anecdotes. I. Newmark, Amy. II. Santa Claus. III. Title: Merry Christmas! : 101 joyous holiday stories

GT4985 .C45 2015
394.2663/02                                                                    2015946949

# Chicken Soup for the Soul

## Merry Christmas!

### 101 Joyous Holiday Stories

## Amy Newmark
## Foreword by Santa Claus

Chicken Soup for the Soul Publishing, LLC
Cos Cob, CT

Chicken Soup *for the* Soul

Changing your world one story at a time®
www.chickensoup.com

# Contents

**❸**

# ~The Perfect Gift~

**❹**

# ~A Different Kind of Christmas~

**❺**

# ~Christmas Spirit Is Alive and Well~

**❻**

# ~Holiday Shenanigans~

**❼**

# ~The Joy of Giving~

**❽**

## ~Traditions Worth Sharing~

**❾**

## ~Around the Table~

**❿**

## ~Honoring Memories~

# Foreword

The elves at Chicken Soup for the Soul have done it again! Mrs. Claus and I have been passing this manuscript back and forth and commenting to each other on our favorite stories. We're enjoying a well-deserved rest up here at the North Pole.

By the time you read this in the fall, the Mrs. and I and the whole gang up at the North Pole will be in full production mode: The factory will be running 24/7, the lists will have been triple-checked, and the reindeer will be practicing their flying maneuvers while their trainer checks Google Earth for new obstructions and those darn satellite dishes.

We know that you will all be rushing about, too. Mrs. Claus and I are not alone in loving the holiday season. We watch as you reunite scattered family members, see the wonder on the face of a child, feel the joy of giving, and remember the true meaning of Christmas and Hanukkah. The rituals of the holiday season give a rhythm to the years and create a foundation for your family lives. We watch you gather with your communities at church and temple, at school, and even at the mall, to share the special spirit of the season, brightening those long winter days.

*Chicken Soup for the Soul: Merry Christmas!* will take you on a wonderful journey through the holiday season. Here's a little tour of what you'll find inside:

In Chapter 1, "Tales of the Tree," you'll discover all the different ways that people handle their Christmas trees — and all the ways that things can go wrong. I laughed out loud at Joyce Laird's story about the first and only time her family cut their own tree and put it up in their living room. When a squirrel emerged from the tree that night, and their dog and cat chased the terrified creature through the house, the ensuing mayhem ensured that Joyce's family would never cut their own tree again!

Chapter 2 is about "The Joy of Family." Mrs. Claus particularly liked Teresa Martin's story about the time she had the flu and her husband and two sons pitched in and saved Christmas Eve. The Mrs. points out that many of you get so stressed about making everything perfect for the holidays, and it really doesn't have to be perfect. *Who* sits around the table is much more important than *what* is on the table!

If you want to talk about stress, remember that I'm the one who needs to come up with new gift ideas every year. With all these new electronic devices that the kids want, it's hard to keep up! That's a lot of pressure for a guy who has a bit of a weight problem and is supposed to be watching his blood pressure. So I loved Chapter 3, "The Perfect Gift," because it makes it clear that there are many ways to give someone a meaningful, loving gift. I was amused by Katie Martin's story about the beautiful, unique Christmas scarf she received from her sister. After she wore it for years, collecting plenty of compliments, she told her sister how much she appreciated it, only to be told by her horrified sister that the "scarf" was actually a table runner.

I know that some of you, especially the kids, worry about whether I'll know where you are if you travel during the holidays. No worries. I'm on top of it. And as you'll read in Chapter 4, "A Different Kind of Christmas," sometimes celebrating Christmas away from home can be a real pleasure, as Karen Robbins describes in her story about how she and her husband went on a Tahitian cruise over Christmas when they couldn't visit their five grown kids scattered all over the country.

I will always find you. In fact, in Chapter 5, "Christmas Spirit Is Alive and Well," you'll read about S.K. Naus's recollection of the year that her family moved from a house to an apartment with no chimney. She was so worried that I wouldn't come, but of course I did. While I find chimneys very convenient, I am always happy to land on the lawn instead of the roof and come in a door if necessary.

The holidays wouldn't be as much fun if we didn't horse around, right? When you gather families together, there will be teasing and silly traditions and "Holiday Shenanigans" as presented to you in Chapter 6. Vince Monical's story about a gigantic creepy snowman made me laugh. After he and his son built the sinister snowman by accident, his son and his cousins all conspired to move the snowman on Christmas Eve, so that it was looking in the window Christmas morning when everyone got up. I think I remember that guy—I thought the abominable snowman had shown up, and I almost jumped right back up the chimney.

While my job is to bring the gifts, we all know that the real joy of the season lies in *giving*, not receiving. The stories in Chapter 7 about "The Joy of Giving" are among my favorites. I loved the one by Paula Maugiri Tindall about how she went to Walmart with a friend and was surprised when he bought a bunch of gift cards and started handing them out to mothers who couldn't afford to buy gifts for their children.

That was an amazing annual holiday activity, and, indeed, there are many similar stories in Chapter 8, "Traditions Worth Sharing." You'll probably pick up some new ideas for your family. It appears that I am slated to start at least one new tradition in the Claus household, as Mrs. Claus has already folded over the first page of Joan Clayton's story. Joan wrote about how she and her husband started a tradition as newlyweds when they couldn't afford to buy ornaments. They wrote each other love notes and hung them on the tree, and they continued doing that for the many decades of their marriage. The tradition continues now through four generations of their family. I guess I'd better get busy writing some notes of my own now, for the Mrs.

As I write this foreword, I know that many of you are sweltering in heat and humidity. It has been a hot summer up here at the North Pole, too. But, despite the heat, the Christmas spirit lives in all of us year-round. Wouldn't it be nice if it were Christmas all the time? How about leaving a couple of those decorations up all year? Mrs. Claus pointed out Roz Warren's story in Chapter 8 about when people take their Christmas lights down. *Never* sounds good to me. And Mrs. Claus agrees, because she finds it so sad when the lights come down after the holidays are over.

Speaking of Mrs. Claus, I won't even tell you what happened

the first time she made Christmas dinner for me after my long night working, but she was tickled pink by Gail Molsbee Morris's story in Chapter 9, "Around the Table." Gail was so pleased by how well her first Christmas dinner was going that she started to relax and enjoy herself, until there was a loud noise in the kitchen. Gail rushed in and saw nothing amiss until she opened the oven and discovered that the turkey had exploded into hundreds of pieces.

Chapter 10 is all about "Honoring Memories," because Christmas and Hanukkah are the time of year when we particularly miss those loved ones who are no longer with us. I highly recommend Daryl Wendy Strauss's story about the instructions her mom left when she died. She asked her kids to continue filling a Christmas stocking for her each year and then give it to a woman in need. Her kids ended up turning this into a charity called Mom's Stocking that has distributed hundreds of filled Christmas stockings across the U.S.

That concludes my tour of the book! This book sure has gotten me into the Christmas spirit. No matter how busy you are this holiday season, I hope you will find the time to curl up in front of the fire and have a good read. And remember that Chicken Soup for the Soul's Christmas books are always appropriate for young readers or listeners — their editors work closely with Mrs. Claus and me to keep the magic alive — so you can share these stories with the young ones.

Now I have one very important thing to tell you, and if you want to go on my "Nice" list you'll pay close attention. *Do not listen to Mrs. Claus about the cookies.* My cholesterol is fine. And I get plenty of exercise on Christmas Eve.

I like the cookies.

I depend on you for the cookies.

She won't let me have any cookies the rest of the year.

So cookies for me — and carrots for the reindeer — okay?

Speaking of carrots, I just love the cartoon on the next page. The Chicken Soup for the Soul folks have sprinkled eleven hilarious cartoons throughout the book, starting with this one. It's just another reason why the Mrs. and I have enjoyed reading this manuscript.

And with that I remain your jolly friend and I look forward to visiting you soon.

~Santa Claus

August 17, 2015

Reprinted by permission of www.CartoonStock.com.

Chapter
**1**

# Merry Christmas!

Tales of the Tree

# White Spruce from Heaven

*Miracles happen to those who believe in them.*
*~Bernard Berenson*

"Mom?" The voice on the phone was tentative, a young man. The question wasn't intended for identification since he already knew it was his mother, but more to gauge her temperament. He was calling with bad news from distant lands.

"Ephraim!" she breathed with excitement. Then she paused, a mother's intuition rising from within her maternal DNA. "What's wrong?"

Ephraim Rogers, a thin, sandy-haired man in his mid-twenties, was an award-winning soldier in the Delaware Army National Guard's Military Police (MP) 153rd Unit. He was the first Army National Guard soldier to have ever won the Army's "Soldier of the Quarter Award" twice. He was ordered to Riyadh, in central Saudi Arabia, in July 2002, just prior to the rollout of Operation Iraqi Freedom, leaving behind a loving and faithful family in Dover, Delaware. His unit's primary mission was to provide security for the American airbase. The unit was projected to return to the States in March 2003, but there was growing hope that the soldiers could return home for the holidays.

"Things are kind of edgy over here, Mom," Ephraim replied with a serious tone. "I can't get into it, you know, classified security stuff. I'm sure it's in the news back home every night."

"You're not coming home for Christmas, are you?" she asked, already knowing the answer.

"Still hoping for March, Mom. It was a long shot for Christmas, you know?"

"Yes," she managed, her hopes dashed.

After a pause he asked, "Did you get my presents?" His voice carried an upbeat tenor.

"Yes, they came today, several large boxes, all wrapped. You did a good job. Who helped you?" She laughed.

"No one, Mom," Ephraim replied lightheartedly. "I wrapped them myself." Then after an awkward period of silence, "Mom, I've got to run. Probably won't talk to you 'til after the holidays so please tell everyone 'Merry Christmas' for me, okay? I'll e-mail when I can, but they're keeping us busy."

The mother couldn't talk, her throat constricted, tears pooled in her eyes.

"I love you, Mom." Then the call ended.

It was a mere two weeks before Christmas Eve. Earlier that same week, Lilian Rogers, the soldier's mother, in preparation for her son's possible homecoming, visited nearby Turning Pointe Farm and selected a striking and splendid White Spruce. The bluish-green needled conifer was immediately decorated with the family ornaments, twinkling lights and some tinsel. It was perfectly shaped, and delivered a visual and aromatic air of Christmas to the house. Ephraim's gifts were strategically placed under the tree's branches where additional gifts would soon join them.

Christmas was quietly and reverently celebrated by the Rogers family, minus Ephraim, but Lilian, after discussing the idea with her husband Al and their daughters Corinne and Louise, decided that all the gifts would remain unopened until Ephraim's safe homecoming. The family watered the cut tree throughout the Epiphany season, often referred to as the "12 Days of Christmas," and for the rest of January. And then they stopped, in view of taking it down.

But as the calendar days clicked away, and February came and went, the family witnessed a strange, unexplainable reality… the White

Spruce had not lost any needles. It continued to look as fresh as the day the majestic tree was sawed down in the field, tenderly carried into the house, and erected in the emerald and burgundy colored tree stand the family had used for decades.

With a sparkle in their eyes, and sympathetic hearts, Corinne and Louise suggested the tree remain in place as long as it continued to look good and retained its needles. They reasoned, "Why take it down?" But they also assumed the tree was on its last leg, especially since they continued to deprive the tree of any watery nourishment.

In the interim they decided to also add yellow ribbons and bows to the branches in preparation for Ephraim's return in March. And each night they plugged in the lights. Could the tree miraculously hold on?

The deployment for the soldiers of the 153rd Delaware Army National Guard unit was about to end; excitement connected the First State to the sandy landscapes of Saudi Arabia when the second Iraqi War violently broke out. Terrorists in Riyadh blew up a hotel where many Americans were staying as guests. Ephraim's unit was summoned to assist in removing the deceased. The work was solemnly and carefully completed, but tensions in the region were understandably high. Ephraim and his dedicated buddies would stand guard in full military armor and garb for shifts lasting fourteen hours, in 120 degrees of suffocating heat. It was a hellish existence, and Ephraim, along with many of his fellow soldiers, relied on prayer and faith in God to survive the challenging days.

And no one went home in March, because their deployment was extended.

April arrived and the Christmas tree still stood proudly in the Rogers' home, like a protective sentry, and like Ephraim and his unit at a barricaded gate in the Middle East. Still not one needle had fallen from any of the branches. The miracle continued.

Ephraim's unit did eventually come home… on May 10th! They received a heroes' welcome when they landed, complete with tears of joy and bear hugs from joyous family members, all captured by local TV stations and newspaper columnists and photographers. The homecoming festivities spilled over to the Rogers household as Christmas gifts were happily shredded open to reveal items purchased by Ephraim for his family while stationed in Riyadh, including diamonds for his sisters and expensive cigars for his dad. Laughter filled the house, Christmas carols wafted through the stereo speakers, cameras permanently captured each precious moment, while outside the neighbors mowed grass and planted flowers.

That evening the tree was taken down and placed outside. Not one needle ever fell from its limbs. The family stood amazed, and praised God. Then everyone went to bed, exhausted but ecstatic.

Lilian walked outside the next morning and took in the beauty of the morning: singing birds busy at work on nests and hunting worms, the fragrant scents of newborn grass and sprouting flowers, and the warmth of rich, yellow sunshine upon her face. Then she noticed the tree.

In less than twelve hours, the green fir tree had turned orangey brown as if it had been dead for months. The needles were dried out, crispy, and hundreds of them now littered the ground. Lilian was amazed. Was this the same tree that looked as good last night as it did five months ago when it was taken from Turning Pointe Farm?

~David Michael Smith

Chicken Soup for the Soul

# Our First Christmas Tree

*The best of all gifts around any Christmas tree: the*
*presence of a happy family all wrapped*
*up in each other.*
*~Burton Hillis*

As Christmas approaches each year, our house becomes a stop for our young grandsons on their way to visit their other grandparents. Our daughter and her husband unpack just enough for a night or two with us and then they are all on their way. Since we are Jewish, our house isn't set up for Christmas, so it is understandable that, in their mixed family, they would want to be where the holiday is celebrated. We don't mind. It is a chance for my husband and me to see them for a few days as they travel back and forth.

Only this year was different. The family came, as usual, a couple of days before Christmas Eve, but it was obvious as they exited the car that something was going on. One of our grandsons was coughing and the other was sniffling.

By the afternoon they were both cranky and in need of a nap. When they awoke, my daughter said both boys felt feverish. They had planned to leave the next day but, not wanting to travel with sick kids, asked if they could stay a little longer.

Of course they could.

In the morning there was no fever but the coughing was worse and both boys had drippy noses. My daughter and I were constantly washing the dishes the boys used, the clothes they wore, the toys they played with — just to keep the germs at bay. I was fast running out of disinfecting wipes. It was not the time for them to leave.

Another day passed and things were pretty much the same. Was it just a cold affecting both boys or was it something more serious? Should we call a doctor? And which one? I hadn't needed a pediatrician in forever so I wasn't up on who was available. We decided to wait one more day and see how things were going.

Now it was the day before Christmas. The boys seemed better but they were still coughing. It still didn't seem like a good idea to travel with sick kids. Could they stay one more day?

They were certainly welcome to stay as long as they liked but the boys were disappointed that there was no Christmas tree.

It wouldn't feel like Christmas Eve without a tree. It was time to make the house holiday friendly. We had a small Norway pine in a planter in a corner of our living room. It wasn't a traditional Christmas tree but I suggested that we decorate it.

Our daughter set up a decoration-making station on our coffee table. Our older grandson made long, colored-paper chains while our younger grandson decorated paper circles to use as ornaments. I found some small, carved wooden birds, which I attached to twine and hung on the tree. We sang as we worked. The whole house came to life. My husband took photos for posterity.

Our son-in-law laid woolen scarves at the bottom of the tree for the blanket where the presents would be placed when the boys were asleep. After such a busy day, they trotted off to bed, happy.

Before I retired for the night, I looked at what we had all created. It was our first Christmas tree, transformed from an ordinary evergreen into something grand, and it graced our house with its simple beauty. I smiled at the thought of how excited our grandsons would be in the morning.

And excited they were. They reached under the tree and eagerly opened their presents. My present was that the boys were feeling much better. They left the next day, finally on their way to their other grandparents, who were eagerly awaiting their visit.

When the holidays were over, I removed the decorations. The tree reverted to its former self—though not quite. I left a little bird on one of the branches for a while longer as a reminder of the joy our impromptu Christmas tree had brought. I later put it in a special place, easily accessible, just in case we decide to do it all again next year, but this time, with healthy grandchildren.

~Ferida Wolff

Reprinted by permission of www.CartoonStock.com.

# Artificial Unintelligence

*Christmas is for children. But it is for grown-ups too.*
*Even if it is a headache, a chore, and nightmare, it is a*
*period of necessary defrosting of chill and*
*hide-bound hearts.*
*~Lenora Mattingly Weber*

A few years ago we bought a co-op Christmas tree. The idea was that one year it would be at our house and the next year it would be at Carl, Christy, Leila and Charlie's house. It was pretty expensive and I probably would have objected had I known this was happening. But I didn't learn about it until I came home from work one day and, there it was, all set up in our dining area.

"Merry Christmas!" they all yelled.

I looked up at the ten-foot tall behemoth tree with its pre-attached lights and perfect branches. A giant ominous-looking white box sat on the floor next to it. It had Chinese writing on the side.

"Carl put it up. It was easy."

I glanced at my son-in-law, but I didn't exactly see "easy" in his eyes.

"After Christmas, we simply take apart the easy-to-assemble sections and pack it away for next year."

There was that word "easy" again.

Christy and the kids started singing Christmas songs. I felt a bit nauseated, I mean nostalgic.

"We'll never have to buy another real tree and watch it die."

I do have to admit, I have had some less-than-joyous experiences with real trees. One year in New Hampshire my buddy Del and I offered to cut down trees for everyone who gave us money. Del brought a chainsaw. Being a logical thinker, Del figured it wasn't worth firing the thing up unless we were going to cut trunks the width of a telephone pole so that's what we did. Very quickly we had cut four huge trees that were exactly twice as long as my K5 Chevy Blazer. I drove home with one hand on the wheel and one arm around the ends of two trees that were resting on my dashboard. I couldn't even see Del. Surprisingly, people were not all that pleased with their eighteen-foot-tall trees that required special tree stands. Plus my Blazer smelled like pine sap for months.

Another time I cut a perfect tree, but the bottom was uneven so it wouldn't fit in the stand. I trimmed a bit, then a bit more, then a bit more, until I ended up with a tree that was six-feet wide and three-feet tall.

So maybe this tree was a good thing. Especially seeing as how just after Christmas — again while I was at work — Carl took the tree down, packed it up and put it in the garage.

Two years later, Carl put it up and took it down again. Great guy that Carl.

Then a few weeks ago it was our turn for the tree again. I called Carl.

"Sorry," said Christy, "Carl's away on business. Should be pretty easy though."

There it was again… easy. Oh well, my wife and I could do this.

"This one must go next," I said as I hefted the metal section up the stepladder. I felt a twinge in my lower back.

"No, that one is larger than this one so it's nearer the bottom."

"Is this the top?"

"That's the part that goes in the stand."

"I already put a piece in the stand."

"That one may be upside down. See how the branches are pointing toward the floor."

"#$@%$#@!"

"Did you just curse at me?"

"No, that was aimed at the Republic of China's tree manufacturing division."

Somehow we finally got it assembled; then we connected the cords that ran from section to section and plugged in the lights. Just the bottom lit up.

"Seems darker than usual," my wife said.

I climbed the ladder and switched plugs. This time the middle lit up.

I switched them again. This time the top lit briefly, then went out. I kept switching them. Top Middle or Bottom. Top Middle or Bottom.

Finally, some four hours, three extension cords, and a roll of duct tape later, most of the lights were lit. We put on the decorations and that was that.

Until today.

"I think it's time to pack away the easy-to assemble pieces," my wife said.

I called Carl. He was away on another business trip.

"How about we just throw a giant sheet over it until next year? We can tell people it's a piece of modern art."

"I'll get the box," my wife said.

Carl, if you're reading this, you have less than two years to find a new job that doesn't involve traveling.

~Ernie Witham

# The Ugly Christmas Tree

*The perfect Christmas tree? All Christmas trees are perfect!*
*~Charles N. Barnard*

I hate our Christmas tree!

Short and spindly, it doesn't look right!
And up on top the star won't light.

The bulbs have blown. The branches droop.
It's bending and bowing and starting to stoop!

Needles are dropping all over the floor.
By tomorrow there won't be any more.

It's skimpy and scraggly. It looks awfully thin.
It's leaning to one side. Half dead! Done in!

One side has boughs. The other is bare.
There's a hole in the middle. No branches, just air!

It's Christmas Eve, so we have to make do.
It's got to be ready for you-know-who.

Santa will come down the chimney quick as a flash.
Deliver the presents; then off he will dash.

He's got millions of children to visit tonight.
We can't hold him up 'cause our tree isn't right.

We'll decorate the boughs with strings of light.
Twinkling red, green, yellow, blue, and white.

We'll hang the ornaments one by one.
And won't stop till the job is done.

Place a red ball here and a blue one there,
A silver bell, an angel, and a teddy bear.

A nutcracker, a Santa, and all kinds of fruit.
Snowflakes, a bird, and a horn that can toot.

We'll hang stars and snowmen and even some mice.
And one or two reindeer would be very nice.

Next comes the garland, all shiny and bright.
Wrapped 'round the tree, it's a beautiful sight.

Now hang the tinsel. Drape every strand.
It always looks pretty, no matter the brand.

My, but this tree is looking quite nice.
So lovely, in fact, that I have to look twice.

Much better than last year's, so stately and green.
It's the prettiest Christmas tree I've ever seen!

~Mary Vigliante Szydlowski

# Let There Be Light

*A woman is helpless only while her nail*
*polish is drying.*
*~Author Unknown*

It is the day after Thanksgiving and merchants are opening their stores early with enticing bargains for eager shoppers. My alarm sounds around 4:15 a.m. I push my snooze button twice and then I reluctantly get dressed for my quick trip to Home Depot to buy a Martha Stewart pre-lit tree. It is twenty-five degrees and dark. I'm sipping my instant coffee while driving to my desired destination. My husband is not with me and this is no accident.

I arrive at Home Depot at 5:15 a.m., walk in and ask where the $69 Martha Stewart trees are located. As I walk toward them, someone is picking up the last boxed tree. I'm visibly despondent and the sales guy says I can have the one on display. This seems good as I can watch him disassemble it and hopefully remember how to put it back together. He helps me load it in my Prius and all is well... for now....

After lunch I decide to tackle the tree assembly. My husband is gone... this is no accident.

I make four trips to the car to get the pieces. I assemble the tree, getting hit left and right by branches. Looks good! All seems well. As I reach to plug in the tree, I notice there is no plug. I search all over the house and car, but still find no plug. I call Home Depot and the customer service representative says she will connect me with the Christmas tree department. For ten minutes I listen to canned music and then I hear a live voice… oh joy! But my happiness is diminished as I realize it is the same customer service person I spoke to earlier. She assures me I will get help this time. Sure enough, after four minutes I finally speak to a guy who doesn't seem to understand what I'm talking about. I share the story of my early morning purchase with him. I'm thinking he may have dozed off because he asked me if I checked the box. I remind him there was no box. He "says" he has looked around and sees no extra plug. He assures me I can get a refund. After all, what good is a Martha Stewart pre-lit tree with no working lights?

I disassemble the tree and make four trips to the car to load it. My husband is absent… this is no accident. With receipt in hand, I'm driving back to Home Depot… all is well for now… a refund is in sight.

I arrive at Home Depot and leave the tree in the car. As I walk in with the receipt, I'm greeted by two employees who cheerfully ask how I'm doing. I tell them I am sad as I purchased a tree and assembled it only to discover that it has no wall plug. They look puzzled, so I go through my story once again and then explain I need a flat cart to load the tree.

One of the employees says we should look in the tree area for an extra electrical plug thingy. He walks over twenty feet, pats a shelf and pulls a plug from a box. It "looks" like it should be a match. Am I going to drive back home with it? I don't think so. This guy offers to go to my car and check it. I open the trunk, and he attaches it to the wire as easily as the famed prince put the glass slipper on Cinderella. I thank him repeatedly and drive off… all is well for now… of course I've had this feeling before.

I arrive home and make four trips to unload the tree. My husband is not home… this is no accident.

I assemble the tree, getting hit and smacked by branches. I plug the tree into the outlet and yes, it is working… except for the top tier. After a jiggle to the top of the tree, the lighting is complete and working! I have the choice of white or multicolored lights. I collapse into a chair to admire the effect.

Only now does my husband walk in… and this is no accident.

~Cindy Willimon Fricks

# Wild Kingdom

*Heav'n has no Rage, like Love to Hatred turn'd, Nor*
*Hell a Fury, like a Squirrel scorn'd.*
*~"Chippy" Congreve*

I was eight years old and I would remember that Christmas forever. It all started when my father made the announcement at dinner that we were not going to do our typical "tree night." We always did the same thing. We would go out to dinner, drive around a bit to enjoy the holiday lights, and then wind up at the same tree lot. We made a big deal out of choosing just the right tree, and then drove home with our prize tied on top of our car. We would spend the rest of the evening setting it up and decorating it. I would get to stay up as late as I wanted, but typically wound up asleep on the couch, leaving my parents to finish the decorating.

Mom and I had already made dozens of cookies with red and green ribbons through them that we would hang on the tree. As the boxes were slowly unpacked there was a bowl of popcorn to munch on while listening to Mom telling the same, familiar stories of Christmases past that were attached to each ornament.

But this year, my father said we were going to cut down our own tree. I wasn't too happy about this. Dad was definitely not the outdoor type. But, he said, business friends of both my parents had recently bought some land that had a lot of Douglas fir trees on it and they offered to let us choose one for Christmas. We could drive out to their ranch early in the morning, enjoy a nice visit and brunch with them, cut our own tree and be home by late afternoon to set it up. It would be fun.

It took some cajoling to get me to go along with it. I didn't like change. I preferred the comfort of our rituals. However, when Dad told me they had horses, I changed my mind. Like a lot of kids, I was horse crazy.

So it was all set. The day came and the trip was long, but the ranch was beautiful and there were a lot of fir trees. They had to drag me away from the horses to actually help choose one, but finally it was done and Dad and his friend cut it down and tied it to the top of the car.

I had to admit that it was a beautiful tree. It was much deeper green and very thick. It was much prettier than the trees on the lots. The ritual at home went as it always had. Dad set up the tree in the stand and attached the lights. Mom told stories as she unwrapped the ornaments. We munched popcorn and hung the ornaments, cookies and tinsel, while the music of familiar carols filled the air.

I don't know what time I fell asleep on the couch, but I do remember it was 3 a.m. according to the clock by my bed when I woke up to hear my parents yelling, a cat screeching, a dog barking and what sounded like a train rumbling and bumping from the living room and down the hall between our bedrooms.

The bumping and banging was the Christmas tree. Our dog Lassie was completely entangled like she had on a harness in the light strings and was now charging up the hall back toward the living room hauling the tree behind her. A terrified squirrel was about two feet ahead of the raging dog, only to be met by Mom's cat, Mr. Mitty, who dove off of the top of the drapes at the terrified animal.

Mom pushed me back into my room and dashed after Dad to help. Of course, I came out and watched from the hall. Dad managed to grab Lassie but she was so tangled in the light strings the best he could do was carry her back into the hall where he and Mom pushed her into the bathroom, tree and all, and shut the door. Lassie, however, was not going to go silently and a volley of barking came from behind the door.

Mitty had the terrified squirrel cornered on the mantel, which was now devoid of all holiday decorations. The squirrel was ready to fight. Dad tried to move between the cat and the little beast, just as Mitty took a leap. He missed the squirrel but landed on Dad's back with all four paws — claws out. Dad screamed, fell over a chair and the cat took off for parts unknown. Now it was just Mom, Dad and one very upset gray squirrel. Evidently, that tree had been his or her home and the branches were so thick that the little creature simply hid away in them until the decorating was done and the lights went out. Then it ventured out, only to be met by a Collie and a Tomcat. It probably jumped back into the tree for safety, but both the other animals had already seen it and jumped into the tree too.

Dad motioned to Mom to open the back door. She slipped past him, opened the door and then she hurried back. Dad picked up a magazine and swung it at the squirrel and started yelling. Mom picked up a throw pillow and did the same. Not to be left out, I ran into the living room yelling and waving my arms. We went through the house like hunters beating the bushes for game until the squirrel took the best path of retreat and dashed out the back door and up a tall elm tree to safety.

It was now around 3:30 in the morning and we all stood looking at a house in total ruin. Instead of getting mad, Dad started laughing, Mom joined in and we all went into the kitchen. Mom made some hot cocoa and we sat at the kitchen table reliving the event and laughing even harder — until Lassie started to howl.

Dad got up to go take care of the poor dog and see if anything at all could be salvaged from the ruins. Mom hustled me off to bed.

Mom and Dad spent the wee hours of Christmas morning putting everything back into place the best they could, and when I got up, although short a few ornaments, and all of the cookies (Lassie ate them), the tree looked perfect to me. The presents were there and all was right with the world — except Mom and Dad were not quite as chipper as they were on other Christmas mornings.

It was our first and last venture into cutting down our own tree. However, it did create a memory that lasted through generations.

~Joyce Laird

# The Perfect Tree

*The pursuit of perfection, then, is the pursuit of*
*sweetness and light.*
*~Matthew Arnold*

Visions of Christmas trees have been dancing in my head for weeks. I dreamed of a glorious tree adorned with lights, expensive ornaments, and topped with a beautiful store-bought angel. I pictured it in my mind: shining ribbon cascading gently from top to bottom, strategically placed porcelain ornaments, and brilliant baubles on every bough. This year, my vision was shattered the moment the tree went up and the kids got their hands on the boxes of decorations.

Untangling the lights is a family event. How can seven strands of lights get tangled up in a box when we only use two on the tree each year? I've come to the conclusion that they must be multiplying in the garage over the summer. As I wound lights and attached ribbon, the children were waist-deep in decorations, fighting over who got to hang what. All four rushed to the tree, hanging ornaments on the same branch, then argued over whose should be moved. I love the way they settle their disagreements. Sometimes, the one who gets there first triumphs. And sometimes they decide by birth order. But when my preschool daughter stomped on her brother's foot and insisted, "Ladies first," she won.

I did my best to squeeze between them here and there to place a few ornaments of my own on the top branches, placing each one in just the right spot. To the left, I hung the tiny porcelain sleigh from the gift shop downtown. And to the right, I tied the silvery bells that I'd purchased while on a trip last fall. I wanted to create a tree like the ones I'd seen in the home and garden magazines. One that even Martha Stewart could be proud of. My kids of course, had other plans.

Fifteen minutes into the decorating process, the tree leaned hard to the left. I took a step back and realized that the children had emptied an entire cardboard box of decorations, all of which were hanging on the front, lower branches. I wanted the tree to be perfect and they just didn't get it. This was supposed to be a Christmas to remember. Why couldn't they be more creative? When no one was looking, I made a few adjustments. The lower boughs still sagged a bit, but at least the tree didn't topple over.

Late evening was upon us, and we were eager to shut off the lights in the room and view our work of art. Just as I reached for the switch, into the living room came the cat, followed closely by the Beast, AKA our Labrador Retriever. The cat found refuge in the tree, just under the angel and the dog stood close by, her boomerang tail wagging furiously, smashing four bulbs. The kids laughed hysterically as I dug in the tree with one hand and tried to hold the dog back with the other. Upon receiving a multitude of scratches, I decided it was easier to let the cat stay where she was and lock the dog in the garage.

I looked at the tree and shook my head in disappointment. It leaned sharply to one side. The ribbon was mussed up, none of the ornaments were hung symmetrically and the angel that sat atop was handmade, not the porcelain one I had counted on. There were no crystal snowflakes and not a single silver icicle. Not to mention the fact that there were three, half-eaten candy canes sticking to the nativity ornament. This tree certainly didn't compare to those I'd been admiring online and in magazines since October. I sighed and plugged it in anyway.

The lights twinkled and danced, and I was instantly overwhelmed. My children's eyes lit up, and mine brimmed with tears. As I looked, I didn't see the same unsightly tree I had just moments before. There, before me, was the most beautiful Christmas tree I had ever laid eyes on. Those low branches that swept the floor were filled with ornaments that my children adored. Ceramic Santas and elves sat side by side and I even spied one that read "Baby's First Christmas." I could see where little hands had placed the paper ornaments that they had lovingly created in school. Cotton-ball snowmen and felt ice skates accompanied the tiny painted pinecones and the ornaments that I had crafted with my own mother when I was a child. And just under the cross-stitch bears from my grandma were the sequined ornaments that were sent to me by my husband's grandmother, whom I had never had the honor of meeting. That tree was a part of every member of my family and the mere sight of it was breathtaking.

I am reminded, during moments such as these, that the most important gifts I could ever receive are the ones that have already been given to me. I am reminded to give more freely of my heart, and to take time to see Christmas as it's meant to be seen.

~Ann Morrow

"We're done decorating...
YOUR TURN!"

# Hope Beneath the Branches

*The wings of hope carry us, soaring high above the driving winds of life.*
*~Ana Jacob*

Helplessly, I watched my husband stagger from the sheer weight of the enormous box, finally hoisting it through our front door and depositing it with a thud on the living room floor. Before even freeing the carton's contents, I knew the truth.

We had seriously overestimated our modest home's ability to host our first artificial Christmas tree.

I remained undeterred.

Eight months pregnant, I was relegated to reading the crisply folded instructions while my husband coaxed each prickly pine branch into its predestined hole. Our living room shrank with each successive tier. Then, like a flag claiming new territory, the majestic top was at last anchored onto its perch. I stood in awe.

Our Christmas tree was larger than life.

Although I couldn't know the significance this tree would hold in my life, the two of us became instant friends. To start, its billowy branches hid my burgeoning belly in our Christmas photos that year. In turn, I lovingly adorned our tree's branches with baubles: a box of red and gold balls and a string of white lights reflected that simpler time of life. Finally, as my due date approached, and my bed became uncomfortably harsh, I retreated to the soft support of the living room sofa. There, under the cozy shelter of my Christmas tree, I slept like a baby — dreaming of my own first baby to come.

And she did. Arriving three weeks early on Christmas morning, my daughter Kelsey Noelle was born.

The days became a blur of joyous chaos, but the nights held a magical calm. I learned that, along with a serenade of "Silent Night," nothing soothes a colicky baby like a midnight waltz under the glow of Christmas-tree lights. Those were precious nights, and I was loath to pack away my pine-tree friend.

Three years later, I relived that charming season of special births when my son Christian was born. But, as I rocked my new baby next to the tree that year, I was unaware that my infant son's first Christmas would be our last of its kind. Like a giant spruce felled by a ruthless ax, life as I knew it came crashing down around me. Before Christmas gave way to Easter, I became a single parent.

Alone with a toddler and a newborn, I faced rapid-fire losses: first my marriage, then my home, and finally, my sense of security. Within months, my children were hospitalized for pneumonia, seizures, and asthma, and my already precarious finances began to crumble. Unable to find solid footing, I sought a safe haven where my children and I could establish new roots. I found one in a tiny rental flat in a quiet neighborhood where we would celebrate the first Christmas in our new life.

Little of our furniture made the cut that move, but our Christmas tree did. Early that December, I dragged the eight-foot carton from our basement storage locker and bumped it up the three flights of stairs to our unit. I felt a shiver of anticipation as I slit open the box.

It was akin to reuniting with a friend.

Impulsively, I hugged an armful of branches, releasing enough tears to water a redwood as a mix of emotions flooded over me.

Kelsey and Christian dove through the box like pirates digging through a treasure chest. Each branch elicited a "Wow" and was then placed reverently into one of the piles scattered around the room.

After fishing out the now crumpled sheet of instructions, I slowly and patiently resurrected my pine. The kids were mesmerized to see the tree take shape, cheering me on as I triumphantly attached the top. If it had been oversized in our house, our tree was gargantuan in our flat. Stepping back for a better look, I watched the kids meticulously place each red and gold ornament — mostly on the bottom two branches.

I stood in awe.

The finished masterpiece filled our living room — and our hearts — to the brim.

That day, we were never further away than a four-foot radius from the tree. We ate under the tree, we read under the tree, we dreamed under the tree. Night fell; I was exhausted.

"Time for bed," I announced wearily.

But my son — in Thomas the Tank Engine pajamas — stood resolutely behind the swell of green.

"Mama," he began quietly and earnestly, "I want to sleep under the tree tonight."

My heart lurched, memories flooding back to the many nights I'd given in to the same desire, drifting to sleep with a baby in my arms.

Dragging train blankets and Barbie pillows, we settled under the welcoming branches, warmed by the pinpoints of twinkling light.

I'm home, I thought. We're going to be okay.

Of course, okay is a relative term. More challenges, more illnesses, and three more moves uprooted my little family and my larger-than-life tree. With each upheaval, I left more and more things behind, but never the faithful fir. Friends thought I was crazy, as they heaved the box over three more thresholds.

"What's wrong with getting a real tree?" they asked, hoping to spare us (and them) the effort.

"Ours is not a friendship of convenience," I defended our tree. "Besides, I don't abandon my friends when the going gets tough," I added, silencing their objections.

The going was tough — but our traditions kept us strong. Our tree became a sacred place for my family, nurturing us in the good times and the bad. Like a living tree that blooms anew following the harsh realities of winter, our Christmas tree, crushed and contorted in a cardboard box, sprang back to life each year, its branches unfurling in a perpetual symbol of hope.

I no longer had babies to rock under the tree. But, as the years marched on, many stories were shared under its branches, worries soothed in its glow, songs sung in its graceful presence. In a life rocked by change our tree symbolized permanence and loyalty, comfort and faith.

As life inevitably spins full circle, my now teenage kids have assumed new tree-raising roles: my son does the heavy lifting and my daughter the expert instructing. I am relegated to leading the parade of ornaments, which now number in the hundreds.

On a recent Christmas, while admiring a forgotten ornament and steeped in memories, I heard a voice from the past mingling with the present.

"Mama," said my son, his deep voice interrupting my reverie. "I think I'm going to sleep under the tree tonight."

I swallowed to hide my tears as my kids formed a circle of sofas. Then, with the cats nestled under the lower limbs, we tucked ourselves under blankets and quilts. Eventually, the flicker of cellphones burned out.

Our Christmas tree lights twinkled like stars.

It was a precious night.

And we slept like babies… under our tree that's larger than life.

~Judy O'Kelley

# I Really Should Take Down the Tree

*I will honour Christmas in my heart, and try to keep it*
*all the year.*
~Charles Dickens, A Christmas Carol

Sitting in the semi-dark
staring at the shorter-than-life
Christmas tree in the corner
(blocking the door to the balcony, useless in this season).
The multicolored lights
warm the room almost as much
as the open candle flame
on the coffee table,
tucked in amongst books,
journals, and photo albums,
awaiting someone to wander through their pages.
I really should take down the tree
since it offers constant temptation to the cat
and it's already January
but I simply can't bring myself
to sacrifice the promise within
its branches.

How many seasons of my life
have I loved to sit like this
alone
in the semi-dark
dreaming of sugar plums and claymation movies and being told
"Yes, Virginia"?
No matter how many Christmastimes I live to see,
I will never be tired of the magic
in the tinsel and lights
of the tree.

~Jen McConnel

# Caught!

*Never say, "Oops." Always say, "Ah, interesting."*
*~Author Unknown*

Our car slid to a slushy halt in the circular driveway of the Park Street Tower. We piled out, bubbling with the joy of the season. The four of us: Ben Hansen and his wife Lynn, and my wife Carol and I lived in balcony suites on the seventh and tenth floors. We were all newlyweds so this would be our first Christmas together as husbands and wives and as friends. We had just returned from cutting our Christmas trees and now we proudly carried them into the lobby.

That was as far as we got! Our progress was halted by Mrs. Watson, the building superintendent. She pointed to the sign posted by the elevator.

"No LIVE Christmas Trees Allowed!"

Oh no! This couldn't be. We did not want artificial trees. And we had already cut these trees and hauled them back to our building.

There was only one solution. Sneak them in!

We couldn't sneak them in through the lobby and take the elevator or the stairs because we would leave a trail of needles right to our doors. But Ben had a long coil of rope in his storage locker, so we formed an outdoor plan. Simple — or so we thought.

Shortly after midnight, we went into action. Quietly, we snuck the trees onto the front lawn of the building, secured the rope to the railing of our balcony and lowered it to a waiting Carol, who attached the first tree. Hauling an inverted Christmas tree straight up, from ten stories above, was no easy task. Ben and I struggled as foot by foot the tree inched upward, brushing lightly against balcony railings as it passed each floor. At the seventh, Lynn pulled it onto their balcony and the Hansens had their tree!

Now for our tree. Panting and sweating, even in the sub-zero temperature, Ben and I were straining, inch by inch, to raise the tree to the tenth floor. Then… disaster struck.

Our tree got hooked on the railing of Apartment 805 and, before we could do anything, dropped onto that balcony and stuck fast. We discussed our options for getting it back, including using the rope to climb down the outside of the building. Thankfully, we had a better idea. We would wake the tenant in 805.

The building's internal communication system listed an R. Pearce as the tenant. Our wives recognized her as a woman they had met in the communal laundry room. Mrs. Pearce was a recent widow. How would she react to being roused in the middle of the night by a couple of nuts who had stranded a Christmas tree on her balcony?

Carol buzzed apartment 805 on the intercom and eventually received a sleepy, "Hello?"

Carol identified herself and thankfully Mrs. Pearce remembered her. She explained our predicament. The intercom went silent, then: "Well, there is a tree on my balcony; I guess you'd better come and get it."

Carol tapped softly on the door of 805. It opened to the length of the security chain and the lined face of an older woman appeared. She smiled at Carol and then her gaze rested on me.

"It's okay." reassured Carol. "He's my husband. May we come in?"

Mrs. Pearce nodded, "Yes, dear."

The layout of the apartment was similar to ours. I sheepishly made my way to the balcony door. Carol paused to chat and to reassure our benefactor. I freed the tree, mumbled "thank you," and left Carol chatting with Mrs. Pearce as I hurried upstairs to help Ben. We hauled away and having no further glitches, soon squeezed our tree through our balcony door and set it in the waiting stand. Mission accomplished!

Carol returned. "Did you notice that there were no Christmas decorations in Mrs. Pearce's apartment?"

I hadn't. During their chat, Carol learned that the lonely widow was quite sad. Her husband Jack had been her sole companion. They were childless and all of their friends now wintered in Florida. Mrs. Pearce explained that she wasn't expecting any visitors so it seemed pointless to decorate. With only a week to go before the big day our helpful neighbour was facing a bleak and solitary Christmas.

It was back to work on Monday, but the last days before Christmas flew by and we soon found ourselves stuffing stockings and placing gifts under the tree.

On Christmas Eve Carol and I gathered some of those gifts and visited the Hansens. Our main topic of conversation was of course our adventure with the trees. We recalled and relived the humour and tension of our escapade, gloating not a little over our success in outwitting the Watsons. Ben and Lynn saw us to the door, where we exchanged hugs and wishes for a Merry Christmas. They would be hosting Lynn's parents for Christmas Day, but both Carol and I had parents who lived out of Province, so we planned to have our own turkey dinner in our apartment.

I noticed Carol was still carrying a gift. She explained we had another present to deliver — to apartment 805. She knocked. "It's me, Mrs. Pearce."

The door swung open. "Merry Christmas!" we said in unison. She motioned us to enter.

"Christmas is for children, young people like you, and families — not old folks like me."

"Christmas is for everyone," said Carol, "including you! And here's a present to prove it."

"But I can't accept a…"

"Nonsense!" insisted Carol. "It's Christmas Eve! Please open it."

She did. It was a ceramic Christmas tree Carol had crafted for our apartment.

"Oh, thank you. It's lovely; but…"

"No buts. You helped us with our tree; this one is for you. It's special. Here, look."

Carol plugged in the electrical cord and the tree came to life, with tiny coloured lights twinkling from the tip of each branch.

"It's beautiful. Thank you."

"And that's not all. We'd like you to join us for Christmas dinner."

"But I can't…"

"I said no buts. You told me that no one would be coming to visit you."

"Well, that's true. But I do have some family here. Actually quite close by."

Carol challenged her claim, "Who?"

"My sister and her husband live right in this building. Now that my Jack is gone, I'll be eating with them, this year." In fact I think you know them — the Watsons? They're our building superintendents.

"The Watsons?" gasped Carol.

I groaned and looked at Carol. We stood to leave, embarrassed, and thinking about being evicted.

Mrs. Pearce was concentrating on her tree. Positioning it just so, she gave a murmur of approval. Then she turned and looked up at us from her chair. Her bright blue eyes twinkled merrily as she grinned from ear to ear.

"Don't worry," she said. "Your secret is safe with me! Would you like some tea?"

~John Forrest

# Merry Christmas!

## The Joy of Family

# Island Bliss

*Time spent with family is worth every second.*
*~Author Unknown*

As a single parent, I didn't have the means to vacation with my three children. After I remarried, my two high-school-age daughters begged their stepdad to take them to an island for vacation. It was a big surprise when my husband agreed. What better time to go to a warm climate than during the Christmas holidays when both of my girls would be on winter break? My son Casey had just moved to California the prior summer to attend college. Even though he had planned to come home for the holidays, with a heavy heart I had to tell him not to come home because his stepdad and I were going to St. Maarten for Christmas... with the girls. I felt like the worst mother in the world. I didn't feel like I could ask my husband to include my son. After all, these weren't his kids and my son wasn't even living with us.

My heart ached that the entire family wouldn't be together during the holidays, or on our first real vacation. My son didn't whine or carry on like I had expected, but that didn't make me feel any better. I knew I'd need an extra large suitcase to help carry the guilt that I would lug around on this trip.

I faked my happiness as we boarded the plane. I knew the girls wanted their brother to be there too and I sensed they faked their excitement as well. But since they were going to an island, I surmised that it wasn't all phony.

We arrived in lush St. Maarten, went through customs, and made our way through the open airport. As I looked at all the people gathered in the waiting area, I had to do a double take. I saw a young man who wore a black hoodie and stood about six feet tall. His hair was a little sparse on top, just like Casey's. I knew my eyes had played a trick on me. My heart again felt the sting of not having him with us; seeing that young man was just one more reminder of the awful mother I was for not having the entire family together at Christmas.

We walked a little further, and I watched the girls as they looked to their left too. Jessica turned to me. "Doesn't that guy over there look like Casey?"

"Yeah, I thought so too. Dresses like him and everything."

Rita chimed in, "Yeah, he does."

My husband walked ahead of us while the girls and I shuffled along as we continued to stare at the young man. I knew we were all silently wishing that Casey was there with us.

By now, we were only about three feet from this young man. Suddenly, and all at the same time, we realized that it *was* Casey! I looked over at my husband who had the cutest grin on his face. The girls and I rushed over to Casey, screaming, "It is you! Yay! You're here!" We all hugged each other as the tears fell.

My husband had schemed all along to surprise us. He'd called and made the arrangements with Casey, purchased a ticket for him to come to St. Louis, where he had spent the night in our hometown. Then Casey flew out of the airport on a flight ahead of us so that he would be in St. Maarten when we arrived. My husband kept it a secret and didn't tell any of us.

That evening as my husband and I snuggled, I wrapped my arms around him and said, "That was the sweetest and most special thing you could have ever done for me!"

It was my first real vacation with all of my children and not only was I surprised that my husband agreed to take us, but I was doubly surprised when he included my son.

On Christmas Day, we all gathered and as the kids opened their gifts, my heart sang. No one knew the pure joy I felt.

"Mom, we don't have a present for you."

"It's okay. My gift is having all of us together." And without a doubt, it was my best gift, ever!

~Lynn M. Obermoeller

# 12

# A Christmas Blessing from the Flu

*Gifts of time and love are surely the basic ingredients
of a truly merry Christmas.*
~Peg Bracken

I love Christmas. I love doing my Christmas shopping, writing Christmas cards, getting out the special china and crystal, and polishing all my tarnished silver-plated serving pieces. But last year, the week before Christmas, I came down with a bad case of the flu. That was not supposed to happen to me. I had too much to do.

Instead, I laid on the couch wrapped in the red and green afghan that my grandmother made for me. I had all the symptoms: a low-grade temperature, aching body, coughing, sneezing, and a splitting headache. All I could think about was what would happen if I couldn't get everything ready for Christmas Eve. I love having the family over for Christmas buffet and look forward to singing carols, sitting in front of the fireplace, and exchanging gifts. How could we keep our Christmas traditions if I had the flu?

"Please, dear Lord, help me get well so I can get everything done, because if I'm sick with this flu, our holiday will be ruined," I prayed.

The phone rang, and it took every ounce of energy I could muster to lift it to my ear and utter a weak, "Hello."

The chipper voice of my husband said, "Hey, honey, what are we having for supper?"

I managed to say, "I have the flu," and that evening he brought a pizza home.

"What are we going to do?" I asked.

Without any discussion, one of our two teenage sons said, "Oh, don't worry, Mom, we'll take care of everything. You just get some rest, drink plenty of liquids, and try to get well."

The next morning, I wasn't feeling any better and spent the day dozing between sneezes and nose blowing. The guys went shopping.

Later that evening, I heard the door open, the rustle of plastic bags, and the happy banter of male voices. The guys were home from their shopping expedition.

"I think we got everything we need." My husband smiled as he headed toward the kitchen with the groceries, followed by our younger son, who added, "I even remembered the cranberry sauce."

Our older son headed toward the couch, holding out my Christmas gift list and juggling an armload of colorful bags. "Mom, we went to the mall, and look — everything you wanted is checked off!" He placed the bags on the floor beside me so I could inspect the contents.

During the week, my husband brought home Christmas stamps and he and the boys finished writing out the greeting cards.

By Christmas Eve, although I began to feel better, I was still too weak to do anything but admire the zeal and creativity of my three heroes as I listened to them scrambling around in the kitchen trying to finish up before everyone came.

That evening, my family put on the best Christmas Eve buffet I ever had. The table was beautifully set and couldn't have been more perfect. Before we ate, we all sat down, held hands, and Marc, the younger one, said grace. I thanked God for hearing my prayers — and, yes, even for the flu.

~Teresa Martin

# 13

# Christmas Eve Dinner Plus One

*Good news from heaven the angels bring, Glad*
*tidings to the earth they sing: To us this day a child is*
*given, To crown us with the joy of heaven.*
*~Martin Luther*

There was the usual hustle and bustle of the Christmas season: the shopping, the decorating, and the planning of the day we would celebrate the birth of our savior. My daughter Francesca and I had spent Christmas Eve day in the kitchen preparing a sumptuous dinner to share with family and friends before heading to a midnight candlelight service.

We were tired, but excited about the evening, sharing the fruits of our cooking, and the gifts that lay beautifully wrapped and waiting to be opened and enjoyed. Little did we know that we would receive a gift far greater than any found under the tree.

We had both gone to shower and dress. I was sitting at my dressing table blow-drying my hair when I found Francesca beside me pointing at a stick at me. Blind as a bat without my glasses, I put them on to find that the stick was a home pregnancy test.

"Mom, look what it says."

Looking at the plus sign in the little window I looked up at her and said,

"Is it the dog's?"

"MOM!"

Now, I know this might sound strange, but my daughter had been fighting anorexia for ten years and in the last year had chosen to use medication to combat this disease. It was helping. So Francesca and her husband Richard began trying to have a baby. Nothing happened. They both went to get checked out. Richard's sperm were strong and virile, but the eating disorder had severely depleted Francesca's estrogen stores. She began a series of drugs to increase her estrogen levels, but other than mood swings, swollen injection sites and mounting debt, only temporarily higher levels of estrogen were present and never long enough for pregnancy to be achieved. Doctors told them she would probably never get pregnant and to think about adoption or surrogacy. They had decided to accept the doctors' diagnosis and once they paid off their debt would begin to put away money to adopt.

Through all of this I had thanked God that my daughter was finally physically healthy. Having a grandchild would be nice but I could survive without being a nana. Losing my own child to an eating disorder was something I did not know how to survive. Also, my husband Thad and I had at one time discussed adopting a child ourselves, so I knew that we could give as much love to an adopted grandchild as to a biological one. I looked forward to watching this time in their lives unfold.

"Mom, are you listening? I think I am pregnant!" my daughter said, bringing me back to present day.

"What made you take the test?" I asked.

"You know how tender my breasts have been. Even though everyone said it was because I was finally getting back to a healthy state, I found the test kit in the bottom of my make-up bag and decided to use it." Francesca stopped talking to catch her breath.

"Francesca, we need to make sure it's accurate."

Bless my husband for he went out and bought not one, but three more home pregnancy kits (the true scientist that he is). Each one showed a very clear and pregnant + sign!

Once we were done cheering, hugging, and thanking God, we decided that we would place one of the test sticks in a jewelry box and wrap it with Christmas paper and ribbon. Francesca would present it to Richard as an early Christmas gift.

Richard was out playing golf with his dad but he should be the first to know!

It was the longest hour of our lives before Richard finally came home, tired and sweaty from his golf game. He was off to take a shower. A shower! No way! Francesca presented him with the gift and asked him to open it immediately. He stated that he would wait until Christmas Day! Francesca assured him that this was a very special gift and he would want it now. He opened it, looked at the test stick and said, "Is this the dog's?"

"NO… IT'S ME! Why can't anyone believe I am pregnant?" my daughter asked.

It was a most joyous Christmas Eve and the best Christmas gift I think any of us have ever received.

~Loretta D. Schoen

# 14

# Three Gingerbread Houses

*Only an aunt can give hugs like a mother, can keep
secrets like a sister, and share love like a friend.*
~Author Unknown

L ily and the table were covered in icing. She had consumed more candies than adorned the gingerbread house. Candies hung in gobs of white icing haphazardly on the house… and it was beautiful. My great-niece was two years old, and it was the first time I invited her to decorate a gingerbread house. My boys, now teenagers, had outgrown the custom but I had not. And it had been many years since my niece had visited Aunt Rose to decorate a gingerbread house.

Over the next few years, gingerbread-house decorating transformed and I learned many lessons. At three years of age Lily insisted on doing all the decorating herself. The following year she stressed about making her gingerbread house the same as the picture on the box and I learned to throw the box out before she arrived.

And then Lily's sister Jaime was old enough to be included and I learned that a five-year-old and a two-year-old could not share a gingerbread house harmoniously. The five-year-old wanted symmetry and the two-year-old was happy with gobs of icing precariously holding the candies onto the house. For one it was about the finished product and for the other it was more about the process. The next year they each had their own gingerbread house.

And then there were three gingerbread houses when their brother Jack joined us. The heck with icing for Jack, he discovered that if you licked the candies first they would stick just fine and the ones that didn't stick could just be eaten.

Lily is now twelve years old and almost as tall as I am. For the time being she still tolerates gingerbread house decorating with Aunt Rose. Jaime now has a plan for her decorating and spends a lot of time completing it. Jack uses icing to make the candies stick now but still manages to eat a few during the process.

Four years ago, when I moved to a new city an hour away, I wondered how and if we would continue the tradition of decorating gingerbread houses. Not only have we continued, but the tradition has grown to include a trip to the local theatre. Their mom and their dad or meme (grandma) make the drive to my place. The day includes gingerbread-house decorating, lunch and theatre. So far we have seen *Mary Poppins*, *Peter Pan* and *The Little Mermaid*.

My calendar is marked early in the season and I anticipate this day with excitement and wonderment. I see Lily, Jaime and Jack throughout the year at family functions, not as often as I would like now that I live farther away, but on this day it is about our tradition, a tradition that has grown as they have grown and changed as life has changed. It is our time — my time to watch how they have grown and changed from the previous year and to enjoy their company and their joy of the Christmas season. It gives me comfort to know that no matter how crazy and busy life gets, this tradition is a for-sure thing. For them it may be about decorating a gingerbread house and going to the theatre but for me it is about the love of family and the feeling that the Christmas season brings.

~Rose Couse

# 15

# Presents or Presence?

*From home to home, and heart to heart, from one*
*place to another. The warmth and joy of Christmas,*
*brings us closer to each other.*
~Emily Matthews

When we moved from California to Colorado, 1,200 miles away from our extended family, my husband and I decided that we did not want to travel with our four children for Christmas. So, one late October day, I had that phone conversation with my mother-in-law.

"When are you coming?" she asked.

I paused, not knowing how to respond, and changed the subject. When she asked again later in the conversation — "when are you coming?" — I knew that we would be abandoning our plan to stay home for Christmas.

The thought of not being in our own home caused me to be anxious. What would Christmas away from home look like? Would we pack presents to take with us? Would we be giving up the magic of Christmas by not being in our own home, with our personal traditions?

I always loved Christmas morning; we would start by reading *The Christmas Story* together before viewing the Christmas tree with all the gifts that had arrived the night before. I loved the excitement of opening gifts — it was like a big birthday party for everyone! And then we had all day to relax and enjoy our new things.

This year would be different. We wanted to prepare our four

children, who were twelve, fourteen, sixteen, and eighteen, since this would be the first time they had spent Christmas away from home.

"How would you kids like to give Grandma Mary and Grandpa Carl the best Christmas present ever? We can do that by giving them the gift of our presence this Christmas," we told them. The kids all agreed we should go and so the trip to California was set.

My husband's large family always kept Christmas very simple. The focus of their celebration was the special meal together and enjoying fun times playing cards or watching old slide shows. My in-laws' faces lit up with joy when our family arrived, filling their living room with our presence. Christmas Eve was filled with laughter, as we played games with aunts and uncles and cousins and the sound of our voices as we sang our favorite Christmas carols.

Sadly, my mother-in-law's dementia was advancing so I was glad that we had made an exception and traveled that Christmas. I didn't know it at the time, but it would be the last Christmas we would spend with my mother-in-law. The gift of being present with her that year was the best gift I have ever given or received.

We have a video of our memories. We view that video as part of our holiday tradition now; we are passing on the value of memory making to our future generations. We listen to the recording of our family singing Christmas carols. We listen to Grandma Mary's voice and are blessed by the gift of her presence, even though she has passed on!

That was a decade ago. Recently, I got another memorable phone call and I found myself wondering again what Christmas would look like this year.

"My job has been terminated," my husband said over the phone.

My husband and I had moved back to California from Colorado for a new job opportunity four years before, and our kids were grown now. Family dynamics had changed so much since they were living at home. All had made lives for themselves. Our oldest son lives in San Francisco and is planning his wedding. One daughter and her husband live in Denver and are pregnant with our first grandchild. Another daughter lives in Los Angeles where she is attending graduate school and planning her wedding. Our youngest son lives in Vail, working in a five-star restaurant during the busy holiday season. We are all living different lives in different cities — including my husband and I. Because of some marital difficulties, he and I decided to separate while working to repair and strengthen our thirty-two-year marriage.

When my children heard that my husband and I were separated and that their dad was out of work, they listened to the Christmas spirit speaking to them. The four of them worked together and made a plan; it would be another Christmas without presents. The money that they would normally spend to purchase gifts for the family was instead used to make travel plans and to pay for accommodations to spend Christmas in a mountain rental home, all together as a family. I am so grateful that our children value the presence of family more than presents. We learned a valuable lesson from our Christmas in California with my mother-in-law, Mary — we aren't always guaranteed another Christmas together.

Presents are fun to give, but having loved ones present in our lives is the most valuable gift we can give each other. Christmas 2014 was another special and beautiful Christmas to remember. My husband and I are now living together again, stronger than ever because of the beautiful gift our children gave us, the gift of family togetherness. Whenever someone asks me what I want for Christmas, I will forever answer, "Presence… it's all I need or want!"

~Casie Petersen

# 16

# Divinely Staged

*Christmas is not just a time for festivity and merry
making. It is more than that. It is a time for the
contemplation of eternal things. The Christmas spirit
is a spirit of giving and forgiving.*
~James Cash Penney

I smiled as I received a compliment from a guest about my high-
necked black velvet dress. I stifled a laugh when her look of
approval changed once her eyes drifted down to my black high-
top sneakers. As the drama director for the church Christmas
event, I would don my heels just before the program started, but
until then I needed the comfort of sneakers to run from problem to
problem.

Crooked angel wings, torn costumes, temperamental cast members,
latecomers, sick singers; no matter how well organized the program,
there were always last-minute glitches. This particular performance
seemed to have an abundance of them.

One of the main characters in the drama approached me. I encouraged her before she even spoke a word. "Ann, you'll do great. You're
a natural."

Her mouth quivered as she fought back tears. "That's not the
problem. You're not going to believe this, but my parents just walked in."

I grabbed her hands. "That's wonderful! You've been praying so
hard for them!"

She gave me a tremulous smile. "I know. But they haven't spoken to me in months. They haven't wanted anything to do with me since we had that huge argument."

I looked at her with a confused expression. "How did they know about tonight's program?"

She shrugged. "I sent them an invitation. I figured at this point I had nothing to lose."

Her tears started to spill over and I gave her a quick hug. I pulled back to look into her eyes. "Well, it's nothing short of a miracle that they came tonight. It's a step toward reconciliation. Just focus on your part and do your best."

She took a deep breath, gave me a tiny smile, and walked off to study her lines one more time.

Now my thoughts were in a whirl. There had been a serious split in Ann's family. Hopefully our performance of a modern-day Christmas drama would make a difference and help to heal the rift. I went back to the business of torn wings, cough-drop handouts and other program problems. The lights flickered as a reminder for people to take their seats. I yanked two little sisters apart before they ripped off their halos, located a Sunday school teacher and handed the kids over to her.

I ran down the hallway to grab my shoes in the coatroom. I teetered on one foot while waving to some last-minute guests. They eyed me with curiosity, shook their heads and walked into the sanctuary.

I flicked a brush through my curls, slipped on a sparkly vest over my velvet dress and stood still for a moment. Before I entered the sanctuary I said a silent prayer: "Here we go, God. Without you this could be a disaster. With you, it will be outstanding. Please bless all our efforts and practice, and use this drama to reach people's hearts tonight with the true message of Christmas."

I slid into a seat near the front. After a brief introduction the drama began. The two main characters opened the scene perfectly. The story unfolded with only minor mistakes, nothing obvious to the audience. The musical performances were perfect. The children were adorable and able to bluff their way through anything. The spotlights came on and off on cue. The chaotic scene was wonderful and the audience laughed at the right times. The soloist presented a moving rendition of the theme song. Finally we reached the climax of the story — Ann's dramatic speech and prayer.

I leaned forward, a bit worried. Ann had not done well in our last rehearsal for this final scene. She didn't portray enough emotion or raw feeling. Something was missing. Yet I had hesitated to push her as she was already stressed.

I had no idea how this crucial scene would play out. On stage, Ann said an absent-minded goodbye to her co-worker as she looked over her great-grandmother's journal. At this part of the story she was supposed to read aloud a prayer of her great-grandmother, written many years ago. She began to read and the fictional tale and present-day reality merged.

Ann's voice choked with tears as she read the written prayer. "God, please bless my family and all those I love and hold dear. Help them to understand and know the reality of Your presence and the true meaning of Christmas. Let them remain close to each other throughout their lives, celebrating all those special moments together." Her voice quivered with true emotion, she broke down several times and the audience sat in complete silence, captured by the performance. Very few people knew the true story of what was taking place.

During all the rehearsals, Ann had no idea that "those I love and hold dear" would actually be in the audience for her that evening. The most difficult scene of the drama turned out to be a divinely staged masterpiece. Ann stumbled her way through the prayer, no longer acting. After the drama, Ann reunited with her family. They shared tears, laughter and hugs and remained for the fellowship after the program.

Ann and I still joke about that drama. I shared with her my initial concern that she would not show enough emotion in the final scene. She assures me now that if she had been any more emotional, we would have had to pick her up off the floor.

At a time when hearts are softened by the beauty of the Christmas story, that staged Christmas drama brought forth another Christmas miracle.

~Cynthia A. Lovely

# 17

# Guess Who's Coming to Dinner?

*Every child comes with the message that God is not
yet discouraged of man.*
*~Rabindranath Tagore*

I t was three weeks before Christmas, and our group of close
friends decided to celebrate with a progressive dinner. We had
four couples involved, so we would have four courses: hors
d'oeuvres, soup and salad, the main course, and dessert. I like
baking, so I chose to have the desserts at our house.

The first glitch in this glorious plan came when my husband, John,
and I found that none of our regular babysitters would be available
on the big night. Fortunately, our friend Bill came to the rescue. His
sister Mary would be coming home from college the afternoon of the
dinner. She was an experienced babysitter and would be happy to help.

The show would go on! I did have a few misgivings, however,
because although John and I had met Mary several times, our three-
year-old, Michael, had not. I decided to overcome this hurdle by talking about her frequently, and thereby fully preparing Michael for his
unfamiliar sitter.

Now, I could launch myself into the party preparations. I have
to confess that I go a little crazy with things like this. We don't have
parties very often, and I go overboard with the cleaning, painting, and
decorating. Fortunately, Michael was probably the most well behaved

child ever, quietly entertaining himself with toys and books whenever Mom went bonkers.

I did slow down enough to make meals (thank goodness for hot dogs and pizza) and to make sure Michael went to bed at regular times. I periodically emphasized the fact that our friend Mary would be coming to take care of him while Papa and I went out to a party. I even reminded Michael to choose his favorite toys, books and food to share with Mary on that special night.

All in all, I felt I had done a pretty good job of juggling everything. By that Saturday morning, the house had been painted, dusted, and scrubbed so thoroughly that I think the walls lost about an inch of plaster. I kept a running list in my head of important, last minute jobs:

- Light the candles and blow them out (so they wouldn't look brand-new)
- Put the wooden manger and figurines back in their assigned places on the coffee table (Michael kept rearranging them)
- Straighten the ruffles on all the curtains
- Tie red bows on the wax apples in the stoneware bowl
- Place sprigs of plastic holly around each picture frame and mirror

Michael had silently moved from room to room, lugging his toys with him, as I attacked each section of the house. Now, I proudly surveyed the results of my labors.

The seven-foot, ornament-laden Scotch Pine stood tall and straight in its water-filled stand, while fake packages lay artfully scattered across the emerald green tree skirt. Michael's handmade red felt stocking hung precisely centered beneath the snow-flocked village atop the fireplace mantel. Cedar swags tied with giant red satin bows wound gracefully up the banister, and had not yet begun to shed — as long as no one breathed near them.

Now, the only tasks left were to bake and decorate the sugar cookies and set the table. This last job would require arranging the Battenberg lace tablecloth and napkins, Grandma Murray's Limoges dessert plates, Mom's sterling silver, our "first-time-out-of-the-box" wedding crystal, and Great Aunt Bessie's brass candelabra.

I planned to finish by 4:00 p.m. so that John and I could get dressed for the party, which began at 6:00. In the midst of this final dash, I again reminded Michael that we would be going out, but that Mary would take good care of him.

Finally, amazingly, everything seemed ready. It was already 4:30 when I raced upstairs to change. Back downstairs by 4:55 p.m., I took a last look to make sure all the bows and baubles were still perfectly lined up in their respective locations. Michael, looking like a little blond cherub in his blue footie pajamas, was perusing his Winnie the Pooh picture book on the couch, his tiny body carefully curled up in the one small corner not filled with a symmetrical grouping of snowmen and Santa bears. Since Mary was due to arrive at 5:00, this was absolutely my last chance to go over the plans for the evening.

"Remember, Michael," I said, as I gingerly perched beside him, trying not to upset the snowmen, "Papa and I are going out tonight, so Mary will be coming to stay with you. She will eat dinner with you and play and read you stories, and take you up to bed before we come home. In fact, Mary will be here in just a few minutes."

While I recited all of this for the millionth time, Michael looked up at me with his big, serious blue eyes. When I was finished, he held my gaze for a long moment, and then finally asked, "Will she be bringing Joseph and the Baby Jesus with her?"

Well, it took me a second to realize what he meant, but then I laughed, cried and hugged him all at once. I had to explain to him that his babysitter wasn't that Mary — although she would have been a great one. When they say "out of the mouths of babes," nothing could be truer. While I was obsessing about plastic holly placement and perfectly blackened candlewicks, my little three-year-old had somehow managed to hold onto the true meaning of Christmas.

Nothing about the rest of that night sticks in my mind now, except that Mary really did turn out to be a terrific babysitter, and that John and I were late for the hors d'oeuvres because we spent a while enjoying more time with Michael before we left.

In the years since that memorable holiday, I can't honestly say that I have become rational about entertaining. I still run around like a lunatic, sweeping and scrubbing and attempting to perfectly arrange bowls of fake fruit. But I do try to pause every now and then to think about what's truly important.

~Mary Kay Bassier

18

# Christmas at the Creek

*The best thing about memories is making them.*
*~Author Unknown*

Back in the late 1990s, after our growing family packed together like sardines for another Christmas in our little house, my husband and I decided a venue change was necessary. Enter the Canyon Inn at McCormick's Creek State Park, just about fifty minutes from our house. When our children were small, we'd taken jaunts to the park for a day of picnics and fun. Sometimes we had even stayed at the Inn during summer vacations. Our kids loved it.

Now, in lieu of presents, we would pick up the tab for the whole stay. When my husband spread the good news, everyone was excited about our first "Christmas at the Creek." For the next twelve months, e-mails, texts, and family conversations centered on the new venue for our Christmas celebration.

Christmastime finally arrived and our destination was Spencer, Indiana. The snow covering the ground was perfect for sledding. The interior of the Inn was adorned with lighted trees, scenes with cotton snow, manufactured musical carolers and forest animals, along with a fireplace that gave the entire indoor area a scent of the woods. It was truly a winter wonderland.

Each family scurried to their suites, unpacked and bundled up, heading for the hill outside the Inn. Sled disks and garbage bags made for a rousing afternoon of frolic. After a couple of hours we went back

The Joy of Family | 57

inside for a change of clothes and hot cocoa with whipped cream or marshmallows.

My husband was a creative genius and he organized activities such as walks on the trails, strolls up to the horse barn, and a visit to the Nature Center along with a stop at the flowing waterfalls on the way back. On another morning we visited the outdoor amphitheater where all the grandkids performed songs, skits, and dances on the stage.

In the evening, there was pizza, sandwiches, and homemade yummy desserts brought by each family. Special games for the young ones and card games for the teens and adults made for fierce competition.

We have been doing this now for sixteen years! Each year family photos are taken, not only in front of the fireplace, but the entire group journeys back up to the stables where there is an oversized maple tree with enormous branches. The kids and grandkids climb to a lower level branch of their choice for the grandkids' picture. Then individual family pictures are shot, as well. We call it the Ely Family Tree.

As time has passed, our traditions have evolved. There are performances, contests, and lots of fun for every age group. Highlights of holiday experiences are now put on DVDs so that each family can watch and enjoy them again later.

This past Christmas our family surprised us. Working with the State Department of Natural Resources and the park property manager, our children and grandchildren purchased a bench in our honor that is now placed out in front of the Canyon Inn. A brass plaque is attached that reads: "Your Legacy: As Sure As It Started Here, May It Endure Forever More." We look forward to many more Christmases at the Creek.

~Cindy L. Ely

# 19

# Eggnog with Pickles

*Human beings, who are almost unique in having the*
*ability to learn from the experience of others, are also*
*remarkable for their apparent disinclination to do so.*
~Douglas Adams

I n the first few years after my mother's death, I was a little bossy with my widowed father. When he didn't seem to be moving on and enjoying his life, I decided he needed a pet. Dad had always taken an interest in my family's cats and dogs so I decided to get him a kitten.

I bought bowls and food, a litter box and litter, scratching post and catnip mouse, and a cat carrier. I wrapped everything and purchased a gift certificate for neutering and three veterinary visits. All I had to do now was select a kitten at the animal shelter and pick it up Christmas Eve morning. My kids jumped right on board with this gift for Gramps. "Great idea, Mom, he'll love it. Maybe we should get two!"

My husband Jim, a practical kind of guy who cares about actual facts, wanted to weigh the pros and cons. "Let's discuss both sides," he suggested. "On the one hand the five of you like this concept, but on the other hand, no one knows how Gramps will feel about the surprise." I assured Jim it would all work out. I knew what he really wanted was a firm guarantee that we wouldn't wind up with another animal. We already had three cats and a snooty Pekingese.

Jim had the last word: "Remember, all of you, this will be Gramps' cat. We have enough mouths to feed around here."

On the blustery, snowy day before Christmas, chubby, fluffy, gray-and-white Pickles (named by the volunteers at the shelter) planted himself on our family room couch. Except for the Peke, who took to his bed, all of our critters welcomed little Pickles and he soon joined in the cat festivities — batting tree ornaments and pawing at the bows on the packages under our freshly cut Scotch pine.

Surveying the cat chaos and the laughter of our kids, Jim's brow scrunched into those deep furrows that indicated considerable concern. "Don't forget, we're not getting attached," he said. "As of tomorrow, Pickles belongs to Gramps."

A beautiful, sunny Christmas Day dawned and shortly before noon Dad arrived. With Pickles hidden in my basement office and cedar logs crackling in the fireplace, we welcomed my father into our toasty family room and gathered around the tree to present him with the preliminary gifts.

"What's all this?" he asked. "You'd think I had a cat or something."

That was the perfect intro, as the kids marched into the family room with Pickles sporting a big red bow on his gray-and-white head.

"You have a cat now, Gramps," said my son Chris. "Merry Christmas."

Pickles took quickly to my father and at day's end the two of them left for home. I was elated that my father had a companion and new chores to add to his daily routine. The next morning I resisted the urge to call and check on the two of them. But I could imagine the scene — an adorable kitty and a dear old man playing and bonding. I decided to wait for our New Year's Day brunch for an update.

Then the doorbell rang. It was my father, cat carrier in one hand, and shopping bag in the other. I opened the door to a litany of complaints: "He's swinging on the drapes, scratching the furniture, scratching me, and that litter box is more than I bargained for. I can't keep him. I love you all for caring about me, but I really don't want a pet right now. Sure wish you had asked me first."

"You have to give him a chance to settle in, Dad," I said. "Oh, please try it for a few more days. He'll be such good company, you'll see."

Dad put his two hands on my shoulders and focused his warm, blue eyes on mine. His voice was gentle. "I need to find my own way, figure out decisions by myself and that includes pet ownership. Now give your old dad a hug."

Jim was first down the stairs. The kids followed right behind. I had my back against the front door, the kitten in his carrier at my feet, and the bag of supplies in my arms. Dad waved as he backed out of the driveway. Jim's sigh was deep and long and accepting.

"How about some eggnog for breakfast, Pickles?" he mumbled, picking up the cat carrier on his way into the kitchen.

~Carole Marshall

Reprinted by permission of www.CartoonStock.com.

# 20

# A Happy Mess

*One of the most glorious messes in the world is the
mess created in the living room on Christmas Day.
Don't clean it up too quickly.*
*~Andy Rooney*

I t's happened again. My husband has removed all his gifts from
the living room, within hours of Christmas morning. He's
already eyeing my pile of gifts and cards, the ones I will stubbornly leave there for a week or two. Being married to a neat
freak has its advantages, but not right after Christmas.

By the time I get through the holidays, I am exhausted, my to-do
list has exploded, and my house is a mess. Between the extra food, the
extra people, and the extra events, I feel myself falling further behind
every day. But it's all worth it, and the key is to relax and enjoy all the
family time. After all, you wouldn't have the mess if you didn't have
so many people you love home for the holidays. And that mess is all
that's left when everyone goes home after the holidays.

There's nothing better than a huge pile of laundry, a dining room
full of special occasion plates that have to be put away, and a kitchen
chock-full of leftovers and wine glasses that have to be washed by hand.
The new stains on the dining room carpet, the pine needles threaded
into the living room rug, the melted wax on the table — they're all
souvenirs of the great time that we had.

We *live* in our house, and that means laughter and trash piling
up and sticky spills and scratches where there shouldn't be scratches.

Our house is a home, not a showcase.

The British poet John Dryden said, "If you have lived, take thankfully the past." And that's how I view the holiday mess, as a souvenir of past good times for which I am thankful. That red salsa stain on the beige carpet happened the year we had almost thirty people for Christmas Eve and some people had to sit on cushions around a low coffee table. The sticky sap on the living room ceiling has been there for years, ever since I bought a tree that was too tall and it scraped the ceiling before we took it back outside to cut six inches off its base. Now that spot on the ceiling shows us where to put tree the each year. The dents in the wood cabinetry by the fireplace are from the heavy, metal Christmas stocking holders that keep falling down and bashing the furniture. They are a wonderful reminder of many magical visits from Santa.

So the debris from opening presents on Christmas morning will sit in the living room for at least a week after Christmas, and I won't care, because I will already be feeling nostalgic. The Hanukkah pillows and the menorah will stay in our library until New Year's, the tree won't come down until the middle of January, and the rest of the decorations will stay up until the Super Bowl. And the lights on the big spruce outside? I haven't taken those down for years; we even turn them on in the summer!

There's actually nothing sadder than a completely clean house after Christmas, because then I know it's all over, and we have to wait a whole year to do it again!

~Amy Newmark

# Chapter 3

# Merry Christmas!

## The Perfect Gift

# 21

# My Christmas Scarf

*I never make stupid mistakes. Only very,*
*very clever ones.*
*~John Peel*

E very winter when the winds blow cold, I take out my scarf. It is affectionately referred to as "My Christmas Scarf."

Before I digress, I will tell you the story of the scarf that brings so much love and laughter into our lives and the lives of people we know. It is hard to believe one scarf could bring smiles to people's faces and tears to their eyes.

I have a sister who has always bought the most wonderful gifts. Anything she buys is great, but the Christmas presents are always the best. One year, it might be a china plate. Another year, it might be a set of miniature lantern lights for decoration.

The Christmas I am talking about was a particularly cold one. You know, the bone-chilling-cold type when it seems like there is no way to ever get warm.

As the wind howled outside, we opened our Christmas presents. I tore open the brightly colored, beautifully wrapped present from my sister with excitement. I knew it would be special. As I lifted the lid of the box, I saw a beautiful but very unusual scarf.

It was bright red, like the color you associate with Christmas. There were Christmas green tassels at the two ends. In between were woven patches of yet another green, and a few small patches of black and burgundy.

All along were narrow ribbon lines of gold. The gold was a bright shiny gold... almost like it was freshly spun gold.

As you can imagine, each time I wore it I received compliment after compliment. Everyone loved the colors. People loved the width of the scarf. Most of all, there were the comments about the ribbons of "spun gold," the bright red color and the Christmas green tassels on the ends.

I loved wearing the scarf. It always made me warm and cozy, even on the coldest days. People would come over to me to talk and admire the scarf. "Where did you get it?" they would ask.

To each of them, I would recount my story. I didn't know where it came from or how much it cost. I only knew it was a wonderful gift.

One Christmas, I decided to tell my sister how much I loved the scarf. I wanted her to know what a wonderful gift the scarf had been and how much I enjoyed it.

As I proceeded to tell her about all the compliments I had received, she had a puzzled and then, HORRIFIED, look on her face.

Finally, in a very serious tone she said, "It isn't a scarf. It is a table runner." She could not believe I had not known.

I still have "My Christmas Scarf." It has never been used as a Christmas table runner.

With tears in their eyes, people laugh as I tell this story. Everyone still thinks it is the perfect Christmas "scarf."

Even now, years later, I realize I could see my scarf as a table runner, but to me, it is still "My Christmas Scarf."

~Katie Martin

# 22

# Santa Claus Rocks the Mills

*One touch of nature makes the whole world kin.*
*~William Shakespeare*

It started so simply, during a walk in the woods. My husband, Bob, stood in front of a massive stone boulder, stirred by its stark splendor. "Wouldn't you love something like this in our yard?" he asked. "It's so magnificent!" And when I saw the deepness of his wonderment, I swore to myself that somehow… I was going to make this happen.

We live in a small town in Massachusetts called Marstons Mills, commonly called the Mills. The land is flat with no large rocks or boulders. I had no idea where to find one. Well, who would?

I called monument companies and gardening centers and got nowhere. Then I called a landscaping company.

Stephen, the owner, didn't act like I was a lunatic when I told him I wanted the largest boulder he could find, delivered on Christmas Eve. Actually, he jumped right in. "How about we have Santa deliver it in a sleigh on a flatbed?" I loved the idea.

"Where is your septic tank?" he asked.

Bob turned pale when I asked him that same question several days later. "Your gift is too heavy to go over it," I hinted.

Three days before Christmas, I called the local newspaper's photo department and told somebody named Ron about the rock. "Why are you doing this?" he asked me.

"It's what Bob wants," I said.

Then I called local TV station. These were not easy calls. Can you imagine explaining that Santa would deliver an 18,000-pound boulder on Christmas Eve? (You got it. Nine colossal tons.) I invited all our neighbors to greet Santa, but I wouldn't say what he was bringing.

On December 24th, at 3 p.m., twelve pizzas arrived. I had bedecked our backyard shed with wreaths and lights and put out plenty of cookies and soda.

"It's time." I said to Bob. We stood at the end of the driveway, alone. Oh no, I thought. Nobody's coming to meet Santa. And I was so hoping we'd have a party in the shed. And then, like an image from a Dickens tale, children with their dogs emerged from the woods. Parents came out of their houses. The TV station van pulled up and the newspaper photographer arrived. I was trembling with excitement.

Then came the air horn, blasting away, as a caravan of trucks filled with families in Christmas costumes came rumbling down the street. Police closed the road to traffic. Over loudspeakers, we heard "Merry Christmas, Bob!" as Santa rang sleigh bells from the front of a giant flatbed that carried wooden reindeer, kids dressed as elves and a bright red sleigh with the rock.

Bob's expression was priceless. He didn't speak for minutes. Finally, he whispered, "You bought me a rock?"

"Why not?" We hugged. "It's what you wanted."

And so, we had our party. Everyone frolicked around the boulder with overflowing plates of pizza and Oreos. Carols filtered through the air. Our story was told on that night's local news. Our picture was in the paper with the words, "Tons of Love" underneath.

It was a Christmas only dreams are made of.

Late that night, Bob and I climbed the rock and sat on the top sharing cookies. I thought of all the people that helped make this fairy tale happen and I pictured my community gathered in awe. We had all re-discovered holiday magic that day, when Santa Claus rocked the Mills.

~Saralee Perel

**23**

# The Christmas Letter

*You don't raise heroes, you raise sons. And if you treat*
*them like sons, they'll turn out to be heroes, even if it's*
*just in your own eyes.*
*~Walter M. Schirra, Sr.*

**W**hat was that? I knew it wasn't one of my secret surprises. My husband had just pulled a white envelope from his stocking on Christmas morning.

A Christmas letter from our son, secretly hidden in the stocking by our daughter, brought a wave of emotions. Our son had dropped out of college, didn't really want to work, and kept thinking that life was going to be handed to him on a silver platter. For four years he had traveled a rough road. We supported him through all of it, lending a helping hand physically, spiritually, financially and emotionally. Still there seemed to be a great lack of appreciation.

Then our son joined the Marines and was deployed to Iraq for a seven-month tour of duty. On Christmas morning he called home to wish us a Merry Christmas. With a sad tone in his voice, he said, "I'm sitting by a lake, watching the sunset." He was lonely, missing family and home. As we said goodbye and hung up the phone, my husband opened the white envelope and read the handwritten letter.

*Dear Dad,*
*It has been long overdue, but I need to say thank you. When I was*
*little, you always pushed me to be better, to be stronger, faster, and smarter.*

*At that time, I didn't understand, but I do now. I wouldn't have become the man that I am today without you.*

*You taught me the value of hard work. You taught me to push myself farther than before. The work ethic that you instilled in me has been more beneficial than you would have thought.*

*Unfortunately, I've had to make my own mistakes to learn valuable lessons. You were always there to help me up whenever I fell. You have done so much for me that I could never repay you. I couldn't ask for a better father. I only hope that I can be as good a father as you.*

*Thank you for everything that you do. I love you.*

Neither of us could get through the words in the Christmas letter without tears running down our cheeks. For everything there is a season. One season can be filled with sunshine and blue skies. The next season can be filled with storms and black clouds. The storms shape us and test our faith. But at the end of it, our son became the man we always knew he could be.

~Sandra Diane Stout

# 24

Chicken Soup for the Soul

# Big Teddy

*Once a bear has been loved by a human being, its
expression is forever marked.*
*~Jama Kim Rattigan*

As a toddler, I was featured on the family Christmas card snug in my jammies and leaning on a huge stuffed puppy dog. A six-foot-long purple snake slept on my bed the majority of my preteen years. Glassy-eyed creatures sat on my bedroom shelves, propped in playroom corners, and served as confidants when needed. Bears, a lion, sheep, and even a turtle were stuffed animals that my mother could not resist. She loved a toy store and could not withstand the lure of plush gifts.

My father would roll his eyes, "Don't the kids have enough animals?" and my mother would respond, "Oh, but this one is so cute."

Hey, the stuffed animals didn't make a mess; they were colorful: and they did bring joy, especially to Mom.

Years later, it was a month before Christmas and I was studying for my first semester exams, writing papers, and working my part-time jobs. I lived at home and commuted to Temple University, so I could still enjoy Mom's cooking and spend time with my eight-year old sister, Lori. Lori was my own live action doll — she walked, talked, and yes, adored me.

One chilly Tuesday afternoon, I decided to stop home for a late lunch. Mom flung open the front door and said, "Hurry! I need your help before Lori gets home."

I ducked inside, dumped my load on the kitchen table, and watched my mom scurry to get the car keys. She was tiny but quick. She was out the garage door in a flash and hollered back, "Follow me. It's in the trunk."

She popped the trunk and revealed a humongous stuffed brown bear wedged inside. His arm, now unhindered by the trunk, stuck up in a friendly wave. An unblinking charcoal eye stared at me and it had a twinkly glow. A cheery grin on his face and a jaunty blue and red striped cap clinched the deal. Big Teddy would be a hit under the Christmas tree.

My mother shuffled from foot to foot as she looked over her shoulder for the school bus. I glanced at my watch; we had a minimum of fifteen minutes to get the job done.

"This was on sale at the grocery store, believe it or not, and I just couldn't resist. One of the bagboys helped stuff him into the trunk. I forgot about food shopping in favor of bringing Big Teddy home. He's too big for me to carry upstairs by myself. I'm so glad you came home between classes." She gave me a hug. "What do you think?"

We stood there and stared into the trunk. Scenes from various mob movies flashed before my eyes.

I deliberated. "We need something to cover him."

"You're right," she said and dashed into the house. I barely had time to pull Teddy from the trunk when she returned with a garish flowered sheet. We proceeded to wrap him tight like a mummy.

"Where do want to hide him?" I asked.

"Your closet, the one with summer clothes. I moved a few things around. I knew you wouldn't mind. We can set him on the upper shelf." I shrugged, picked up my unwieldy bundle, and proceeded to waddle into the house. The bear wasn't heavy, but he was bulky and the sheet was unraveling already. I struggled up our narrow stairs and into my room. Mom opened the closet door and I could see she'd moved some luggage and other non-essential items to make room.

"I think I hear the bus. Darn. It's early. Can you get the bear up on the shelf yourself? I'll go distract Lori." With that, my mother zoomed out of my room and closed the door behind her. Man, she was wired. She loved Christmas and worked hard to surprise us all with the perfect gift.

I tucked pieces of the sheet back into the mummy wrap and proceeded to heave Teddy into the closet. He kept wanting to tumble off the shelf and I had to give him an extra shove to ensure he stayed up there.

I could hear Mom ask Lori questions about her day, and the fridge door open and close. With a final reassuring pat to Teddy, I shut the closet and then rearranged my face to not reflect the last half hour of excitement. As I rounded the kitchen doorway, my mother caught my eye and I gave a slight nod. She smiled and turned back to Lori's spelling test, while I fixed a sandwich before leaving to go to my night class.

At any other time of the year, Lori wouldn't be around when I opened closet doors. The countdown to Christmas proved tricky, however. She lingered. She hovered. I think she sensed a magical being encased in a cloth garden, a magnetic pull from Teddy's chocolate brown eyes.

The buildup was excruciating. By Christmas Eve, my mother could barely contain her glee, and even my father was ready for Christmas Day. He was happy he didn't have to assemble anything. Finally, Lori was tucked into bed and Mom and I tiptoed to my room. I pulled on the sheet and dislodged Teddy from his winter's nap. And down he came. His ear was slightly scrunched, but other than that his eyes sparkled and his open arms beckoned for a hug.

Mom inspected him for matted fur or any other imperfections. Teddy had to be perfect. With muffled whispers and a slight stumble on my part, I hauled Teddy downstairs. Mom placed him in the corner. "Do you think that's the right spot, George?" she asked my father. Dad stood munching on a Christmas cookie and watched her walk back and forth. Mom tilted her head, scrunched down to see Lori's sightline, and angled Big Teddy one last time. When she was satisfied, she straightened his big red bow and patted him on the head. It was bedtime.

I slept longer than expected and was surprised that the house was so quiet on Christmas morning. I stretched, slid out of bed, donned my robe, and peered out my window. I padded down the steps and joined my mother on the landing. "Ssh! Take a look." Nestled in Teddy's arms, Lori was asleep. She had celebrated Christmas morning early.

~Joanne Faries

# 25

Chicken Soup for the Soul

# The Twelve Dates of Christmas

*A wise lover values not so much the gift of the lover*
*as the love of the giver.*
*~Thomas á Kempis*

**M**y husband Peter grinned at me with the enthusiasm of a little boy as I reached for the last present under the tree.

"Really?" I thought to myself. "What's he so excited about? It's obviously a wall calendar. He makes sure I get one every Christmas. Maybe he personalized it with family photos or something."

When I opened the wrapping I was confused. It was just an ordinary calendar with mountain scenes — beautiful but nothing exciting. I glanced over at Peter.

"Thanks! It's great," I stated with forced enthusiasm.

"Yes, it is great!" he grinned even wider. "Open it."

I flipped open to January and there, taped on the first Friday of the month, was a gift card for Starbucks.

"You complain I never plan anything! Now I'm good for the next twelve months, and paid in full up front too! Our first date in the new year will be coffee and scones at Starbucks," he announced proudly.

I grinned back at him, very impressed with my groom of twenty-five years. He and I have firmly believed in the necessity of a date night at least once a month, when the two of us go out for an evening without any of our four kids tagging along. As romantic as that sounds, lately that had been reduced to meeting for an hour at our local diner and had basically become just another obligatory appointment.

Peter's excitement on this Christmas morning was contagious. I flipped to February and saw a gift card for our favorite seafood place taped to the 13th. After our reservation had gotten "lost" at a horrifically busy restaurant on our very first Valentine's Day together, I swore to always celebrate the day before. It was sweet of him to take my vow into account.

I looked at March and on the 4th was a gift card for my favorite Mexican restaurant. My eyes started to tear up. That was our middle son's birthday and since he had just moved away from home for his first real job, I wouldn't be able to celebrate it with him in person. How considerate of Peter to keep me busy that evening.

April 23rd was Administrative Professionals Day and since I work as an Executive Assistant, on the 23rd was taped a gift card for our favorite steakhouse. May 14th is our wedding anniversary, and on that date was taped a gift card for my favorite buffet.

For June we had been planning a road trip to visit my mom who lives 1,000 miles north of us, and on the departure date he had taped a gift card for our favorite road-stop restaurant. July 29th is my birthday and on that date he had taped a gift card for McDonald's and had written "Big Macs and Sundaes on the Beach!" which is my very favorite kind of picnic.

And the rest of the year was every bit as romantic, sweet and thoughtful. Peter brought a whole new meaning to "Personalized Calendar." When I looked up from the most perfect gift ever to stare at my amazing, if not always perfect, husband, I definitely planned to renew my lease on him for another twenty-five years.

~Jayne Thurber-Smith

# 26

# Chicken Soup for the Soul

# The Big Gift

*Having a sister is like having a best friend you can't get
rid of. You know whatever you do, they'll still be there.*
~Amy Li

veryone was looking at me, expecting something. My
mom and dad had their beaming "learning moment" grins
on; my seven-year-old little sister was on the edge of her
seat, wide-eyed, eager, and nervous.

I was fourteen and had decided I was beyond Christmas. I had
proclaimed myself too old for hand-knit stockings that embarrassed
me, men in red suits with whiskey-breath, afternoons spent trying to
remove sticky icing from my fingers, and days spent with my family,
who constantly displayed their inability to understand the struggles
of teenage relationships.

As the smells of the evergreen tree danced in the air, I was too
preoccupied to notice. I was thinking of the concert tickets I was
trying to save up for and wondering how soon I could begin my daily
hour-long phone call with my best friend.

But here we were, Christmas morning, and everyone in my family
was staring at me. I blinked, clueless.

"What am I missing?" I thought. I looked at the present in my
hands, ready to open it.

My brother smirked in the corner, shoving dry cereal into his
mouth at lightning speed. But my sister had a look of pure anticipation.

The present was taped up messily with silver paper. This gift seemed tattered, torn, and lost. The little tag read, "To: Allison, From: Saundra."

I looked across the tree at Saundra, my little sister, who still sat nervously.

My brain worked hard to assess the situation. Eventually, with the logic innate only to a self-centered teen, my heart quickened and I thought, "This is IT! This is going to be my biggest and best Christmas gift of the year!"

You know, the Big Gift.

Every Christmas is defined by one gift we either receive or give. It is the gift that elevates the holidays and makes us feel loved. It is the gift we fondly remember year after year.

"This is going to be the exclusive set of CDs I've been dying for!" my head deduced. I was set to get the Big Gift.

The nervous tension in the room now felt good and I started to ride on adrenaline. I had the spotlight and I was excited! I began to tear off the paper, slowly, from one corner, always a performer who knew how to work a crowd.

As the big unveil happened, all I had was confusion.

I peeled back the paper to reveal... a puzzle I already owned!

That first second when the gift receiver peers under the paper is the most critical second in the history of all holidays and major events. So much rides on that first second. It is then that relationships are broken or undying gratitude extended. It is that first second that makes gift giving worth it, or a terrible mistake. That first second that reveals your true feelings: "Wow, I love it!" or "Wow, I don't like it at all."

That first second never lies.

I was now in that first second, and it was nothing but confusion.

My sister was crushed.

"Why would she get me a puzzle just like one I already own?" I haughtily thought to myself.

I looked closer as I removed the rest of the wrapping. It was open, worn, and the box was ripped.

I quickly realized that this WAS my puzzle, pulled from my own closet!

I looked up, confused as to why I was getting my old, used, worn out puzzle rewrapped and presented to me on the holiest of gift-giving days. What was I missing? Was there a hidden message that would lead me on a scavenger hunt to my new CD set?

Mom and Dad were still giving me The Look, still waiting for me to do something, to learn a lesson, to say something beautiful.

My sister just stared at her slippers, tugging sadly at a piece of string sticking to her flannel pajamas. I had let her down. That first second crushed her; my follow up reaction of nothingness was worse.

My dad swept in to clear the ugly silence. "Your sister really wanted to give you something this year, specifically just from her to you, with no help at all."

It turns out that my little sister, the youngest of three, was determined to keep up with the rest of the family. She was going to give each person in the family a unique gift, from her to each of us. This was the first Christmas where she understood that giving meant something.

But she was seven. She didn't have transportation, a big enough allowance, or the maturity to form a plan. So two days before Christmas, gift-less, she got resourceful.

She hunted through the house, looking for something I treasured. She found this dusty old puzzle, wiped it off, and wrapped it. She proudly placed it under the tree, ready for me to open it.

That puzzle was her heart. She had boxed up all that she could give, her hope and gratitude and seven-year-old memories of my time loving the puzzle, and wrapped it. Determined that I would get a gift from her, she sat there on Christmas morning, excited to watch me open the very first gift she had ever independently selected and prepared for any one.

And in that first second I failed.

I would like to say that I sat with renewed interest in that puzzle, lovingly putting the jigsaw pieces back together, basking in memories of times past sitting on the floor doing puzzles. Even more, I would love to say that my sister and I worked that jigsaw puzzle together every Christmas since.

But I was fourteen. I gave her a hug, said a polite "thank you," and began to patiently wait for the CD set to appear from somewhere under the tree.

More than two decades have passed since that Christmas. Interestingly, I don't remember what else I received that year. I certainly don't currently own the CD set I so desperately wanted, I can't even say for certain that I received it.

But I do remember that puzzle. I remember the shiny paper. I remember the worn out box. I remember the look in my sister's eyes as my selfish reaction failed her. I remember Dad giving her a consolation hug afterward, saying he was proud of her.

Since that Christmas, I have learned to control that first second. I have also learned that the Big Gift is never the one you expect or ask for. That Christmas I had received the Big Gift. I was just too blind to realize it.

~Allison Barrett Carter

# 27

# The Perfect Giver

*While we try to teach our children all about life,*
*Our children teach us what life is all about.*
*~Angela Schwindt*

A few years ago, as a Capuchin-Franciscan, I was living in a rectory that was also a friary, an abode of brothers. There were a couple of associates for the parish, a retired priest and three others who served at mission churches attached to the parish, and we all lived together.

On this Christmas Day all the other friars were gone, visiting their families for the holiday. The services for Christmas had all been completed and I was left home alone to cover possible emergencies.

In the middle of the afternoon I answered the doorbell to find a mother and son at the door. Sandy happened to be a member of one of our Bible study groups and she had Steven with her. He was just a little over three years old.

"Steven would like your permission for something he wants to do," Sandy began. Without waiting for further introduction Steven exclaimed, "I want to give my Teddy to Baby Jesus so he can sleep."

"We were praying at the crèche just a little while ago," Sandy explained, "and Steven became agitated because there was no teddy bear in the crib."

"Okay," I hesitated. "You want to lend your teddy bear to Jesus for a while?"

"I want Teddy to stay with Baby Jesus all the time, so he can sleep," was his reply. Sandy explained that Steven used a teddy bear instead of a special blanket at bedtime.

"A few months back I decided that Teddy needed a bath. He wasn't dry when Steven went to bed and Steven ended up coming for a hug about four times during the night. Now he believes that a teddy bear is essential for a child to sleep."

Trying diversion, I said to Steven, "Did you tell Baby Jesus that you love him when you were visiting?"

Instead of answering he blurted: "He needs a teddy bear so he can sleep."

"Did he tell you he wanted a teddy bear?" I tried to delay.

"No, but he needs one. I know because that's how I sleep. I'll give him my teddy bear so he can sleep."

"But Steve," I persisted, "don't you need to keep Teddy for yourself?"

"That's okay," Steven insisted. "I have the old one Mom washed. It's dry now." Sandy explained that she saved the older teddy bear as a spare when needed and Steven was ready to fall back on that one.

"Okay, Steve. You want to come and have a cookie first?" After a snack and a look at the friary's Christmas tree, Steven and his mother went to take care of their errand in church.

Later, when I went to lock the church for the night, I stopped to check the crèche in the sanctuary. There was Steven's teddy bear, bigger than the image of the Christ Child. It actually looked as though the teddy bear was hugging the infant and keeping him warm.

When we were taking down the Christmas decorations I checked but Steven did not wish to reclaim his Teddy. He figured that it belonged to Jesus. So I had it packed with the crib set and stored for the following year.

In the meantime, my Capuchin-Franciscan superiors transferred me to another parish and I was not there for the following Christmas.

Judging by the response of the parishioners, they would have chosen to have the teddy bear do an encore. As lopsided as it looked, it also looked appropriate, as though a master decorator had made the decision.

Wherever Steven is, he must be a grandfather by now. I pray that he and his children and grandchildren are enjoying the cuddly blessing of Jesus this Christmas. I know that I am blessed just to remember how Steven shared what he treasured most with his little brother.

~Bonaventure Stefun

# 28

# The Message Behind the Gift

*The heart of a father is the masterpiece of nature.*
~Antoine-François, Abbé Prévost d'Exiles

I never wanted a gift more in my life. It was a simple gift, really — a record player. It was before the era of component stereo systems, and as a fourteen-year-old I wanted total control of my music. I was still riding the boom of the Beatles and the British Invasion and was tired of painfully waiting for the radio to randomly play my favorite songs. If I owned a record player, specifically the model I pinpointed in the Sunday newspaper sales circulars, I could listen to "my music" any time — in the privacy of my bedroom. That is, in whatever privacy exists in a bedroom shared with two brothers.

I was one of six children in a single-parent home. My mother had died two years earlier after a short but brutal bout with cancer. We were an average middle class family before that. But now, although my father was a successful accountant for a major automobile manufacturer, six hungry mouths to feed on one income changed everything. We weren't scraping by but there weren't many extras. Hand-me-down clothes were a way of life. Yet, we were a solid family run by a disciplined man with rigid schedules, strict rules, and daily routines that kept life organized, efficient and predictable.

In the weeks leading up to Christmas, I pored over the sales circulars every Sunday to ensure my record player was still being advertised. If it went on sale, I would have one more reason to pitch my father on why I needed that record player.

Looking back, my father must have felt overwhelmed, or worse, inadequate, doing the Christmas shopping alone for three sons and three daughters. I wonder if he asked himself: How will I ever make everyone happy? How can I make each gift equitable? Will this Christmas be meaningful? And most importantly, will the finances stretch far enough?

This particular Christmas he asked my aunt and uncle to help him shop. And on that Sunday afternoon I showed my aunt that my record player was advertised in the newspaper again. Maybe she would lobby on my behalf.

I had great expectations for Christmas that year, despite my father's noncommittal reaction to my entreaties. After church, we assembled around the tree in the living room in our quaint Cape Cod home. I don't remember which one of the six of us was selected to hand out the gifts while the rest of us watched and waited — I was too busy surveying every package under the tree. There was good news. Plenty of gifts for everyone. And bad news. No gift large enough to be a record player.

I enjoyed watching my brothers and sisters receive what they hoped for on what was probably our first Christmas of significant healing after our mother's death. Still, we felt her absence — none more than my father. For me, the thought of receiving my special gift was a healthy diversion from the pain of what remained our family's greatest loss.

As I watched the presents quickly disappear and it became clear I would not receive my coveted gift, I felt the rejection you feel when you're the last one chosen for a team. I guess I knew it was simply too much to ask. Yet, I wondered how to question my father.

I looked over at him. "Dad, I think something is missing," I said.

"Really, what?" he replied.

"Well, I was hoping for…" my voice trailed off.

"Have you checked under the tree?" he suggested.

"Yes, but…"

"Have you checked *in* the tree?" he added.

"*In* the tree?"

I rifled through the branches, careful not to disturb the ornaments. In the back of the tree near the bottom I found a sealed envelope with my name on it. I ripped it open. There was one sentence scrawled across the middle of the page. "Look in the basement near the clothes dryer." I ran to the basement and looked around the dryer. Nothing. I popped the door open and looked inside the dryer. Another envelope. I opened it. "Look in the closet in Mary and Joanie's bedroom." I ran back upstairs to my sisters' bedroom closet. I found another note with the next clue. This process continued until my father had me run all over the house. The thrill of the hunt intensified with every note. At last, I discovered the final note. "Look under your bed." I raced upstairs to my room and looked under my bed. There, wrapped in newspapers, was a large gift.

I shredded the newspapers. Beneath this crude wrapping paper was the gift — a record player. I paused. It was not the one I wanted. It was *better* than the one I asked for. Far better. I was stunned. I knew I didn't deserve it. It was a major name brand. It even carried the two words that symbolized quality in that era: Solid State. I excitedly plugged it in and spent the afternoon with my siblings listening to our favorite records.

My father would never know the full impact of what he did for me that Christmas. I used this cherished gift all through high school and college. In fact, I used it long after technology had passed it by. I'm sure my father would've been satisfied if I had gotten just a few years of use out of it. I used it for ten years. Eventually, I replaced it and carefully put it in storage. It survived numerous spring cleanings, rummage sales and moving days.

In the end, I kept it for thirty-seven years. This Christmas, it's been forty-seven years since I opened the gift. It remains the most memorable gift I've ever received.

Why did I keep it so long? I suppose it's because of the powerful message behind the gift that my father unknowingly sent me: The value of a gift is not what it's worth; it's what it says about your worth to the giver.

~James C. Magruder

# 29

Chicken Soup for the Soul

# She Knew

*We should all have one person who knows how to bless*
*us despite the evidence. Grandmother was that*
*person to me.*
*~Phyllis Theroux*

The house was filled with people: my father-in-law, my husband's sisters and their spouses, our nieces and nephews. The tree with its colorful decorations was surrounded by piles of presents. We had enjoyed a delicious Christmas dinner and now it was time for the gift exchange. My father-in-law was busy handing out the gifts. Rachel, our fourteen-month-old daughter, sat on my lap, excited by all the bright wrappings, bows and activity. Gifts were being unwrapped, paper was flying, and laughter filled the room.

My father-in-law handed me a gift. "For Rachel from her grandma" he said to me. I quietly took the gift and looked at my husband Marvin with a puzzled expression. It had been almost three years since his mother had passed away. Rachel, with our help, tore the paper off the big box. Inside the box was a beautiful blond curly-haired doll with blue eyes. She wore a pink gingham dress with a white apron. In her arms she held a baby doll that wore a matching pink romper. Marvin removed the doll from the box for Rachel. As we admired the doll, we noticed a knob on the back of the doll. I carefully turned the knob. The doll started to sway back and forth, the motion causing her to rock the baby doll in her arms. A lullaby accompanied the movement. Rachel looked at the doll with wide eyes and reached her arms out to take it.

I was still puzzled. When my mother-in-law passed away, Marvin and I had been married for eight years. Those years were filled with infertility treatments, adoption agency interviews and paperwork. At the time it had seemed that we were no closer to having a baby to call our own than we had ever been.

Now almost three years later we had our precious daughter. I wondered about the story behind the gift of the doll. Thinking of my mother-in-law's love for shopping I thought that perhaps she had bought the doll and stored it away for one of her other granddaughters. After all, she had already had twelve granddaughters among her twenty grandchildren. Rachel's grandpa must have found the doll in the back of a closet and selected it for her.

As the Christmas celebration continued, Marvin's sister Barbara shared with me that she had been shopping with her mother when the doll was bought. Barbara had asked her mother whom she was buying the doll for. Barbara was surprised when Mom replied that it was for Marvin and Donna's daughter. "But Mom" she said, "Donna and Marvin don't have a daughter, and even if they have a baby it could be a boy." Mom insisted on the purchase and Barbara knew that it was better not to argue with her mom.

Later Luella, another of my husband's sisters, told me her story. One day she had been helping her mom clean out a closet. Finding the doll, she had asked her mother whom the doll was intended for. Again the reply was that the doll was for Marvin and Donna's daughter. Luella, not wanting to press the issue, carefully put the doll back in the closet for safekeeping. I now understood that this doll was for Rachel, a special doll picked out for her, before she was born, before we even knew if she was ever to be.

Once home I thought about putting the doll away, safe from little hands, a keepsake for her to have when she was older. But then I decided that it was more important for Rachel to have the doll now. Over the years, the white apron tore, the doll's hair was messed up and her leg even fell off. In time I came to realize that the real gift was my mother-in-law's faith, her belief that one day her son Marvin and his wife Donna would have a daughter to love and raise. Even if Grandma was not there to share in the joy, her future granddaughter would have a precious gift from her grandmother.

~Donna Welk Goering

# Passing Storm

*I would maintain that thanks are the highest form of*
*thought; and that gratitude is happiness*
*doubled by wonder.*
*~G.K. Chesterton*

"Hello," I said into my phone as I hurriedly swallowed my cereal.

"Mrs. Grumbein, this is the Captain. Would it be convenient if we deliver today about 1 p.m.?"

"Yes, that would be fine." Both apprehension and excitement flooded my heart as I hung up the phone. Someone had given our name and phone number to a marine squadron, and they were bringing us Christmas presents. I made sure the house was as spotless as could be with four children living in it.

As one o'clock drew near, I perched myself on the edge of the couch. Each time I heard a car I jumped up to see if they were here. Each time it wasn't them I was relieved yet disappointed.

Finally a huge SUV pulled into the driveway, and four marines in dress blue uniforms got out. One of them glanced at the inoperable station wagon sitting by our driveway. I was even more embarrassed, but so grateful too. I greeted them with a smile, wondering if they could hear my heart pounding.

"Mrs. Grumbein, we're here on behalf of a squadron on base. The marines have collected toys for families who might be having a difficult time this holiday season."

"Please come in." Two came in and two went back to the SUV. They made several trips and soon my living room was full of boxes and bags.

"We hope you have a blessed Christmas, Ma'am," the oldest marine said.

I tried to say "Thank you," but my throat suddenly closed up and tears welled up in my eyes.

He looked uncomfortably at the floor, hat in hand, and turned toward the door.

"Thank you," I managed to squeak, when they were halfway down the porch steps.

"Yes, Ma'am," he said, putting on his hat and smiling at me.

"What squadron are you with, so I can send a thank-you card?"

"We can't tell you that, Ma'am. No thanks necessary."

I watched through the window as they drove away, wondering what they thought of me.

I had always donated, not received. We weren't always like this. My husband had been laid off this year, and we were struggling. I'd wanted to say this to those marines, but the words wouldn't come out. I felt ashamed.

I quickly wrapped the gifts so I'd be finished before the school-aged children came home. I stashed them in closets and under beds as quickly as I could.

On Christmas morning I felt a twinge of guilt as our four children tore open the gifts with gusto, thinking they were from us.

My nine-year-old son opened a game box and taped inside the lid was an envelope.

"What's this, Mom?" He handed it to me.

I opened it and read aloud, "May the joy of Christmas be with you all the year through." All around the card were the signatures of all the men and women in the squadron, except instead of their real names, they'd signed nicknames, like Pug, Buck and Ace. They had done this kindness for us and we would never even know who these men and women were, or who had given them our name.

At the bottom of the card, written in small, succinct letters, it said, "Although the sea gets rough, no storm lasts forever."

All those thousands of emotions came flooding back.

I was suddenly ashamed of being ashamed.

I finally understood.

~Sharon Palmerton Grumbein

Chapter
**4**

# Merry Christmas!

## A Different Kind of Christmas

# Yuletide in Florida

*There's nothing that makes you more insane than*
*family. Or more happy. Or more exasperated.*
*Or more... secure.*
*~Jim Butcher*

'Twas the week before Christmas, and at JFK
My sisters and I flew off to Del Ray.
We've traveled each year since two thousand and one
To visit our aunt and sit in her sun.

We tell her each time "We want nothing to do
But sit by the pool and hang out with you."
And yet on arrival, agenda in hand,
Our aunt told us all of the fun she had planned.

Monday we visited her friends to play cards,
Their condo was gated, the entrance had guards.
They're serious players, we anted up nickels
They served us egg salad on rye with some pickles.

On Tuesday a bird walk where we saw a flamingo,
On Wednesday a free film, On Thursday, yes! Bingo!
But Friday's the night that my aunt liked the most
A party for forty where she starred as the host.

She hired some helpers who knew what to do,
The house looked like Christmas when they were all through.
And what to our wondering eyes did appear,
But a wet bar set up with wine, scotch and beer.

The hors d'oeuvres were plated and the room was all set,
Guests were arriving, all people we've met.
The Kellys, the Weinsteins, the Dailys, of course,
And Patty, the neighbor, who just got divorced.

Then Morris, who had to replace his left knee
Topped by Henry who just replaced hip number three.
Enter Myrna and Hilda and Rosie and Gwen,
There seemed to be far more women than men.

The men had on shorts and a Polo or Tee,
But the ladies were dressed as if diamonds were free.
Their eyes how they twinkled, 'tis Botox for many,
While others had crow's feet and wrinkles aplenty.

The bedroom TV was playing the game,
So we lost half the men, which was kind of a shame.
But there was a piano and this guy, Tommy Farrell,
He played all night long and taught us to carol.

There were cheese balls and salsa and hummus and dips,
Scallops surrounded by sweet bacon strips.
Chicken piccata, roast beef au jus,
Cheesecake and cookies and tiramisu.

Strawberry daiquiris and wine, white and red,
Went into my stomach and straight to my head.
By now the clock said it was way past eleven,
Going to bed became my kind of heaven.

Those octogenarians sure knew how to party!
I started to dance with this old guy named Marty.
He cha-cha'd away as the music grew loud
While I quietly slipped away from the crowd.

In all it was such a successful affair,
But as I fell asleep I whispered this prayer:
Auntie, at eighty you're still pretty cool,
But next year can't we sit by the pool?

~Eileen Melia Hession

# An Unforgettable Christmas Eve

*Gratitude is the music of the heart, when its chords are
swept by the breeze of kindness.*
~Author Unknown

I stared out the front window of our home. How would I survive Christmas without my family and friends?

My husband had transferred with his Highway Patrol job and we had moved to Eagar, Arizona, a town of only 5,000 people, from bustling Scottsdale. We had left the dry desert for the towering pine trees, meadows, brooks, and lakes that surrounded our new home. And now there was snow in the forecast!

I missed Scottsdale, which glittered with Christmas lights and decorations by November each year. The stores were busy and packed with gifts, bells tinkled on street corners, and churches were putting on special programs. Christmas was in the air. Year after year I expected and looked forward to these things.

This year, however, in my new small town, I quietly decorated a fake tree, shopped in the one store in town, a kind of "five and dime store," and tried to get used to the bitter cold and the absence of our friends and family.

My daughter, Lindsey, on the other hand was excited. She hounded me. "When is it going to snow?" She wanted to play in the piles of snow that forecasters assured us would arrive in time for Christmas.

We lit the pellet stove and snuggled together on the couch. Christmas carols played on the radio. We resigned ourselves to a quiet Christmas Eve; just the three of us along with the Golden Retriever and Saint Bernard dogs that lay curled at our feet.

When the doorbell rang, I hoped to open the door to the sound of carolers, something I always loved when we lived in Scottsdale. Wendell, the only neighbor we knew so far, stood at the door. His smile reached the corners of his eyes. "Hey, we just wondered if you, your hubby and your little girl would like to join us in our traditional Christmas Eve hayride.

Caught off guard, I stammered. "Uh, uh, well, I guess so. Yes."

I turned and looked into Ray's wide-eyed expression. He stood behind me nodding his head up and down. Lindsey jumped around like a kangaroo. "Can we? Can we go, Mom? Please." We dressed quickly in warm clothing and joined Wendell on the porch. We piled in his car and he took us down a narrow dirt road and stopped in front of a roaring bonfire. Twenty or more neighbors surrounded its blaze. A horse-drawn wagon stood off to the side, already filled with laughing children, teens and adults.

Total strangers hugged us; men slapped Ray heartily on his back and shook his hand. A group of young people handed out cups of hot chocolate and warm donuts. The sky seemed bigger and the stars shone brighter than I'd ever remembered. A group of teens strummed "Silent Night" on their guitars and a flutist trilled alongside them.

My tears of joy fell softly on my cheeks. Children surrounded Lindsey. They grabbed her hands and pulled her into their game to play. Before long she roasted her first marshmallow on a straightened wire clothes hanger and enjoyed her first s'more.

"All aboard," someone shouted. We squished shoulder-to-shoulder onto the hay wagon. The fresh scent of newly cut hay was in the air. The driver, a burly cowboy type with his giant hat pulled down over his ears, hollered "On Donner!" He snapped a long whip and we lurched ahead.

We arrived to a scene that took my breath away. A lit stable with a live nativity brought my trickle of tears to a flood. Three young ladies played violins with precision. "Oh Come All Ye Faithful" penetrated the still night. Baby Jesus cooed in the arms of a young Mary. A deep voice flowed from behind the enclosure that represented the manger. "And to this night, a babe is born. He will be called Jesus."

I knew right then that God had placed us right where he wanted us for this season in our lives. Yes, we missed the family and friends that we left behind for this new adventure, but right here, this night, these people were a promise of new friendships, new beginnings and memories that could last a lifetime. I knew that Christmas Eve in Eagar, Arizona presented a new truth to me. Good things can come through change and trial.

I've never forgotten that Christmas. Most of our families are close by once again and we make new traditions as the years go on, but that one Christmas Eve instilled forever in me the belief that change is always accompanied by new blessings as long as we are open to them.

~Alice Klies

# Our Home for the Holidays

*The purpose of all major religious traditions is not
to construct big temples on the outside, but to create
temples of goodness and compassion inside,
in our hearts.*
~Tenzin Gyatso, 14th Dalai Lama

Some years, explaining the differences between the holidays is a struggle. After all, Christmas is Christmas. It's everywhere. Where wouldn't it be, right? It's fun, it's beautiful, and it's festive.

It's the stuffed snowman that sits in a small flower-pot-like container atop my unread and unclipped magazines. It's the shiny one over my left shoulder, hanging next to the bright and shiny Star of David. And my other shoulder? Over to my right? Our tree. Our beautiful Christmas tree in all of its glory.

It's gorgeous. I mean, it really is. A beautiful, breathtaking tree that my husband decorated in blue and white lights for me.

We've avoided an abundance of ornaments. I like it simple, with candy canes strewn about and a few ornaments. One ornament is a snowman. I love snowmen. Always have, probably because they connote holiday cheer without naming a specific holiday. The second ornament? A Yankees hot air balloon that my Jewish mother bought my not-Jewish-Yankee-fan husband many years ago. And the third ornament? A star of David. Yep. On the Christmas tree.

A handprint menorah hangs beneath a handcrafted Santa Claus. The tiniest of Christmas trees sits atop our Hanukkah tablecloth at the kitchen table. It's decorated more intensely than anything you've ever seen.

Our house couldn't be more balanced.

My heart is trying. My husband doesn't mind either way. Supporting me. My methods. Goals. Whatever it is we plan for our little Jewish Southern girl.

She learns slowly what Hanukkah represents. We read books, sing songs, dance around the living room with garland and tinsel flying everywhere.

She knows, happily, that Santa comes on Christmas. And she states that she knows that not everyone sees him. She's gone so far as to say that maybe she wouldn't see him this year. But we'd take the dogs to see their Santa. Of course.

How beautiful, caring, sweet.

She sings Christmas songs and seasonal songs she's learned at school. But she knows the words to the blessings we share over eight nights. "Nine," she says, pointing to the ninth candle. I explain gently, with a reminder of what that tallest candle is for.

The other night she put her Hanukkah presents beneath the Christmas tree. Maybe it's actually easier when the holidays are together. Maybe it's not? I'm not sure. One year I thought it was better. The next, maybe not so much?

She's so young. Easily confused. Am I supposed to have taught her all of my religious beliefs yet? Or is it enough to explain that I am Jewish, her daddy is not, and she is. And she's also both, but we don't get into the particulars. We celebrate. We observe. I talk about my memories. We Skype with my family. The whole family is there. Blessings stream over telephone wires. There are speakerphones and cellphones and three-way-calling and more. Technology brings us together and we laugh as our chorus of words jumble and overlap from 500 miles away.

It's confusing. But I wouldn't change it for the world.

~Andrea Bates

# Christmas Afloat

*I can't control the wind but I can adjust the sail.*
*~Ricky Skaggs*

I spent the first Christmas of the 2000 millennium afloat on my sailboat in Beaufort, North Carolina with my husband Tom and our Cairn Terrier, Chip. Our New Jersey house had sold within days of being listed the previous spring. In the whirlwind of moving from house to boat and with the limited space in our floating home, the only thought I gave to Christmas was to pack a small plastic container with unbreakable tree ornaments to take with us. The other ornaments were either sold or given away. I could not have a tree on the boat, but I could decorate the cabin.

Now with the holiday weeks away, I found myself far from family and in a town where I knew no one. The few people I did meet would gradually leave town to spend the holiday with relatives. I craved some Christmas on the boat. I eagerly unpacked my decorations and hung them one by one in front of the portholes: a plastic candy cane, a tiny metal stocking with gifts poking out of the top, a wooden rowboat, a brass tree, a stuffed green-fabric Terrier, and a miniature hobby-horse with a red fabric head, a white yarn mane, and a candy cane–striped pole. Compared to the way I used to decorate my house, the result was pathetic — forlorn orphaned ornaments in a barren landscape.

Then I remembered seeing a notice asking for volunteers to help decorate the marina for Christmas. On the designated morning, I met three other women on the dock and received a red and white fleece

Christmas hat, complete with pom-pom. Our hats made us official elves, and we spent the rest of the morning attaching red bows and live garland to the railing along the marina boardwalk. Outside the dock master's office, other locals decorated a tall tree next to the temporary small house where Santa would hold court for children every Saturday afternoon until Christmas. At least I now had Christmas outside, if not inside, the boat.

As Christmas cards arrived, I tucked them in various places like the wooden louvers on cabinet doors and over the handrails above. I purchased small red bows and tied one by each porthole. I knew the bows could squeeze inside my ornament box after the holiday. Then two Christmas gift baskets arrived — one with fruits and cheeses from my cousin and another with snacks and teas from Tom's brother. My boat décor transformed from pathetic to festive as holiday traditions adapted to life on the water.

A Christmas tradition in many waterfront towns is the flotilla — a parade of boats decorated for Christmas. Often competing for prizes, boaters use generators to power the light displays and sometimes add music. Never having seen a Christmas flotilla, Tom and I eagerly anticipated the parade.

The night of the event, locals and tourists crowded the marina boardwalk to see the show. Like others with boats at the docks, I enjoyed a "front row" seat at the end of my pier.

"Here they come!" someone shouted.

Not wanting to miss a minute of it, I leaned out to watch the parade come up the creek until it finally reached my pier. Timed lights on one boat mimicked animated dolphins leaping from stern to bow. Lights depicting a giant palm tree with live hula dancers below floated by to Jimmy Buffett's tune, "How'd you like to spend Christmas on Christmas Island?" Fortunately for the dancers, the night was warm. Another boat sported a team of reindeer outlined in lights with red-nosed Rudolph in the lead pulling a sleigh with a live Santa ho-ho-ho-ing. I heard "Hark the Herald Angels Sing" as the outline of a giant angel appeared. A total of fifteen boats, each with a different theme, paraded by to applause and shouts of appreciation from the onlookers.

The flotilla inspired the rest of us to decorate our vessels. Every evening when I walked Chip I scanned the marina to see what was new. Most people used simple lights outlining hulls or sails at night, but I wanted something visible during the day. I hung large red bows along the side of our boat facing land, on the anchor at the front, and on the stern. I wound newly purchased silver garland around the boat's lifelines. The marina became a floating Christmas village.

Christmas morning appeared warm and sunny, but the temperature was only in the twenties, unusually cold for December in North Carolina. After a special Christmas breakfast of cheese omelets shared with Terrier Chip, plus mimosas, homemade oatmeal-raisin muffins, and fresh-brewed coffee for Tom and me, the outside thermometer read thirty degrees. We bundled up and headed to the beach with Chip.

Walking onto the bare winter sand, I raised my collar against the unwelcome wind and tried to imagine the sand as snow. Looking up and down the strand, I realized we were the only ones there. Chip would have an extra Christmas gift — a rare chance to romp off-leash. When I unclipped his leash, he just stood there staring at me.

"Run, Chip," I said. Tom and I started up the beach ahead of him.

Not about to be outdone by his humans, Chip soon overtook Tom and me, then circled back. A wind-blown mass of brown fur streaked past Tom's feet, came around behind, and overtook us again. Out of breath, Tom and I gave up the race. When my panting Terrier returned to my feet, I picked him up for a group hug. Sand clung to his muzzle, framing a big doggie grin. I couldn't help but grin back and think a Christmas morning beach walk would make a fine new tradition for a family afloat.

~Janet Hartman

# A Diversity of Holiday Traditions

*We may have different religions, different languages,*
*different colored skin, but we all belong to*
*one human race.*
*~Kofi Annan*

Eight beautifully wrapped gifts, each labeled "Lisa," sparkled and glittered where they lay on the red bricks of our living room fireplace. The Hanukkah gifts, sent from New York by Grandma Sylvia, rested just beneath the Christmas stockings and a little bit over from the Christmas tree. My eyes shone as I eagerly anticipated both holidays.

My mom was from a Midwest Protestant family, my dad from a family of New York Jews. With such a merging of diverse cultures and influences, we managed to develop and maintain more than the usual number of family holiday traditions — including multiple gift exchanges, lighting the menorah, visits from Santa, playing dreidel games, singing Christmas carols, preparing many delicious meals, crafting holiday projects, putting up a plethora of decorations, and hosting various family parties and social gatherings.

When I married a man, who'd been raised Catholic, in Panama, by an American father of Polish descent and a bilingual, Spanish-English speaking, Panamanian mother — well, let's just say that things got even more complicated. Our wedding ceremony, for example, was a mishmash of religions, languages, ethnicities, nationalities and cultures. All this combined to enhance our relationship and we embraced the diversity — much as I imagine both sets of our parents had also done with each other, a generation earlier. In time, we started our family and began to build our own family traditions with our two boys.

Since both of our extended families are geographically scattered, it makes it difficult to say what we "usually" do for the holiday season. Some years, we travel to spend holidays with my husband's family, and others with mine. Some years, we just stay home on our own. Other years, his family joins us, and others, mine do. Despite the fact that every year is different, we — my husband, our two boys, and myself — have managed to develop quite a number of our own family holiday traditions.

When we do stay home, things are pretty "standard."

Each year, to commemorate the eight nights of Hanukkah, we light the candles on our menorah. We play dreidel games, eat beloved gelt (chocolate coins) and make delicious latkes. Grandma Sylvia is now gone, but I always give each of my precious boys eight gifts.

Each year, to celebrate Christmas, we hang stockings for Santa and decorate a Christmas tree. We make chocolate chip pancakes or waffles for breakfast on Christmas morning, and then enjoy exchanging gifts. The boys play with their new goodies, we lounge around in our pajamas most of the day and eventually cook a big dinner — usually a turkey, sweet potatoes, and vegetables — along with Mom's mouthwatering corn-pudding dish and chocolate silk pie, both recipes passed down from the Midwestern side of my family.

A couple of years ago, when Thanksgiving and the first night of Hanukkah coincided on "Thanksgivukkah" we found ourselves cooking latkes, shopping for Christmas gifts online, and putting together a Thanksgiving feast — all on the same day. It was a bit confusing, but it was also good, meaningful, family fun. My husband flipped the latkes while musing, "How did a Catholic boy from Panama end up making latkes on Thanksgiving Day?"

When we travel for the holidays, things get even more interesting. Last year, we visited my husband's extended family in Panama, eating *platanos* and *arroz con pollo* while enjoying traditional neighborhood fireworks displays at midnight on Christmas Eve as we called out, "*Feliz Navidad!*" to the crowds and partied in the streets. Afterward, in the very wee hours of the morning, we exchanged gifts before we went to sleep, exhausted but happy.

Also, not having wanted to abandon any of our "standard" home-holiday activities because of travel plans, we opted to celebrate "Pawlakmas" before we flew to Panama. This new holiday, involving the usual number of pancakes, presents and pajamas — fell right in the middle of Hanukkah and just a few days before Christmas.

Perhaps the best way to explain our family's holiday traditions is simply to say that we embrace a spirit of adventure, along with the richness of our family's cultural diversity and absolute certainty of our underlying love for each other. So wherever we happen to be, with whomever else we are fortunate enough to be with — we are always able to experience and treasure the warmth of the holiday season.

~Lisa Pawlak

# 36

# A Borrowed Christmas

*Every house where love abides and friendship is a*
*guest, is surely home, and home, sweet home for*
*there the heart can rest.*
~Henry van Dyke

Due to my husband being out of work our little family had been living with friends for a few months. At the time, our son Max wasn't quite two. As the holiday season approached I found myself growing anxious. What would Christmas be like in someone else's home? The couple we were living with had grown children who would be visiting during the season. Would we be in the way?

I couldn't help feeling a little sad. Everything in our lives felt borrowed. It wasn't easy to be a family in need, relying on the kindness of others to make it through. I feared being a burden. Especially at Christmas.

I soon found I needn't have worried. We were warmly included in their large Thanksgiving celebration, becoming an extension of their family. In the following days our friends naturally included us in Christmas planning. Rarely had I felt more welcomed into someone's life.

One night in early December the talk over dinner was about getting a Christmas tree. Our hostess asked if I wanted to put some of our decorations on the tree. The offer touched my heart. The next day I rummaged through our boxes looking for our family Christmas ornaments.

A couple of days later we set up the tree. Snow blanketed the little white cottage in the woods, and a fire crackled in the stone fireplace, giving us a cozy, tucked in feeling. Christmas music played as we decorated. I brought my little box of ornaments out to add to the tree.

Sitting on the floor with my toddler I handed him our decorations to hang on the fragrant branches. But Max didn't stop with our ornaments; he went between our family's box and our friend's box of decorations, hanging ornaments without discrimination. His happy chatter and enthusiastic admiration of the Christmas finery lightened our hearts.

As I watched the tree fill up with two families' Christmas memories I realized what I thought was an unfortunate circumstance was really quite the opposite. Christmas had taken on a new meaning. The gift of love we celebrate at Christmastime became a tangible reality to my little family that year. Our need was met with kind generosity. Max's life was enriched by more love than we could have imagined.

On Christmas Day I understood in a new way why a "weary world rejoices." Our need sets the stage for receiving great gifts.

~Beck Gambill

# 37

# The Twig Tree

*When you look at your life, the greatest happinesses*
*are family happinesses.*
*~Dr. Joyce Brothers*

I looked at the big living room of the cabin we had rented. It was two weeks before Christmas and I had flown up to Wisconsin to be with my sons, grandsons, and new great-grandchild. My brother and his kids joined us. We were a rambunctious group of sixteen and were no strangers to celebrating Christmas on whatever weekend we could in December.

But this year we had forgotten the tree.

My two teenage grandsons ran to the cabin door dressed in heavy jackets, mittens and woolen hats. "We'll be back," they said.

Ten minutes later they reappeared. They stomped their feet to shake the snow off their boots and threw off their heavy clothes.

"Look what we found, Grandma," Colton exclaimed. "A Christmas tree!"

They dragged in something brown and lifeless. A large, dried up tree limb with stick arms branching out in many directions.

"Oh, my," I exclaimed with a grin.

Colton's cousin Brandon rummaged in the kitchen cupboard and found a tall plastic pitcher. They put a little water in the bottom and then stuck the dead limb in and propped it up against the wall next to the fireplace to keep it from falling over.

My brother Peter walked into the room. "Good job. What about ornaments?"

"I've got one," grandson Nick claimed. He took his empty soda can, pulled up the tab, and hung the can on a small nub on a branch of the tree.

"That's pretty good," Peter declared and laughed.

I laughed too. It was a Charlie Brown tree if I ever saw one. And what could be better than a stick tree for Christmas?

The first soda can was a root beer can in a rich brown and white. The next one added was green and yellow from a flavor of Mountain Dew. Then there were the red and white Coke cans, and the blue, red and white Pepsi cans.

That weekend we sat around the kitchen counter and watched as granddaughter Kaitlyn tried her hand at making pancakes for the very first time.

"I don't know if they're brown yet and ready to flip." She peeked under another one. "Am I doing this right?"

"Just right," we all sang out. "Hurry up, we're hungry."

Someone else browned two pounds of sizzling bacon and added that to the family breakfast table. The smell of scrambled eggs, bacon and pancakes brought the last of the sleepy heads to the kitchen. Later that day, we frosted and decorated sugar cookies, with the children choosing the colors they wanted and sprinkling the colored sugars over the top of the frosting. Plate after plate of cookies was gobbled up in no time.

The tree twinkled in the light of the fireplace as we opened our gifts the second night, the shimmering light of the flames dancing off the brightly colored cans.

Curled up on the sofa with my legs tucked under me, I watched my grown sons gather up the wrapping paper torn off the presents. "Perfect," I whispered, and thought no one heard me. But my brother did.

"What's perfect?" he said.

I looked at the whole family — so full of life, of laughter, of ingenious creativity. "Everything. And especially the twig tree."

Peter laughed. "It is pretty cool. Who would have thought we could make something so special out of what was on the ground behind the cabin?"

Just then another child delicately hung a bright orange can on the tree. It dangled from the pull top tab, bent the branch and dipped low. He watched it settle into just the right spot.

I was filled to the brim with love for all of my family, and thankful that I could fly up to Wisconsin and we could all be together.

That twig tree became the focal point that year. There has been no other tree like it. Sometimes memories aren't planned. They just happen. We had gathered to share Christmas and our love for one another and we made a memory that would last a lifetime.

~B.J. Taylor

# 38

# Confession of a Christmas Cruiser

*I'd rather regret the things I've done than the
things I haven't done.*
*~Lucille Ball*

Who skips out on Christmas? The Kranks tried it in both a novel and a movie but didn't succeed. So what made us think we could? And why would we?

All of the five Robbins kids had left the nest. They were scattered across the country, making it next to impossible to visit all of them at the holidays and a bit expensive for them to travel back home with their children. Bob and I truly didn't want to intrude on their family celebrations either. We remembered how much fun it was to celebrate on our own with them when they were little. Facing a Christmas with an empty house did not inspire a lot of Christmas decorating or cookie baking spirit. What to do?

The cruise brochure arrived just in time, filled with dreamy pictures of beautiful Tahiti and the French Polynesian islands. We sat at the kitchen table sipping coffee and watching the last of the autumn leaves swirl past the window. It wouldn't be long before the snowflakes fell. The brochure sat between us, already dog-eared and wrinkled from our perusal. A big grin spread across Bob's face.

"Let's give each other a cruise for Christmas!"

It didn't take long to sell me on the idea. But questions still arose.

Would we mind being away from home for Christmas? Would we miss not having a white Christmas? What would the kids say? We moved ahead with the idea anyway and made our reservations.

The ship was the Paul Gauguin, a beautiful elegant mid-sized cruise ship. We were welcomed aboard to a venue decorated with Christmas trees, gingerbread houses, and nooks and crannies filled with all the traditional decorations of the season. It was a ten-day cruise and Christmas fell in the middle of it. Bob decorated our mirrored vanity with a string of mini-lights and stuck a Santa hat on the small decorative bust that was in our room. I think our cabin steward giggled every time she saw it.

Christmas Eve we caroled and Christmas morning we awoke to another gorgeous view of luscious tropical greens draping the hills and mountains of Raiatea. In preparing for our trip, I had packed a couple of small Christmas stockings and some candy. Playing Santa's helper, I filled them and gave two to our cabin steward as she began her morning chores.

"One is for you," I said, "and one is for you to give to a friend."

Her eyes lit up and she clutched them to her chest as she ran down the hall hailing her friend in her own language to give her the second stocking. I didn't realize such a small gesture would be so welcomed.

After breakfast, we went on an excursion through the countryside. I was impressed that the driver of our open-sided truck had given up her Christmas morning to show us her beautiful island. Even more impressive was the young boy who quietly played with his Christmas present, a new truck, on the front seat next to his mother.

At noon we were tendered over to a private beach where there were picnic tables, a large barbecue pit, and plenty of beach chairs. Our Christmas dinner consisted of grilled lobster, steak, chicken, tropical fruits, and lots of delicious side dishes. I don't recall missing the usual pork roast with sauerkraut and dumplings that was a tradition at home for so many years.

After our dinner, we were treated to a visit from Santa. I'm sure he must have come to begin his vacation after his long night out delivering his presents. You see, he was dressed in a short-sleeved fur-trimmed red shirt, Santa cap, red shorts and flip-flops. He ho-ho-hoed his way down the beach and greeted all the passengers, gave a little extra treat to the children he met, and then disappeared to begin a long deserved rest.

Did we miss Christmas at home? Not in the least. As a matter of fact we enjoyed our time away so much that we have made it part of a new tradition. Every other year our kids know that we will be off cruising somewhere warm. They don't have to worry about Mom and Dad being alone at Christmas and we don't have all the work associated with the holiday season. I must confess, I love it.

~Karen Robbins

# 39

# Chicken Soup for the Soul

# The Gift of Song

*Blessed is the season which engages the whole world*
*in a conspiracy of love.*
*~Hamilton Wright Mabie*

Christmas at Mémère's house was always an event to look forward to, and not because of the presents. Since my dad's family was so big, we had decided at one point when I was little that there would not be a big gift exchange. The best gifts were my grandmother's stuffing, a fine breaded delicacy, and the aroma of cooked ham, squash, mashed potatoes, and cranberry sauce filling the house. Apple pie and endless treats always followed, no matter how full our bellies.

In the living room, the tree sat in the corner adorned with lights and ornaments of all kinds. The nativity scene always sat before the window, peacefully looking out to the greenhouse. The best part? My aunt's hands moving across the piano, the living room alive with singing and dancing. There was something about the whole family gathering for a sing-along of Christmas carols and French-Canadian songs that completed the day. This was Christmas.

But this year would be different. This Christmas, my grandmother was in the hospital with pneumonia.

This year, we ate dinner just the four of us — my mom, dad, sister Renée and I. This year, we would still get to see Mémère, but it would only be for a short hospital visit.

"What about carols?" I asked my mom.

"No carols this year," she said. "Guess we'll just have to wait 'til next year."

I couldn't help but feel disappointed. It would be nice to see my family, but seeing my grandmother in the hospital did not really put me in the Christmas mood.

When we arrived, we stood in a half circle around Mémère. She seemed to be in good spirits as she sat propped up in her hospital bed. Between my aunts, uncles, cousins, and immediate family, there were probably more than twenty of us gathered around. The hospital was certainly not Mémère's house — there were no lights or decorations, no aroma of delicious cooking, no Christmas tree or piano, but suddenly, this Christmas began to change. Our family's love filled the small room, and so too did their gift of song.

Auntie Rachel started to sing, and then Auntie Gena and Corinne chimed in, along with Joanne and Annette. My Uncle Paul sang alongside my Uncle John, accompanied by my cousin Holly, her voice sweet and soothing. Softly, I joined in too. I had always been somewhat afraid of singing aloud, hearing my own voice, but something about my family's music that night gave me confidence.

The carols did not end there. Slowly, we made our way out into the corridor, our melody drifting through the hallway. We visited other patients. As we sang, it was as if the void of spending the holiday in the hospital disappeared. The woes, disappointment, and sadness fell away, and Christmas was saved. In this moment, everything was well.

I later learned that many years ago Mémère had led my aunts and uncles in a similar fashion around nursing homes, churches, and civic centers, just like this, sharing their gift of song. Now, with my grandmother in her hospital bed, the Soucy Family Singers were at it again.

I will never forget that Christmas. Not only did it remind me how thankful I am for my family, but also how important it is to bring joy to others — making this day one of the best experiences I ever could have asked for. A true gift.

~Danielle Soucy Mills

# Christmas Presence

*Besides the noble art of getting things done, there is the
noble art of leaving things undone. The wisdom of life
consists in the elimination of non-essentials.*
~Lin Yutang

It was 4:30 on Christmas Eve and we had no presents, no decorations, and no food for a proper Christmas dinner. It was the best Christmas ever.

Until that particular year in my early forties, all my adult life I worked hard at "doing" Christmas. Weeks of planning, baking, shopping, crafting, and decorating. Christmas music was the soundtrack to my Decembers, because that's what I remembered. I wanted desperately to recreate the magic of my childhood.

To be honest, I never succeeded. No matter how lovely the decorations, how scrumptious the treats, how perfect the gifts, the magic never arrived.

This time, I couldn't do it. I was overwhelmed by my graduate studies. It was a busy time of year at work for my husband, too. We had little money to spare and our families were a thousand miles away. By that late afternoon, I was exhausted, blinking back tears at the prospect of having no Christmas at all, when my husband said, "We're in New York. It's Christmas Eve. Let's go see what the city is doing."

We took a crosstown bus to Fifth Avenue and then walked the avenue south from Central Park. I was astonished at the crowds and the cameras. We must be extras in dozens of home videos of people all over the world. The store windows dazzled. The scent of sweet roasting nuts from street vendors' carts spiced the frigid air, and it was lightly snowing. We played like children with the toys at FAO Schwarz. At Rockefeller Center, trumpeting angels made of white lights guided the way to the iconic Christmas tree. Carols played for the ice skaters below. We sang along out loud.

These classic Christmas scenes cheered me, but they were not what made that Christmas so special. It was the unexpected things.

Who would have expected a bongo-playing busker in Times Square on Christmas Eve? Or the two rotund elves who turned a doughnut shop, where we took refuge from the freezing weather, into a party?

We decided to get turkey sandwiches as our "Christmas dinner." Through the pass-through window into the kitchen I could see the older gentleman who was preparing them. It made me grateful that at least I didn't have to work on Christmas Eve. I wanted to cheer him, so I got his attention. "Merry Christmas!" I said, smiled and waved to him. He came out to where we were sitting, shook our hands and wished us the same with great enthusiasm. I've never seen sandwiches so enormous. My cheeks hurt from chewing.

By ten o'clock we had walked all the way down to Chelsea and across to Ninth Avenue, to a church we had recently discovered. As we entered I inhaled the familiar resin scents of pine and balsam fir. I let the gentle candlelight and the music of the string quartet soothe me. The sermon? "No one is ever ready for Christmas. Grace comes when we let our expectations go, and allow ourselves to be present to the moment. That's how the wonder gets in."

The moment the service ended, people brought out tables and loaded them with a feast. There was lamb stew, ham, roast beef, salads, sweet potatoes and noodle kugel. For dessert there were brownies, cakes, doughnuts, and of course, cookies. It was an extension of the everyday mission of this congregation, which hosts New York's largest soup kitchen each weekday. They knew that not everyone has a Christmas dinner to go home to. Still stuffed with sandwiches, we could only nibble at the delicious bounty.

If we had known this was going to happen, we probably wouldn't have eaten an earlier meal. But then, we would have missed that moment of human warmth with the cook. So all was well.

I still "do" Christmas. I'll bake the special Swedish Christmas bread my mother-in-law used to make, and maybe a couple of batches of cookies. If we're not travelling to see family I'll decorate a little around the house; for several years this meant hauling in a scruffy pine tree from our field. I keep gift giving deliberately simple. I do what I can enjoy rather than trying to live up to some ideal of perfection. I try to stay open to the unexpected, the opportunities to share a moment, especially with those who might be lonely or hungry or lost.

Because, to this day, I remember a man with a megaphone who stood on a New York street corner that cold Christmas Eve, challenging harried and mostly oblivious shoppers with the words, "Go home! Your children need your presence, not your presents!"

Our eyes met, and from that moment Christmas became magical again.

~Nancie Erhard

**Chapter 5**

# Merry Christmas!

## Christmas Spirit Is Alive and Well

**41**

# Finding Christmas in Tokyo

*Christmas waves a magic wand over this world, and*
*behold, everything is softer and more beautiful.*
*~Norman Vincent Peale*

I stood outside the supermarket pretending to look for something in my bicycle basket. The other shoppers who came and went from the popular little grocery store next to the station in my Tokyo suburb pretended not to notice the tall, curly-haired foreign woman who was crying.

I was running a few errands on Christmas Eve, which was exactly the problem. I was in Japan, where Christmas is more akin to Valentine's Day, an evening of romance, where cake with white frosting topped with strawberries (not in season) is served right after the fried chicken.

I scowled. Christmas isn't fried chicken and strawberry cake. It's cookies and ham, turkey and fruitcake, eggnog and homemade Chex mix. It's my mother's house and my annoying nieces and nephews. It's my husband Richard's grandmother's dining room and the annual family talent show. It's snow and bitter cold and navigating icy driveways in high heels. It's Christmas specials and carols and shopping for presents. That's Christmas.

Back home, I got a text from Richard saying he was going to the gym. That was at 4 p.m. Keiko, my Japanese tutor, had invited us for 5:30 p.m. So now we would be late. "Typical," I harrumphed.

*Christmas Spirit Is Alive and Well* | 135

"Santa's helper had some shopping to do," Richard said coyly when he arrived. "That's why I was late."

"Santa's helper should have planned ahead," I thought, but said nothing.

We boarded the train for Keiko's in silence. I was angry that he was late, and he was angry because I was angry for no apparent reason. "She said between 5:30 and 6:00," he reminded me.

"*Dozo, dozo!* (Come in, come in!)," cried Keiko from somewhere deep inside the house. We let ourselves in just as she arrived to greet us. She beamed when I introduced Richard, and then opened her arms wide and stepped forward to hug him. I was astonished at how utterly perfect and natural it seemed.

The invitation to dinner and the Christmas service all came about when I had spotted a flyer on Keiko's table a few weeks before. It had been five years since we moved to Japan and been home for the holidays. I jumped at the chance to see what Christmas in a Japanese church might be like.

Shortly before 7 p.m. we left the apartment with Keiko and her husband, Masa. A few minutes later we turned onto a small street where a Christmas tree glowed.

"Here's the church," said Masa as we arrived. The windows were dark, but the doors were open, and children in white robes mingled by a reception table where we each received a candle: a thin white taper with a carefully fashioned aluminum foil candle ring. I remembered these, along with the smell of musty hymnbooks, from my childhood, and I grinned, already feeling better. Two more steps and we entered the sanctuary, lit only by a few candles on the altar and the Advent Wreath where four bright red candles burned around a single white Christmas candle.

Masa led us to a pew in front. The tiny church held fewer than 100 people, its interior packed with pews, a small wooden altar, a baptismal font, and an organ. The choir, about fifteen people in white robes, crammed in behind it. We immediately began wrestling off coats, scarves and hats in the overheated space, another familiar holiday ritual.

Shortly after we sat down, the music began. As the children came forward in pairs to light their candles from those on the altar and then turned to light ours, a lump rose in my throat. A member of the congregation seated near the front walked to the lectern and began to read. At first I assumed it was a welcome message, but when I heard "*David no machi* (City of David)," it dawned on me that I was hearing The Christmas Story. As the organist played the introduction to the first hymn, "Oh, Come All Ye Faithful," my tears started flowing. So happy to hear this music again after so long, I turned to Richard to make sure he knew, and saw his face wet with tears and felt his hand groping for mine.

It didn't matter that everything was in Japanese or that the congregation was small. I'm not particularly religious, but sitting there I realized that this tradition was such a part of me... my identity and culture. For this moment it was simply peace and joy, a feeling of home when I needed it most. I cried more and smiled and sang the words in a mix of Japanese and English, so happy just to be there, to celebrate. For the first time in a long, long time, it felt like Christmas.

~Joan Bailey

# 42

# The Big Squeeze

*It is the personal thoughtfulness, the warm human*
*awareness, the reaching out of the self to one's fellow*
*man that makes giving worthy of the Christmas spirit.*
*~Isabel Currier*

In 1990, our church congregation was in the process of having a new sanctuary built. We had hoped that it would be finished in time for Christmas. Our membership had more than qua- drupled, and we had to start having three services on Sunday mornings to accommodate everyone. There were many occasions when worshippers would be standing along the walls and seated in the vestibule, especially if we were having a program in the evening or a concert. As it sometimes goes with construction schedules, we were not going to have our building completed in time for our annual Christmas concert.

The night of the concert, my daughters and I arrived early in order to get a seat. The church was already filling up. By 7:00 p.m. the church was packed. There were many people standing when one of the deacons went up to the pulpit. His face was somber.

"Fellow members," he announced. "I regret to tell you that there will be a delay in our Christmas concert tonight. There is a representa- tive from the fire marshal's office here, and, due to fire safety laws, we have been told that all persons standing and/or blocking the doors or aisles must leave or the concert will be cancelled." The groans and moans that went through the church that evening were mingled with the many expressions of disbelief and disappointment. Then strangely, for a moment, everything became very quiet.

I then was a part of, and witness to, what I feel was a most extraordinary demonstration of true Christmas spirit. People started squeezing together in those pews just as tight as they could get. Parents pulled children onto their laps, wives sat on husbands' laps, sisters on brothers' laps, and more and more until everyone who had been standing could squeeze into the already crowded pews. Soon, there was not one person left standing! A round of applause went through our church that night that brought a little tingle to my heart and tears to my eyes.

That fire marshal representative just shook his head in disbelief as he turned and walked out of the church. And somehow, I enjoyed that Christmas concert better than any other.

~Jackie Smith-Thrasher

# 43

# All Aboard the Polar Express

*"Well ya comin'?" asked the conductor. "Where?"*
*replied the boy. "To the North Pole, of course!*
*This is the Polar Express!"*
*~The Conductor, The Polar Express*

I t's five o'clock and I finish off my elf trappings by making my cheeks pink with my lipstick and sticking a candy cane tattoo on each. Mine is not the wackiest elf costume on the block. In fact if you were to rate it with ten being the craziest, mine would probably be a one. But it fits me. After all, as I tell my passengers on the Polar Express, I work in the stables at the North Pole. You can't be fancy when you're shoveling reindeer you-know-what. That always makes the kids giggle.

Bob, my trainman husband, has already donned his uniform. He looks quite handsome in it and the brass buttons we added to the vest and jacket have really set it off. He tops it off with the special hat he's earned with all of his volunteer hours on the Cuyahoga Valley Scenic Railroad.

I grab my large holiday bag and check to be sure I have crayons and the reindeer games I've printed out as well as a roll of paper towels. The towels are for wiping up the hot chocolate drips and spills that might occur in the excitement of visiting the North Pole. They also help to wipe off the windows of the train when they begin to steam up from all the eager little children whose one wish is to see the big guy in red.

Arriving at the train yard, I park my car, say a silent prayer of thanks that it's dark early and no one saw me driving in costume, and scurry off to check in for my assigned car. The Cuyahoga Valley Scenic Railroad becomes The Polar Express for the month between Thanksgiving and Christmas. It is quite a transformation.

I join the other elves in my car and we ready everything for the storytelling, the hot chocolate and cookie partaking, and all the fun and games along the way. It isn't long before our car begins to fill with kids. Their eager voices and spirited Christmas energy are what fuels an elf for the adventure ahead. Along with two assistant elves and an elf in charge of the hot chocolate and cookies, I keep the energetic little ones — and big ones — entertained with reindeer games and jokes as we wait for all to board and be seated. Most, including the adults, are wearing their pajamas. It is quite a flannel sleepwear fashion show.

Our trainman in the car informs us that all are aboard and the conductor has given the signal for the train to begin moving forward to the North Pole. As a storyteller it is my job to get everyone's attention and introduce the other elves before beginning to read the story written by Chris Van Allsburg — *The Polar Express*. During the telling, the assistant elves and trainman add sound effects, illustrations, and lots of cheering.

Meanwhile back in a little cubbyhole, our server elf is pouring hot chocolate into cups, adding lids, and wrapping packaged cookies (straight from Mrs. Claus's oven) with napkins. As soon as the story is finished, they will be handed out.

Between the refreshments and our arrival at the North Pole, we break out in song, but soon the lights in the car begin to dim. It's the signal that we're getting close. All the children are asked to move to one side of the car and the adults to the other as the "Northern Lights" begin to give the landscape a festive glow.

"We're here! The North Pole!" I announce with glee. We pass the hobo warming himself by the fire and then we see them — the North Pole elves! They are surrounded by thousands of Christmas lights and displays. There's Frosty and the Gingerbread Man and Rudolph (who said he could stay up late?) and Mr. and Mrs. Jack Frost with their dog, Snowflake! We pass the train cars that are holding all the gifts that Santa will deliver on Christmas Eve. As the train pulls through so that all the cars get a view, I point out the Winking Lizard, the watering hole for the North Pole elves.

We stop and wait a few minutes and sure enough, there's Santa! His sleigh is being pulled by a smaller version of the Polar Express and next to him sits Mrs. Claus. Is that a little flour on her nose from all her baking?

It is at this point that all the hours of volunteering become worth it. There is nothing so special as the faces of little ones who are magically transported to the North Pole. Faces pressed against the windows are softly lit by the glow of the Christmas lights. I get to relive my own wonder as a child at all that was magical about the season. But our adventure isn't over yet.

As the Polar Express pulls away from the North Pole there is a distant jingle of bells. The lights in our train car shine brightly now and everyone has returned to their seats. We sing "Santa Claus Is Coming to Town" and suddenly the door to our train car opens and there he is himself — the man in the red suit trimmed in white and ho-ho-ho-ing as he is welcomed with squeals of delight.

Santa makes his way through the car, stopping to hear the wishes of all the little ones. As he greets each child, I hand him a sleigh bell and soon the whole train car is alive with jingle bells. The car is full of believers, since only a believer can hear the bells jingle.

Upon Santa's departure, we of course must sing a chorus or two of "Jingle Bells." Then it is on to "The Funky Chicken," "The Twelve Days of Christmas," and other popular requests. Some nights there is even a fashion show of pajama ensembles.

Little ones and some big ones begin to fade and eyelids flutter on the ride home. As we pull into the station, coats are gathered, little ones hoisted in arms, and thank-you's ring out all around.

When the last passenger has left, elves get busy cleaning up the train car for the next night's run. It's been a great night as always and the memories will last a lifetime for the children. The memories for the volunteer elves will last a lifetime as well.

~Karen Robbins

# 44

# Santa's Secret GPS

*They err who think Santa Claus enters through the
chimney. He enters through the heart.*
*~Charles W. Howard*

"How will Santa ever find me?" I leaned the tip of my nose against the cold pane of glass as I watched the lacy snowflakes dancing in the wind. I felt heartbroken.

In September, my parents had split, and now I was living with my mother and brother in an apartment building. The house we once lived in as a family was an old brick two-story with a fat chimney on the roof and a fireplace in the living room. It was the perfect accommodation for Santa.

However, not only had I forgotten to include my new return address when I'd written my annual Christmas letter and wish list to jolly Saint Nick, I'd also completely overlooked the fact that there was no chimney on top of our four-floor apartment building. Instead there were several tall TV antennae on the roof. Their presence made me pray Rudolph would be able to keep the sleigh and reindeer flying high enough through the sky to avoid getting caught up in them.

With a heavy heart, I pressed another Christmas stencil to the glass and carefully sprayed the artificial snow between the lines to create the image of a sled. Now my window was complete with a tree, a star, a bell and a sled. But when I went to bed that night, I fell into a restless sleep, still so very worried that this would be the year Santa would not visit.

The next day was Christmas Eve. My brother was very excited and his energy was running high. I could practically see the sparks as he bounced excitedly on the kitchen chair and talked a blue streak.

Our apartment was decorated with festive Christmas things and we had a real Christmas tree in the living room. It was beautiful and every time I passed by, I would inhale the fresh outdoor scent. To me it smelled of winter and Christmas together — the most special aroma of all. My favourite moment of the day was when my mother turned on the fairy lights in the evening and the colours twinkled throughout the room. Truly a splendid sight!

Seeing my brother's inability to contain himself, my mother suggested we dress warmly and go outside to play. In our tradition, Christmas was celebrated on December 24th and Santa always managed to deliver the gifts while everyone was enjoying Christmas Eve dinner.

Instead of feeling excitement like my brother, I only felt my nerves eating away at me. Since he was younger, I dared not tell him my fear. I could just envision how his face would crumple and how he would cry. Then, no doubt, he'd run to our mother and be inconsolable and then it would be me who would be responsible for ruining Christmas.

While we played out in the snow, I knew Mom was busy preparing a delicious meal and that my grandparents and other family members would be arriving shortly. My mouth started to salivate as I thought of the delicious food she was making for us, but my stomach began to churn as I realized I would be far too on edge to even eat a bite, knowing that once we were done, there would be nothing to look forward to afterward.

We finally went back inside, changed into our good clothes and the guests began to arrive. Mom had a bowl of her homemade eggnog and was ladling out cups for everyone. For the grown-ups, she would add a splash of rum. After we had greeted everyone and posed for the annual photos taken in front of the tree, Mom told us to go into our rooms for a bit until dinner was ready. However, not more than a few moments later, she called us. There'd been a knock at the door.

Coming down the hallway, I saw the apartment door was open; my mother stood to one side, her hand resting on the doorknob. There was a mysterious smile on her lips when she saw us.

"I think Santa just arrived."

My heart lifted in my chest and I pressed a hand over my mouth. Could this be true? Then she opened the door wider and we could see brightly wrapped gifts in the building corridor. My brother flew past me, as I stood frozen to the floor. I couldn't believe my eyes. So many questions rushed through my head. How had Santa found us? Who had told him? Did my mother have a direct line to Santa Claus?

With knees feeling like jelly, I helped bring the gifts inside to put under the tree. When I saw my name on some of them, I knew for a fact that Santa had remembered me!

~S.K. Naus

Reprinted by permission of www.offthemark.com.

**45**

# The Christmas Shoebox

*It isn't the size of the gift that matters, but the size of the heart that gives it.*
~Quoted in The Angels' Little Instruction Book
*by Eileen Elias Freeman*

When I think of Hanukkahs past, I remember my parents' kitchen, the smell of crisp latkes fried in oil, the glow of colorful candles burning in the menorah, and the gold foiled chocolate coins attached to each small present every night for eight nights. I remember singing *Rock of Ages* at my local Jewish Community Center, spinning plastic dreidels for hours, and eating so many jelly doughnuts that my stomach would ache.

When I think of the true meaning of the holiday season, my mind always takes me back to the time when I was a law student in Boston. As a Midwesterner in a distinctly New England university, I was often teased about my accent and my lack of knowledge of all things Bostonian. But, I was enamored of the city, its rich history, neighborhoods and cosmopolitan feel. Each day I relied on the gold dome of the Capitol to help me find my way to class.

It was a time I felt most alive, because everything was new. As I made the daily trek up and down the sloping cobblestone streets of Beacon Hill, my backpack weighed down by several thick law books, there was a purpose in my step. With so many colleges and universities nearby, it was a great city and a great time to be a student.

One December, however, I found myself all alone in Boston over the holidays. Our law school had finals after winter break and I didn't have the money or time to leave town to visit my parents. I decided that this was my penance for getting behind in Constitutional Law and I would spend the next two weeks huddled in the library revisiting the law of search and seizure. Still, as my friends talked about their visits home and their vacations, I became increasingly blue.

When a friend offered to take me home with her for Christmas for a couple of days, I didn't hesitate before saying yes. I knew that it wasn't an easy decision for her. She was from the Northeast tip of the state and she had told me that she came from a very poor family. Her dad had been disabled for many years and her mom worked several jobs to keep the family afloat. My friend had cautioned me that her house wasn't much to look at and that what little furniture they had was old and tattered. None of that mattered to me.

It was my first time celebrating Christmas and I didn't know what to expect. Talk about being a gefilte fish out of water! As our bus rolled into town, I saw the tired, grey clapboard buildings, one after another, and had to admit to myself that it seemed a world away from my middle class enclave in suburban Chicago. The bit of trepidation I had dissolved when I met her mom. She was warm, with kind, brown eyes just like my friend's. She immediately gave me a big, welcoming hug, something my own mom would have done for any friend of mine.

The tiny kitchen was already full with pans of baked goods, Christmas cookies and presents. There was lasagna in the oven and sausage and peppers on the stove, a nod to my friend's father's Italian heritage. I had purchased a small gift for the family, but noticed that the tree was adorned with dozens of beautifully wrapped gifts. Perhaps I should have brought a few more?

On Christmas Eve, I accompanied the family to their local parish for Mass. I hadn't spent much time in church and didn't want to stand out. I had no idea what the customs were, but I arrived in my holiday finery and nervously smiled at the other congregants. My friend ushered us to the back of the church so that it wouldn't be so obvious when I didn't kneel or take communion. I remained seated in the pew throughout the service on the holiest day of the year. My friend later told me someone asked what had happened to "that lovely young lady's legs." Everyone there assumed that I couldn't walk, not that I wasn't Catholic!

The next day, we exchanged gifts. I certainly didn't expect anything from my hosts. After all, they could hardly afford their own presents and I was grateful that they had taken me in on such short notice. I was surprised when my friend's mom handed me not one, but three, gifts. The first was homemade banana bread wrapped in aluminum foil and a blue bow. Next, was a beautifully wrapped shoebox. I opened it carefully and inside was a small, golden menorah. The third present contained the candles to light.

This little Irish Catholic lady had knocked on the door of the only synagogue in town and had spoken to the rabbi there. She told him that a young, Jewish woman would be staying with her over the holidays and asked what he thought she would like for Hanukkah.

I learned many lessons that day about the true meaning of giving and I learned that simple acts of kindness can remain in your heart forever.

The sweetness of that Christmas so many years ago is the benchmark by which I measure each and every Hanukkah.

~Shari Cohen Forsythe

# 46

# The 129-Year Snow

*Snow provokes responses that reach
right back to childhood.*
~Andy Goldsworthy

People have long thought me crazy because of my love affair with snow. When I was a kid my dad said I only liked it because I didn't have to drive in it. As an adult, my husband says I only like it because I don't have to shovel it. But I think they're both wrong. I love it because of that bit of childhood magic that lives inside me, quiet and sleepy, until awakened by a fresh snowfall.

And Christmas? Well, Christmas just isn't the same without snow. I love the way a heavy snowfall wraps the view outside my window like a sparkling gift. I love bundling up to search for the perfect Christmas tree, and I love shaking fresh snow from the branches before we string lights and hang ornaments. I love the cozy feeling of burrowing under the covers on Christmas Eve while the winds howl outside, and then waking up on Christmas Day to find a million diamonds glittering in the snow. I love the drifts, piled to the rooftops in places, and the icicles, crystal clear and as tall as I am.

There was a time I couldn't imagine Christmas without all these things, and I never thought I'd have to. But then, one day, everything changed with a single phone call. My husband accepted a job offer down south, and before I knew it, we had packed up all our household things in Wisconsin and moved to Georgia. Amid all the craziness and excitement over our move, a small thought crossed my mind: Would Christmas in Georgia be white? It was one of the first questions I needed an answer to, and shortly after we arrived I asked a friend at church. Her smile brightened, and for a minute I was hopeful. Then she said, "Oh, you'll love it here. We hardly get any snow! One year it was seventy degrees on Christmas Day!"

Seventy degrees? On Christmas Day? I smiled and tried not to show just how disappointed I felt. I could handle a mild winter, but this news nearly broke my heart. I decided that even though she had lived in Georgia her entire life, she had to be mistaken about this. I stubbornly waited for my Georgia White Christmas.

But of course, it never came. The years passed and each Christmas was greener than green. Shiny magnolia leaves waved against a bright blue sky. There were times it was so warm that I wore shorts and flip-flops while I decorated the house and left the windows open to let in a balmy breeze. It felt wrong. All wrong. My northern family and friends, as well as my husband, continued to think I was crazy for missing snow. But to me, it always felt like something was missing.

Then one year, when I least expected it, I got my Christmas miracle. It was late afternoon, an hour or so before sunset. I sat on the couch, crumpled balls of wrapping paper and empty gift boxes at my feet. Giggles and happy squeals sounded as the kids tried out their new toys, but I still felt sad. Christmas, my favorite time of year, was coming to a close.

I stood and tried to shake my sadness off. I turned on some Christmas music, pulled the curtains open so I could see the colorful lights outside, and set to cleaning up my living room. As I cleared the trash off the floor, my mind cleared a bit, too. By the time I plugged in the vacuum and ran it over the carpet, I knew that there was still more of Christmas Day to enjoy. And that's when I looked outside. Giant, fluffy flakes of snow fell in the twilight sky. I ran to the window, heart beating fast, and pressed my face against the glass. I hadn't imagined it. It really was snowing! On Christmas Day! In Georgia! Real, heavy, completely beautiful snow. That feeling I'd missed for so many years washed over me and filled me up with a thousand memories of

Christmases past.

"Everyone! Come here! Quick!" I yelled, afraid the snow would disappear any moment. The kids came running and soon all Christmas gifts were forgotten as they scrambled to find their coats and hats. We had no boots or mittens, so they covered their hands in work gloves or socks and raced outside. As it grew dark, I turned on the porch lights so we wouldn't miss a moment. The kids raced around outside, pelted each other with snowballs, and built snowmen in the yard. All the while, the snow kept coming, each flake filling my heart until it was full to bursting. When the snow slowed, and finally stopped, I stayed by the window marveling at its beauty. And, of course, its magic.

The next day I discovered one more bit of magic. It was like a surprise gift waiting beneath the tree. The last time Georgia had seen a white Christmas was 129 years earlier. I suddenly felt honored, humbled even, that I was there to experience what hadn't happened in well over a century. And let me tell you… it was worth the wait.

~Debra Mayhew

# 47

# Home for Christmas

*I dream of giving birth to a child who will ask,*
*"Mother, what was war?"*
*~Eve Merriam*

I watched as a handsome young man came through the airport terminal late that night with self-assurance and confidence beyond his years. He must have been the last person off our plane, which was so late in arriving that the terminal was all but shut down for the night. Perhaps he waited for the pineapple-toting vacationers, some college kids, and the rest of us to disembark and clear out of the public area, or he took a minute to compose thoughts and feelings, or to wash up and look at his reflection in a mirror on the men's room wall.

Wearing civilian clothes, he could have been mistaken for a student, a musician, or a junior partner in some law firm. He was none of those; he was a soldier coming home for the holidays.

I was privileged to watch.

Family members that included an anxious mom, a preteen girl holding a hand-drawn WELCOME HOME poster, and a few other adults and children had been waiting for a long time. They were restless. A gentleman in a suit and tie waited with them. He wore medals of combat on his chest and a VFW hat was on his head. An honor guard of sorts. They were positioned where they could see the passengers descend on the escalator, head for baggage claim, and then to the cars waiting at the curb.

I stood back, unnoticed, to wait with them.

The kids saw him first and the excitement grew. He rode the escalator down and saw them waiting. Hugs, tears, and camera flashes from the family, then a quiet handshake from the older veteran said what words could not. The young man then turned to his mother. She fell into his open arms. I am sure this was the moment she had waited and prayed for, the hope that kept her strong. He lifted her off the ground and hugged her for a long time. Their laughter and tears collided.

As they all began to walk away, I touched his arm and when he turned to me I thanked him for his service, welcomed him home, and wished him a Merry Christmas. I'm sure he will not remember me, but I will never forget him.

~Jana Tritto

# 48

# Our First Noel

*No one is useless in this world who lightens the
burdens of another.*
~Charles Dickens

"We'll be home all day on Christmas if you need us!" When there's a pastor in the family, you tend to stay home for Christmas — at least that was true for our family. After topping off a very busy Advent season with two Christmas Eve services, my husband was not in any shape to travel on Christmas Day. Knowing that Mary's baby was due on December 25th and that she didn't have any family in the area, I threw the offer out there, pretty confident that my services wouldn't be needed. I mean, how many babies are actually born on their due date?

Mary said, "Thanks, I'll keep that in mind," and to be honest with you, I really didn't. Keep it in mind, I mean. Christmas morning dawned bright and clear. Our two kids woke us up well before dawn, and gifts and breakfast were all done by 7:00 a.m. The Little Tykes dollhouse and new action figures were a huge hit with the kids, as I knew they would be. We were lounging in our PJs and robes, watching them play, when the telephone rang. I picked it up, fully expecting to hear my mom or sister on the other end wishing us a Merry Christmas. But instead I heard a man's voice, "I'm sorry to have to ask this on Christmas Day, but we don't know who else we can ask. Remember that offer you made a few weeks back?" Mary's husband sounded a bit sheepish.

"Bring them right over!" I exclaimed, "No problem!"

Within a few minutes there were three sleepy children clambering up our front steps, and a harried dad quickly passed a diaper bag to me and headed off to take Mary to the hospital. Sometimes kids can be hesitant to share their brand-new toys — but not ours that day. I saw their hearts open wide to welcome the children in. The new dollhouse, new action figures — everything was shared generously with our young visitors.

The kids had Christmas dinner with us, and then supper. I was just starting to figure out the sleeping arrangements when the phone rang again — the baby had been born, a little girl, and her name was Noelle. Dad would be by soon to pick up the kids.

We always remembered that Christmas Day as particularly special. I realized how special it was to our kids when the dolls in the dollhouse were permanently named for the three children who spent that Christmas Day with us. And the tiny baby doll? She was named Noelle, of course!

~Laurie Carnright Edwards

# 49

# Christmas Connections

*This time of year means being kind to everyone we meet,*
*To share a smile with strangers we may pass along the street.*
*~Betty Black*

"T he eighteenth bus was delayed a bit, but don't worry, the police are waving it through." It was December, dark and raining. I was a very new coordinator of volunteers in a large hospital for children with mental or physical problems. I had some experience with people issues — fleets of buses were another matter entirely. But this was the evening of the Christmas lights tour.

The head of recreation, his suit covered by a bright yellow slicker, consulted his sheet and directed bus after bus — full-size city buses — to different entrances where the drivers whipped them around in impossibly small spaces so that patients could get aboard without getting wet. Besides the transit buses, we had a fleet of wheelchair buses — they had arrived earlier because they took longer to load.

Most of the drivers were dressed as Santa Claus; some had brought their wives along dressed as Mrs. Claus, carrying baskets of candy. As we loaded patients, bright-eyed and eager, I noticed that the drivers were all mature men. When I asked about that they said, "You need a lot of seniority to get this volunteer spot."

When every last person was on board and settled down we were waved on our way. The lead bus bore a large sign with the name of the hospital and "Christmas Lights Tour" on it. I had wondered, with so many buses, if we might get separated at traffic lights. No worries! At every traffic light in this busy urban area police were stationed. Our entire convoy was waved through together.

I was on a bus with young boys, and having cops wave them through red lights was the highlight of their evening. Never had they imagined a privilege as great as that. Life could get no better. They eagerly looked forward at each intersection, hoping the light would be red, cheering as the cop on duty waved us through.

When we came to the brightly decorated houses, we saw that the owners had been alerted. Street after street had organized for the evening. Our patients might have been rock stars based on the way the groups of homeowners cheered our arrival. Neighbours, family and friends had been roped in to help bring every young person hot chocolate, nuts, and candy.

Smiles and hugs were the currency of the evening. We arrived at one street after another to see people smiling and waving. Once in a while I spotted someone a little uncertain about greeting young people with handicaps. It took only a little encouragement to bring them onto the bus, where they connected and made friends.

We left to more vigorous waving and to wider smiles, to mums and dads and grandpas holding up their little ones to wave or knock on bus windows to say goodbye up close and personal. Every barrier had been broken, smashed by the Christmas connection.

On our return we sang carols on the bus. We had all learned something that night. The boys counted their loot as if it were Halloween. Back at the hospital we collected candy wrappers and hot drink cups and told the lads to make sure to say "thank you" to the driver.

When we got back the drivers spun the great buses into place before the hospital entrances as if they were driving toy cars. The boys appreciated their skill. Their "Wow! Cool! Can you do that again?" was an even better reward than the "thank you."

It was part of my job to send letters of thanks to all the drivers, police, and homeowners. The transit dispatcher phoned me back two days before Christmas. "I thought I'd let you know. All the drivers have signed up to volunteer for this shift again next year."

~Valerie Fletcher Adolph

# 50

# Being Santa

*Everyone has been made for some particular work,*
*and the desire for that work has been put*
*in every heart.*
~Rumi

"Here you are. I found you!" exclaimed a young woman as she rushed toward my husband as we were browsing in a toy store. "Flowing white hair, a kindly smile," she continued. "You even have a twinkle in your eye. I'm the president of a local costume house and I've been on the search for a Santa Claus to model our line of Santa regalia for a new catalogue. I knew the moment I saw you that you were perfect. And to find my Santa in a toy store! Wow."

So began our journey into all things Santa Claus, and what a fantastic adventure it's been. As my husband took on the persona of the man in red, children began to flock to him, no matter where we were or what we were doing. Even in shorts and a T-shirt or playing the fiddle in a country band they thought he was the real deal.

Often, in a restaurant, we have heard "Santa" and a child will make a beeline for him. He puts on his glasses, tilts his head, and with a twinkle in his eye, chuckles a hearty ho-ho-ho. "You found me," he says, "but I'm in disguise. I can't fool you, though!"

"Are you the real Santa?"

"Are you the real you?" he replies. "What does the real Santa look like? Does he have a white beard?"

"Yes."

"Well, I have a white beard. Does he wear glasses and laugh ho-ho-ho?"

"Yes," chorus the children.

"I wear glasses and laugh ho-ho-ho. Let's see. How can we tell if I'm the real guy? I know. There's an official test to solve the question. If I were really him, I would know all the names of the reindeer. Right? Okay, let's see if I know them. There's the famous guy with the green nose."

"No," the children shout. "He has a red nose."

By this time, the whole restaurant is tuned into the conversation.

"Right. I can't fool you. That's Rudolph. Who are the others? There's Sleepy, Bashful and Doc."

The children giggle. "No, Santa, those are the seven dwarfs!"

Santa chuckles. "You're right again! Let's see, there's Dasher, Dancer, Prancer, Vixen, Comet, Cupid, Donner and Blitzen. I know them all. I guess I must be Santa!"

From there, the conversation goes anywhere from "Where are the reindeer?" to "We've moved. Will you be able to find me this year?" Santa always answers their questions with gentleness and warmth. Often adults stop by our table to say, "You've got me believing you're the real Santa."

One of my husband's favourite memories is of the time that our granddaughter phoned and asked for her grandfather.

"Bucka," she said. "Will you come to my school in your Santa suit for show and tell?"

He was blown away. Never in all his life did he expect to be the subject of show and tell for a kindergarten class.

"I would love to come," he said. "Let me call your teacher and make arrangements."

Donning his Santa suit, he walked into her class with a hearty ho-ho-ho. Some of the children squealed and rushed to him for hugs. Some had never seen Santa up close before and were shy and anxious. He shared songs and told stories. He listened, really listened, to each and every child. Those who were scared soon learned there was nothing to fear. The children and adults all left the school happy and laughing. Once again, his fun and gentle demeanor brought the magic of Christmas to a small corner of the world.

Another time, at a company's children's Christmas party, Santa was giving out gifts to the children and laughing with them. A small girl had jumped to her feet as soon as he entered the room. She tugged on her mother's hand and pulled her away from Santa and out the door. As she was leaving she looked back and glanced at Santa from under her lowered eyelids. Her face had gone white and she wore a frown.

I followed them. She was shaking and crying. I approached her mom and asked if I could speak with her. Her mom told me her name was Maddy and that she didn't want to go into the room as long as Santa was in it.

"Are you afraid of Santa?"

"Yes."

"Do you know why you're afraid of Santa?"

"No."

"Is it because of the big red suit or the loud ho-ho-ho?"

"No."

"Is it his beard?"

"Yes."

"Well, Santa is my very best friend. He's very gentle and won't hurt you, I promise. The beard can make him look a little scary, but it's really quite soft. I'm sure he'll let you touch it if you'd like. Would that help you to not be afraid?"

"No, I don't want to go in there."

"Okay. You can come and meet him when you're ready."

"Okay."

I left Maddy and her mom and returned to the party. A short while later, I noticed them enter the room. Cautiously, Maddy moved closer to where the children were sitting. Her name was called to receive her present. Taking her mom's hand, she guardedly approached his chair. She stood so that her mom was between her and Santa. He sensed her fear and gently began to talk to her.

"What would you like to do?"

"I would like to sing 'Feliz Navidad'."

"Do you know that song?" asked Santa. "I know that song too! Let's sing it together."

They began to sing and she started to smile. When they were finished, Maddy's mom said, "Wasn't there something you wanted to ask Santa?"

"Oh, yes," replied Maddy. "Santa, can I touch your beard?"

"Of course."

Maddy moved closer to him, reached out her small hand and gently touched his beard. Santa lifted his hand and softly touched her hair.

"See, it's just like your hair, only yours is brown and mine is white," whispered Santa.

Maddy's eyes widened and she started to giggle. She and Santa smiled at each other for a long time. Then they laughed and she gave him a big hug. Maddy's mom gave him a hug also and whispered, "Thank you so much for helping my girl."

Being Santa is magical. My husband loves to make the children laugh and smile. To think it all started because a young woman found him in a toy store! He is grateful for that day and the circumstances that brought them together. Coincidence? He doesn't think so.

"I love keeping the dream alive for the little ones," says Santa. "That's what being Santa is all about, not just at Christmas but throughout the year. To be able to share hope, laughter and joy with people is awesome. I'm a lucky man."

~Maighread MacKay

# 51

# No Planning Required

*Christmas is a necessity. There has to be at least
one day of the year to remind us that we're here for
something else besides ourselves.*
~Eric Sevareid

"What do you mean, no rehearsal?" I asked. "You have to have a rehearsal, otherwise how will the children and the organizers of the Christmas pageant know what is expected of them and when?"

"Well, things operate differently in the north, but be assured that all will work out in the end and the show will go on." was the answer.

My husband and I had only been in Iqaluit, Nunavut (Canada's Arctic) for six months and I was still adjusting to life "north of 60." Ron had been posted to St. Jude's Cathedral as a first year student minister; and as I was already a volunteer Sunday school teacher, I asked if the children put on a pageant during the Christmas season. The priest-in-charge told me that the children of the community generally presented it at the 7 p.m. Christmas Eve service. When I told him I was interested in assisting he said, "By all means, it's a great experience!"

A couple of weeks later I inquired as to when the first rehearsal was going to take place and the reply was "What rehearsal?" At first I thought I had heard wrong—but no, I hadn't. I started getting stressed out… I'm a very organized person who likes to have everything in place well ahead of the actual event. "I can't do this," I thought. But, what could I do? I had already volunteered and it wouldn't look good for the new minister's wife to back out of something at the last minute. Like it or not, I had to go through with this.

As the countdown to Christmas began I kept asking leading questions about the pageant hoping to catch an indication of how it was actually carried off, but there were no clues. Two days before Christmas, I still saw no signs of preparation for the Christmas Eve service. There was nothing I could do at this point except "wait and see" as neither Ron nor I were in charge of anything. But, I kept thinking — "how can you put on a pageant without weeks of planning and rehearsing?"

December 24th arrived! It was Christmas Eve and three services were scheduled for the church that night. We were both looking forward to seeing how the services would all work out; but, still there was no word about the pageant or even if it was happening at this point. Maybe it got cancelled, I thought. I was hoping so because I had no idea of what was expected of me.

While wrapping Christmas gifts, I was listening to the radio. CBC Radio is a staple of community life north of 60 and everyone tunes in for the latest news. In both English and Inuktitut, they keep everyone informed as to what is happening in their particular community. It could be news of a blizzard blowing in, road closures, flight cancellations, school and business closings, or it could be good news such as someone's birthday, the sealift ship arriving or other special events. Lo and behold, I heard an announcement that St. Jude's Cathedral would be holding their annual Family Christmas Service with a presentation of The Nativity and if any child in the community would like to come and be part of it, just show up at the church at 6:30 p.m.! I couldn't believe my ears! How on earth could you present a nativity with just anyone who showed up at the church? Some of these children would not be regular churchgoers and yet expected to act out The Nativity? And at 6:30 p.m. when the service was starting at 7 p.m.? All of a sudden I wanted no part of this fiasco, but it was too late to back out!

At six o'clock Ron and I went over to the church. The priest-in-charge was there and had brought out a huge box of clothing from the furnace room that was to be used to dress up the children. Another lady had volunteered to help me and our instructions were that as the children arrived, we were to choose who was to play a part by their age and whether or not they would fit into the costume! Any child that arrived late would have to be a shepherd or an angel as we had lots of white sheets. Once the children were dressed, it was our job to keep them quiet (that was a TALL TASK)! It was a scene of mass confusion and bedlam! Many children arrived at the church, but despite their enthusiasm to be part of the nativity scene, some were very shy and needed a hefty load of encouragement.

When the church was filled and it was time for the service to start, a few of the children got very nervous and decided they didn't want to do it. We had to do some fast-talking to persuade some of them to stay in the play. With others, there was just no coaxing whatsoever. So, we sent them off to sit with their family while we did some fast recruiting for someone else to fill the spot. At this point, I still wasn't convinced this method was going to work and I felt a huge headache coming on!

Finally, the service got started with a welcoming carol. A prayer was said, the candles were lit and then the organist started to play "O Little Town of Bethlehem." That was the cue for Mary and Joseph to walk down the aisle toward the front of the church. There was no elaborate set, just a simple, wooden manger filled with straw, which was the central figure at the foot of the altar. Mary and Joseph made their way to the front of the church and stood behind the manger. The stage was set! With all eyes on a doll wrapped in swaddling clothes, the children made their way down the aisle at the appropriate time as the old carols told of shepherds watching their flocks on the hillsides, wise men on a quest following a star and angel choirs at midnight. When all were in place and the scene was set, a sign from the head angel indicated the lights were to be dimmed as the congregation joined the children in singing "Silent Night."

It was very touching. Many people in the congregation were moved to tears as they watched The Nativity unfold in story and in song. I was now convinced that all the elaborate sets and costumes, weeks of planning and rehearsing, could not have made a statement like what we had just witnessed. The children's faces were radiant from the unpretentious offering of love that they had given to make this happen.

It was truly a "holy night" and one that I felt so blessed to have been part of.

~Carolyn McLean

# 52

# The Cannons

*Worry never robs tomorrow of its sorrow, it only*
*saps today of its joy.*
*~Leo Buscaglia*

My childhood home was the only magical haven I knew of where I could dig into the Christmas spirit and forget my troubles. Unfortunately, as the best-laid plans sometimes do, since I'd arrived home, nothing had gone right. I had a decision to make and it buzzed me like a swarm of gnats that wouldn't go away. In fact it ruined everything I'd ever loved about Christmas.

Like a frazzled rope in a tug of war, the two men in my life were pulling me apart. I had planned on spending Christmas with my children, parents, and sister. At that time I was married to my first husband, but we were separated. After I'd made my plans, he had broken off his other relationship and wanted back in our lives. He insisted on spending Christmas with us. Meanwhile, the new man in my life had moved to my hometown with the hope that it might speed my decision-making along. What a mess.

Two men. The stronger they pulled, the more confused I became. My dad had done his best to keep them both at bay. Yet between a husband who suddenly begged me to stay with him, and the phone calls from the other man, I found no peace, no joy, and no goodwill toward man.

As always, Mom and Dad had transformed my childhood home

into the perfect Christmas wonderland. I stared at their magnificent tree, with its sparkling lights and the ornaments from my childhood. Yet instead of brimming with Christmas spirit I felt empty inside. My father had always played beautiful carols on his piano. But instead of reveling in his music, I found myself in tears. Mom had gone overboard with her usual Christmas goodies. Dad had even made his secret-recipe divinity fudge, but I didn't have much of an appetite. I found no Christmas cheer this holiday season, only a deepening obsession with the decision I could not make.

Christmas Eve found me acting like Scrooge. While the flames crackled in the fireplace, the children excitedly hung their stockings over the mantel. Yet none of it mattered somehow. Lost in my own depressed state, I couldn't even muster a smile. My parents tried their best to be festive, but I'd have none of it. Then the doorbell rang.

"Would you mind answering that, Jill?" my mom asked. Mindlessly, I opened the door and found a miracle known as the Cannon family. Their voices resounded with familiar carols as their sweet music floated magically through the frigid night. They stood amidst the freshly fallen snow while the warm-colored glow of the outdoor Christmas lights brightened their faces. Behind them snow-covered mountains jutted against a dark, but star-filled sky. I had never seen a Christmas card more perfect or more beautiful than the one before me. It left me breathless.

"Who is it?" asked my dad.

"The Cannons," I whispered, choking with emotion as my family joined me at the door.

Like a much-needed slap in the face, this wondrous scene awoke me. Sweet childhood memories rushed through my head. Every Christmas Eve for as long as I could remember our family had eagerly awaited the moment when the doorbell would ring. When it did, we'd open the door and find the Cannon family — eventually reaching ten in number — who went door to door caroling throughout the neighbor-hood. Always a treat and a highlight of the holiday season, they nestled together on the sidewalk, harmonizing in the night air. Of course, my best friend was in this family so that had always made it extra special.

That night, as the sweet melody of "Hark the Herald Angels Sing" rang out through the darkness, a feeling of overwhelming love washed over me. The cloud lifted. My heart opened. This was Christmas Eve. It came once a year. It had nothing to do with my troubles or problems. As I searched through the family's faces I noticed a few of their family members were missing. Others had spouses with them. Among them I found my dear friend. We rushed to each other and embraced. It had been many years since we had seen each other.

This was what Christmas was about: love, family, friends, traditions, and so much more. I'd forgotten. I'd almost missed it. Who knew if I'd ever be home for Christmas again? I had no guarantees that my parents would both be with us next year. My problems would still be there in a few days, but this moment — this Christmas — would not. Tears of gratitude ran down my cheeks as I watched the Cannon family, still softly singing, stroll on to the next house. As their beautiful voices sang, "Silent night, Holy night, All is calm, All is bright," it was.

~Jill Burns

**Chapter 6**

# Merry Christmas!

## Holiday Shenanigans

# 53

# A Christmas Made in China

*I once bought my kids a set of batteries for Christmas with a note on it saying, toys not included.*
*~Bernard Manning*

I can't wait for Christmas. There is nothing like seeing your small children bursting with excitement, running to the Christmas tree and tearing open their presents. However, I am a veteran mom now. My children are older. I still love watching their excitement but they try to hide it a little. This is because they are teenagers and to admit such excitement is uncool.

When they were young I made an error in judgment. I wrapped the presents. Isn't that the best part? Opening the presents? Why yes, it is. Except that children's presents usually come with instructions that say, "Some assembly required." I'm sure whoever wrote the word "some" laughed hysterically while doing so.

Picture the scene: My twin two-year-old daughters and three-year-old son running to the Christmas tree and tearing open the wrapped gifts, all of them bursting with excitement to play with the toy in the box. They tear into the box and guess what? The insides of the box do not look like the picture on the box. Then there is crying. "Hurry! Hurry! Mom! Dad! Put it together! Hurry!" The words come out of all of them at the same time.

So in the aftermath of that year, I sat down to gather my thoughts.

And I decided I am going to China. I am going to China to find the persons responsible for my misery. I know they live there because they stamp where they live on their paraphernalia: "Made in China."

I am going to find the people who package children's toys and torture them. Not like making-them-watch-reality-TV torture. Just a little packaging karma will do. I will take these people, put them in a cell, and tie them up. Oh, no, not with rope. With little silver twisties. A whole bunch of them. The kind you can't get off when you try to separate the gift from its cardboard backing.

I will not just tie their arms and legs either. I will twist them around the waist, neck, ankles, and any other place on the bodies I feel might slightly sway in the wind.

Will I give those twisties a twist once, twice? Of course not! I will twist them 300 times each. Then I might twist those together for good measure. I will leave one of their hands untwisted so they can spend eternity untwisting each other. If they have long hair, I will sew a plastic strip in it.

I will then put 3,000 two-year-olds in the cell with them. While they are untwisting forever, the two-year-olds will whine, "Hurwie yup! Hurwie yup!" over and over. If they do manage to untwist themselves before going insane, I will allow a way out of the cell. The door to the cell will be screwed on by tiny little Phillips-head screws. A whole bunch of them. I will give them all Phillips-head screwdrivers to unscrew the door to freedom. But its head will be too large for the tiny screws.

I will provide a map for an escape route… because I have a heart. There are 4,000 parts to it. Actually 3,999; one part is missing but they won't know that until they are almost finished. Here's the instruction book on how to put it together. They can see how the finished product is supposed to look on page 1250, after step 601. When they are done putting together the map, they will notice it doesn't look quite like the picture on the box. That's because they haven't put the stickers on it. Here are the 785 stickers. Where do they go? I think that instruction manual will be accidentally left out. Sorry.

For their entertainment, I will put a TV in their cell. The TV takes twenty D-sized batteries. They will have nineteen. And *Teletubbies* is on just about now. I'll mention that to the two-year-olds. I will leave them some food in the cell. It will be shrink-wrapped in molded plastic that neither teeth, hands, nor feet can tear open. I might put some Goldfish crackers in there too and let those horrible people hear the two-year-olds yelling "FRISH FRISH!" for eternity. I will leave some unwrapped toys out for the kids to play with — I'm not a monster. Oh, but after the toys do something really cool one time, they will break. The kids will cry — a lot. So sorry. The other toys that I leave in the cell will have 1,000 parts per toy. Pieces will get lost. The terrible people will live in eternity looking for the dolly's lost red shoe. It is 1/8 inch x 1/8 inch. The kids will cry until it is found.

We laugh about this now that my kids are grown. These days they ask for just one present. They tell me exactly what to buy. It is electronic. It is expensive and I don't know what it does. But they are happy, even though they still try to hide it so as to appear cool. And I am happy.

~Shannon McCarty

# 54

# A Clue for Christmas

*Our hearts grow tender with childhood memories
and love of kindred, and we are better throughout
the year for having, in spirit, become a child again at
Christmas-time.*
~Laura Ingalls Wilder

My parents didn't go out on dates, not even on their anniversary. Their once a year exception was to my mom's Sunday-school class Christmas party. It was a major event for my mom, who would dress up in anticipation of the party and then regale people with stories about it for years after. But one year my two brothers and I had an even better story — one that we never shared with anyone.

My parents left that evening with the usual attitudes: Mom was excited about going and Dad didn't like social situations. We were old enough to be left alone, although they felt compelled to warn us not to fight or set the house on fire. My twelve-year-old brother Trent, three years my senior, was officially in charge as he was the oldest.

With the parents out the door we settled in for a binge of once-a-year Christmas television shows starting with *A Charlie Brown Christmas* and ending with *How the Grinch Stole Christmas*.

We enjoyed the annual shows but were distracted by the Christmas tree in the corner of the room. Not actually the tree, but those wrapped gifts underneath.

It was family tradition for our mom to take us each shopping separately so we could buy a gift for each of our siblings. Sometimes we bought what the other wished for, but more often we were influenced by our own wants. That year Trent had wanted the board game *Clue*, so he bought it for my middle brother, Tracey.

It seemed like an impossibly long wait until Christmas morning. And it was as if all those brightly wrapped gifts were calling to us. One in particular was a rectangular box whispering over the sound of the television, "Play me. Play me now."

And so we did.

Trent carefully unwrapped the gift, being ever so careful not to tear the paper and then oh-so-gently pushed the wrapping to the side. And there it was... *Clue!*

For the next hour we clandestinely played *Clue*. Every few minutes we would panic, thinking we had heard our parents' car pull up. One of us would run to the window to check.

For the first time ever, we didn't have a single argument. Not once did I threaten to call Mom. Not once did my brothers threaten to kill me if I did.

It was a Norman Rockwell Christmas Card evening as three angelic children gathered around the coffee table rolling dice and wondered if it was Colonel Mustard in the billiard room with a candlestick or Miss Scarlet in the dining room with the lead pipe.

When we couldn't bear the fear of getting caught any longer, we re-wrapped the gift, putting it on the backside of the tree just in case our mom could tell we had tampered with it.

On Christmas morning it was the first gift Tracey opened, not because he was eager to find out what was in it, but rather to undo any likelihood of Mom noticing its shopworn wrapping. I'm surprised to this day she didn't catch on that something was amiss, as he gave the worst overacting enthusiastic surprised performance ever displayed for a board game.

Forty years later, I have somehow inherited that *Clue* game. While deducing with my own children whether the killer was Professor Plum in the conservatory or Mrs. White in the kitchen I remember how, long ago, three co-conspirators played all evening without a clue as to how special that Christmas together was.

~Christine Jarmola

"What's all this 'naughty or nice'
jazz? — Haven't you ever heard
of situational ethics?"

## Picture Perfect

*Santa, Please define Good.*
*~Author Unknown*

In a festive red vest with a matching bow tie and corduroy trousers, Zachary was going to look like a little angel for his first Christmas photo.

Too bad he had other ideas.

I guess I should have heeded the warning when he bawled as I buttoned up the dress shirt. Maybe I should have stopped when he kept ninja-kicking the shiny black shoes off as fast as I could put them on his chubby feet. I definitely should have realized that I was in for nothing but trouble when he tried to eat the tie.

But I was a new parent on a mission. If I couldn't get a thirteen-month-old to look nice for five minutes in order to pose for a few photos, what kind of mother was I?

My husband, bless his heart, snapped pictures like he was wielding a rapid-fire machine gun in hopes that he could catch Zachary displaying a half-smile while his mother belted out "Frosty the Snowman" and made a steady stream of stuffed animals perform moves that would win the Mirror Ball Trophy on *Dancing with the Stars*. But seeing his parents yell at each other to "move this way" or "try the Cookie Monster toy" only resulted in more tears.

After a miserable half hour, I looked worse than Zachary's drool-soaked collar. Admitting defeat, I took off the precious clothes. My husband, meanwhile, took the roll of film in for developing — hoping that somehow one of the pictures he snapped might be usable. He returned looking like a kid who received a hand-knit sweater from Grandma instead of the super deluxe racecar he craved.

As we flipped through the proof of our parental ineptitude, Zachary played happily with his trucks. How could this sweet, smiling child be the same one as that Grinch who stole our photographic dreams?

My husband reached for the camera. Sure, Zachary was now clad in a pint-sized football jersey and sweatpants, but he was babbling and laughing. The photos turned out so well that we had difficulty choosing just one.

While it was no fun at the time, Zachary's day as an uncooperative model provided a good lesson. Children don't always share the same visions as their parents, no matter how much we may try to convince them. To have a happy household, I was going to need to pick my battles and learn to go with the flow.

And maybe even let my baby (now a teenager) pick his own clothes.

~Beth Braccio Hering

# 56

# Christmas Ornaments

*Our most treasured heirlooms are the*
*memories of our family.*
*~Author Unknown*

"How long do you think it'll take Mom to break an ornament this year? I'm taking bets," I announce.

"I'd say definitely before the cookies are even ready,"
says Alexandra.

"I bet she drops the first one right out of the box," Jen replies.

My sisters and I are no longer surprised when we hear glass crashing to the ground this time of year. Every Christmas season begins the
countdown to when my mother will accidentally break an ornament.
It inevitably begins as we bring in the tree and unpack the decorations.
We all forget it's coming, though, as we are entranced by my father
lugging in the freshly cut pine, aromatic needles carpeting the dark
hardwood floors, and by the living room being transformed into a
miniature forest. My two sisters and I pass the boxes down to each
other from the attic, creating an assembly line of lights, tinsel, generic
silver and gold ornaments, and the more special ornaments that tell
the story of our family.

"Remember last year when she broke the Mickey Mouse ornament
we got at Disney World?" I ask. "His body shattered and now he's just
a floating head on the tree. Not exactly festive."

"The only ornaments never in danger are those crappy ones we
made in elementary school out of plastic spoons and felt. I can't believe

she's saved those for fifteen years," Jen comments.

"Of course I saved them!" exclaims our mother as she shuffles into the room with the big box of ornaments. "They remind me of a simpler time when you girls were sweet and didn't make fun of your poor mother."

"Sorry," Jen replies. "I just don't want to see any more casualties this year."

"I'll be extra careful then."

The tree is now up and dressed in lights. Every bulb miraculously works, and we begin to slowly add the ornaments, each hanging his or her favorites.

"Dad, what are you doing over there?" I ask.

"I'm taking the crystals from that old broken chandelier in the attic and turning them into ornaments. I'll put the hooks in and pass them to you."

"Great. More broken things to put on the tree," I mumble.

"A Christmas tree is like a big chandelier if you think about it," says Alexandra. "It's decorative and lights up the room. Except it goes up to the ceiling, not down from it."

"You just described a lamp," I reply.

"Well, you know what I mean."

"Why aren't you hanging any ornaments?" I ask her.

"I'm supervising from the couch. You missed that spot in the back there."

The house is filled with the sound of laughter and the soundtrack from *A Charlie Brown Christmas*. Cookies are baking, hot chocolate is on the stove, and the smell of cocoa mixes with the scent of pine. It is an unmistakable combination that envelops us and transports us directly into the Christmas season. Suddenly, the sound of shattering glass brings us all back.

"Uh oh. Someone grab the broom," my dad calls.

"I win! The cookies aren't even out of the oven yet," says Alexandra.

"Which one was it?" Jen asks.

"Maybe it was Minnie Mouse and now she and Mickey can be disembodied together," I suggest.

"It was the blue and gold one your great aunt gave your father and me for our first wedding anniversary."

The disappointment is evident on all of our faces and seems to hang in the air.

A moment of silence for our lost ornament.

"It's okay. We've had many anniversaries since, and we have a lot more ornaments," my dad responds. "Next year we'll just give you a cheap ornament to smash right away to get it out of your system."

After the tree is decorated, we all place our presents underneath. I put my smallest gift right on top — an ornament for my mother, as usual, so she doesn't feel as bad about the one she broke. I like to think we don't lose or replace our memories when the ornaments break, but we build upon them every year with new ones. Like our memories, the ornaments are jumbled together with very little rhyme or reason, but they twinkle and catch your eye as you walk by, almost as if to say, "Don't forget me."

~Victoria DeRosa

**57**

# At the Kids' Table

*It's like being at the kids' table at Thanksgiving — you
can put your elbows on it, you don't have to talk
politics... no matter how old I get, there's always a part
of me that's sitting there.*
~John Hughes

Another festive holiday season draws near and I fondly
recall a tradition hardly unique to my own tribal group:
The Kids' Table. We've all witnessed this common rite of
family passage wherein the children are not placed at The
Big Table and the motley mismatched siblings, cousins, and kids
belonging to parents' friends may even be relegated to a side room.

Every Christmas my father opened his dining room to a large
assortment of his cronies and their wives and various offspring and
guests. And every year there was an overflow of kids destined for
the annex table that was set up in the family room far away from the
main body of revelers. Here, our jubilant racket wouldn't disturb the
solemn and peaceful merrymaking of our elders. My younger sister
and I, five years apart, were the primary overseers of the kids' table.
We have a brother eight years younger than I who was never required
to complete a tour of duty at the kids' table. We'll get to him in a bit.

When we were in our twenties, my sister and I were dismayed
by the seeming injustice of being consigned to this annex away from
the world of grownups we were hoping to join. The worry that we
would still be out there would ignite a few weeks in advance of the

big day and smolder and die as the event receded in our memory. The curious thing, to me anyway, about this whole reminiscence is that my sister and I never did graduate from the kids' table to the main event; we were never invited, as it were, into the Big House. It took us many years and post-graduate degrees to finally make sense of this, during which time we entertained countless theories and conjectures. It required even more years to finally accept and then enthusiastically embrace our position.

You see, my sister and I never produced kids of our own, while our brother, yes, we're getting to him now, decided from an early age to experiment his way through a series of wives, leaving a trail of children in his carefree wake. At first, his place at The Big Table was ensured because he was the only son, and this successor to my father's seniority needed representation at the main table.

At the young age of twenty, the time of his first marriage, my brother and his young bride were ushered ceremoniously and with great fanfare to the main table on their first Christmas as a new franchise of the family name. My mother wanted to afford this young woman the full dignity and privileges of adulthood and, as I later came to realize, a reward for having married. My sister and I were still out in the family room with the kids.

As the three of us entered our thirties, and my brother's starter marriage gave way to a second incarnation, he retained his seat at the main table, while my sister and I retained ours at the kids' table, now accompanied by, among other kids, our nephew. It all started to become, somehow, sort of comfortable. You tire of worrying over the same issue after a few decades.

My parents sensed after so much time that it was unlikely my sister and I would be producing children of our own, and the boyfriend I lived with for a decade wasn't an actual husband, so we never did earn a place at The Big Table. But this boyfriend's presence at the kids' table all those years added an ironic and almost wacky spin to the mix, as our relationship outlived two of my brother's marriages.

Later, when the second brotherly marriage failed and more of his offspring took their rightful places at the kids' table, the whole program assumed the manner of high theater. My sister and I, comfortably into our forties, still unmarried and childless and therefore not qualified for the grown-ups' table, were finally able to enjoy the laughter and riotous merriment of this wonderful assortment of kids.

Eventually we came to notice the odd silence or occasional grunts or complaints about the news of the day that wafted in from the morose enclave of "grown-ups." After three decades of this ritual, my sister and I, both in our fifties, finally resigned ourselves to our proper places as the celebrity hosts of the kids' table where we held lively court among the more enthusiastic of our holiday guests, noting with great pride the trickle of "grown-ups" who picked up their plates and wandered out to join us where they claimed it was more fun.

So there was our success, if a long time in coming. It has been ten years now since I held court at the kids' table, having been finally released from my duties as overseer by the deaths of my parents. And as I prepare my own Christmas meal for myself and a collection of oddball friends and comrades, I think back on that dreaded kids' table, and wish I were sitting there again.

~Aaron Vlek

# 58

# The Sinister Snowman

*The moments of happiness we enjoy take us by surprise.*
*It is not that we seize them, but that they seize us.*
*~Ashley Montagu*

"Hey Max, the snowfall from last night is perfect for building a snowman!" I said, perhaps a little too eagerly. Each year we spent Christmas in Sun Valley with my wife's family, and each year I had to try a little harder to convince my twelve-year-old son to put down his iPhone or Xbox and play outdoors with me. As the beloved youngest of eight cousins at Grandma's house, Max always had many readily available playmates. Still, I knew Max was my best hope for a snowman-building buddy, so I was selling hard. "All right, I guess," Max finally mumbled. Not the excitement I hoped for, but good enough. We bundled up and went out into the snow.

"Let's build a huge one!" I offered, trying to appeal to the boy's natural enthusiasm for larger-than-life things. Max began to show a little more interest, and we used all of our combined strength to roll what turned out to be a massive snowball for the bottom of the snowman. By the time we finished, it was well over four feet tall, almost as tall as Max. "How the heck are we going to lift the body and head to put on top of this?" my son inquired. "We'll figure it out," I said confidently, despite not having the foggiest idea.

Next, we rolled the middle ball. Easily three feet tall, and heavier than we could possibly lift. "Now what?" asked Max, looking crestfallen and glancing at the imposing snowball. He was beginning to eye the window to the warm indoors. "Uh… hmm… let's see…" I said, clearly befuddled. "Well I guess we could break it in half and put it back together after we lift it up," Max offered logically. "Of course. Brilliant!" I said, revealing both relief and fatherly admiration.

After finishing the middle part of the snowman, we set to work on the head. We quickly rolled a sizeable but still lift-able snowball, and I was able to reach up and set it on top of the snowman's body. We found rocks nearby for eyes and buttons. A quick holler to Grandma inside the house resulted in the perfect carrot for the nose. We grabbed some long sticks for arms, and a bendable stick for the mouth.

Finally, the snowman had all the standard snowman features, but there was one problem: He looked kind of creepy. Something about the misshapen black rocks for eyes and wide stick smile made him look a little less like Frosty and a little more like The Joker from *Batman*.

Me: "Whaddaya think?"

Max: "I think I'm cold."

Me: "Well he's awesome and huge, right?"

Max: "Definitely awesome."

Me: "Uh, do you think maybe we might want to take another shot at making him a little cuter, maybe a little less creepy?"

Max: "I'm good."

Me: "You sure?"

Max: "Yeah, I think he looks cool like this. I'm heading inside."

We went inside and found Max's older cousin Connor sitting at the breakfast table. "How do you like the snowman?" I asked.

Connor replied with intense enthusiasm. "It's amazing! Huge, and just a little bit sinister! I get this strong feeling that this snowman is going to move a bit closer to the window every day until his carrot nose is pressed right up against the window and he is poised to attack us. Simply awesome!" I looked at Max's face to read his reaction. He was on cloud nine, smiling ear-to-ear and shaking his head slowly up and down as though he had planned the sinister effect the whole time. Enthusiastic approval from his older cousin. Life was good!

Over the course of the next few hours the rest of the cousins, aunts, uncles, and grandparents cycled through the kitchen.

"Oh my God, who built the monster snowman?"

"It's enormous! We have had a lot of snowmen up here at Christmastime, but that is by far the biggest."

"Is that thing going to come eat us for breakfast?"

Max's snowman stood guard peacefully and uneventfully for the next few mornings as the family viewed him from the breakfast window. Then came Christmas morning. Every year at Grandma's house, the cousins sleep in while aunts, uncles, and grandparents finalize presents and prepare Christmas breakfast. As the older generations busied themselves with Christmas Day duties, nobody noticed that the window shade next to the kitchen table was mysteriously closed.

Eventually one of Max's uncles lifted the window shade. Aunts, uncles, and grandparents were all shocked to see that the creepy snowman had moved toward the house during the night. His carrot nose and stick arm hands were now pressed tightly against the window. His mouth and one of his eyes appeared to be bleeding. Two signs, written on cardboard and taped to the window, used eerily familiar holiday lyrics to announce:

*He sees you when*
*you're sleeping!*

*He knows when*
*you're awake!*

Aunts, uncles, grandma, and grandpa began laughing hysterically. Who had done this? Whose idea was it? Clearly the younger generation had decided on a Christmas prank.

As it turned out, all of the cousins had been plotting for days. Once the idea struck them, they couldn't resist. They simply had to pull off this prank. It took all of the cousins working together late on Christmas Eve to pull apart Max's snowman, move and rebuild it where it would have the maximum impact. Max was right in the thick of it all, cheered on by his older cousins who suggested ketchup as fake blood and the signs using familiar, but in this context, creepy, lyrics.

Surprises are a delightful part of the Christmas tradition. For our family, this year will always be remembered as the year that Max and his cousins brought a fresh element of surprise to Christmas. This year, it was the older generations' turn to be surprised and to laugh wholeheartedly. It was the year of the giant sinister snowman.

~Vince Monical

Reprinted by permission of www.offthemark.com.

# 59

# The Re-Gift

*Well, if he can re-gift, why can't you de-gift?*
*~Jerry and George,* Seinfeld

Now, since it is Christmastime and thus the season of forgiveness, I must confess, I have a dirty little secret. Before any of you get worked up, you better know that you all probably have one too. I am a closet re-gifter. (Gasp!) I know. Not only am I a closet re-gifter, but I actually have a closet that is just for my gifts to "Re"!

Don't judge me. Re-gifting is a longstanding Southern tradition. I mean, waste not want not, right? Most of you probably have a shelf or a drawer at home that houses some things that are nice but just aren't for you. SO, rather than throw them away, you save them for a rainy day when you realize you need just the right thing for that person you totally forgot about.

My re-gifting is an inherited trait. My mom keeps a cabinet above the washer and dryer filled with goodies to give. And my grandmother? One year she gave my mom this really interesting sweater on Christmas Day. After dinner we pulled the videos and we watched everyone open the gifts from the year before. What did we see? My grandmother receiving the exact same sweater that she had just given my mom! Coincidence? No. Certifiable? Yes. So see? There was no way I was gonna be able to avoid my re-gifting dysfunction.

You would think I would learn my lesson since I have had a re-gift or two backfire on me. Once, I sent my cousin, who lives in

California, a wedding present from my stash... a clock that was given to me on my birthday by my crazy Aunt Nadine. It was... unique. I truly thought she would love it. Weeks later I received a thank you note for my thoughtful gift:

> Dear Erica,
> Thank you so much for the wonderful clock. I was a little confused when I opened it up and there was a card inside that said, "Happy Birthday Erica. Love, Aunt Nadine"

Busted! But even after all that, my affliction remains. I mean, I promise I'll quit someday. First, I just have to get rid of the whistling key finder, light-up shower mirror, cupcake-scented bath gels and the leopard-print long johns. Any takers?

~Erica McGee

# 60
## Chicken Soup for the Soul

# Santa's Joke

*Nothing's as mean as giving a little child something useful for Christmas.*
*~Kin Hubbard*

W e lived in St. Louis when I was six years old. There were five of us, ranging in age from five to ten, so you can imagine the flurry of excitement on Christmas morning. The five of us woke very early and hurried to wake Mom and Dad.

Mom insisted that we all brush our teeth before bouncing into the living room where Dad was checking to see if Santa Claus had visited. As we ran in, we stopped and stared at the beautiful Christmas tree and the mound of presents underneath.

In our house, presents were opened systematically. Typically, Mom would hand one package at a time to whichever child was named on the label. Everyone would watch as the presents were opened one by one. This particular year, as we continued to open one present at a time, everyone was opening clothing. There were dresses, boots, hats, scarves, gloves, jeans, and even less exciting that that — socks and underwear. Even our stockings were stuffed with shampoo and soap and other hygiene products.

The five of us tore open these presents at record pace, thinking that with the next gift there surely would be a toy, a game, or even a book. Alas, as the pile continued to dwindle, and the last present was opened, socks if I remember correctly, there was not a toy to be found.

We were all disappointed but tried not to show it.

Mom said something about thanking Santa and suggested that we all head into the kitchen for breakfast. We did indeed mumble a thank you and slowly followed Mom and Dad to the kitchen.

As we sullenly went around the corner and into the dining room we were suddenly amazed. There in front of the dining room window was a second Christmas tree. Even more, there was another mound of presents underneath. I can still hear our high-pitched squeals. There were claps and jumps and oohs and ahs everywhere!

Mom and Dad were equally surprised and said something like, "Well — I guess breakfast can wait a little longer! What did Santa do?" With that we again began the process of opening presents one by one so that everyone could see the wonderful Christmas gifts. And in this room, full of our second Christmas, the presents were all toys, games, coloring books, crayons, play-dough, dolls, paints, and racing cars. There was not a pair of socks to be found!

As we finished opening gifts, we again thanked Santa (with much more enthusiasm this time) and happily skipped into the kitchen for breakfast. As I've grown older, I consider how practical that first Christmas tree and the gifts underneath were and I also think about how tricky Santa had been! That joke he played on all of us made for a very memorable Christmas!

~Lil Blosfield

# 61

# Saint John

*Santa Claus has the right idea: Visit people once a year.*
*~Victor Borge*

y husband doesn't fit with my family. Never is it more evident than at Christmas. The men are testosterone-driven sports nuts who huddle near the TV ranting and raving, oblivious to the rest of the world—until dinnertime. It drives him nuts.

The first time he was introduced to my dad, he was asked, "What's your favorite sport, John?"

"Golf," he said.

"What about other sports?" my father countered. John wasn't interested in any other sports, so that was the beginning and end of their bonding.

Being an only child, John covets his privacy. He was born to older parents who were stoic Germans. They lived a quiet life, so crowds make him nervous. He enjoys being alone.

I, on the other hand, have two brothers and one sister born of parents who married as teenagers. She nagged and he threw temper tantrums. Noise and upheaval were constants in our life.

In order to be accommodating on Christmas, however, when it's our turn to have the family gathering—and to please me—John has learned to cope. This brilliant, self-effacing, only child takes on a whole new role for the day.

He begins this new role when the first person pulls up and ends it when the last person pulls away from the curb. He rehearses his lines thoroughly and knows exactly what his mission is. To hide.

The first place he hides is in the kitchen. As guests start to arrive, he plants himself near the counter with open bottles of Chardonnay and Zinfandel and shouts, "Come right on in. What's your pleasure?" He knows he can spend ample time there pouring, dabbing up spills, and refilling the wine glasses. The men bring their own beer.

When it comes time to tackle the garlic-mashed potatoes, he digs in with fervor, retrieving the large pot and peeler. Mom, in her eighties, feels somewhat slighted. For years it was her job. "Don't you want some help, John?" she whines.

John dismisses her with a casual, but loving, "Oh Lois, you just go back to the family room and spend time with your family." Is he good, or what? Mom looks up adoringly and coos, "John, you are a saint."

John finishes the potatoes, then takes the hams out of the oven and places them on the counter, along with the side dishes brought by the rest of the family. So far, so good.

"Time to eat," shouts Saint John, and all twenty-two family members rush to the counter. Except the ones with testosterone, who are supervising their sports teams. They have to be called twice.

John hands out the plates so he can go through the line last. Comments that he should go first fall on deaf ears. He knows that by the time all twenty-two get through the line, some of them will be finished eating and he can eat — alone.

Saint John does the cleanup afterward, taking his time. He even takes out trash bags that are only half full.

When he can stall no more, he heads upstairs to the master bedroom to read *Outdoor Life* and *The Rifleman*. If anyone notices he is missing, my mom quickly comes to his defense. "Oh, I hope he's taking a nap. He's worked so hard getting dinner ready," she purrs. If she only knew.

He comes out of his cave only when he hears my brother-in-law Jerry go outside to smoke. Mind you, John doesn't smoke, but outside is another place to hide and he can bond with Jerry. They are the only two males in the family who don't live for sports.

As it nears 4:00, my dad stands up and announces, "Well, Lois, let's get going. It's a long way home and I'd like to get back before dark!" It's a two-hour drive for them, the others about the same, so they all leave together.

No reason to stay any longer. The football games are over and there is no gift exchange anymore since the children are grown.

When the last family member walks out the door, John and I give each other a high five and streak to the kitchen, stumbling and laughing. We fill two wine glasses with Chardonnay and head for the sofa. I feel giddy from one too many glasses of wine already.

I give a toast. "The award for best actor in the family festivities category is... Saint John." We clink our glasses and I quickly add, "And, the award for best supporting actress in the family festivities category is... me! To add to the drama, we hurl our glasses into the fire.

~Rosemary Barkes

# 62

# The Brown Pants

*At Christmas play and make good cheer*
*For Christmas comes but once a year.*
*~Thomas Tusser*

The voices from the playroom downstairs were getting louder, and I was now able to distinguish the words as I slid the lasagna into the oven. "Stop touching my stuff! Look what you did… you've wrecked it. I'm not giving you a doll for Christmas, Becki, I'm giving you brown pants!"

"What? No! I don't want brown pants."

Heavy thumping up the steps accompanied the heartbroken wail, "Mommmmy." This argument would need to be settled.

My distressed eight-year-old daughter burst into the kitchen and stood before me. Her lower lip trembled and two big tears teetered on her dark lashes, ready to spill over. Words tumbled out.

"Mommy, Pete said for Christmas he isn't gonna give me a doll, he's gonna give me… brown pants!"

Her howling started in earnest now and I did my best to hide the smile that was threatening to escape. Apparently this was the worst thing that could happen to an eight-year-old girl. Brown pants. How did my son even think of these things?

Calling her brother upstairs, I waited for the explanation. He came into the kitchen with a huge grin on his face and I struggled to keep from responding in kind.

"Pete, why are you giving your little sister brown pants for Christmas?"

"Well, she keeps breaking my Lego buildings, and I've warned her over and over to stop." With a shrug, he said, "I don't know, it just came out."

Our twelve-year-old son was somewhat of a Lego protégé, creating elaborate and intricate structures that astounded us all. They took him days to complete. His sister, seeking his attention, always got it by attempting to rearrange them. I took the opportunity to sternly warn her. "Becki, you must not touch Pete's buildings. They take a great deal of work to make."

With Christmas only two weeks away, she promised to obey, but her devastation over the brown pants was just too funny for her brother to ignore. Over the next few days he continued the horrid threat every chance he got, thoroughly enjoying her tearful reaction.

It was time to give him a taste of his own medicine.

Digging around in my husband's closet, I found an old suit he had been hanging onto since the 1980s, with a perfect poop brown, pinstriped pair of pants—exactly what was needed. Finding a large box, I rolled them around an old wrench, wrapped the box in bright cheery paper, signed the tag "to Pete, from Becki" and stuck it under the tree.

For the next week and a half Peter shook, sniffed, and listened to that box, trying to figure out what was inside. It was all I could do not to laugh out loud and give away the surprise.

Christmas Day dawned crisp and cold, but the house was warm and cheery, with the crackling fire in the fireplace, the aroma of cooking turkey, and six excited children gathered around the tree sorting stockings that bulged with goodies. Peter could hardly wait to open his big, colorful present, but stockings were always first, then breakfast before presents. His excitement knew no bounds.

The time finally arrived for presents to be distributed, and like every other year, we opened them one at a time so that everyone could see and be properly thanked. Pete chose the one from Becki to open first.

We watched as he tore the paper off and ripped the packaging open. Staring into the box, his face was a picture of confusion and intrigue. He slowly pulled the pants out of the box. Holding them high, he looked at Becki with the strangest expression.

A great roar of laughter rippled around the tree as we all yelled out, "The brown pants!"

Enjoying the joke, Pete good-naturedly put them on and modeled them for us as we clapped and whistled. My mother especially found the whole thing hilarious, cheering Pete on with enthusiasm.

The next year, a strange box appeared under the tree, wrapped by a young boy's hand, addressed to his grandma, and that morning we all laughed once more as my mother opened the brown pants and managed to model them for the family.

The following year they materialized again, this time finally given to Becki, now ten years old and able to appreciate the humor.

Those old brown pants have shown up under our Christmas tree now for twenty-two years, each time rewrapped in brightly colored paper and always surprising the recipient.

Our reaction remains the same as it was the first year, but instead of a family of eight, we are now a family of twenty-five enjoying this never-ending prank. We really need a bigger room now, and perhaps a smaller tree, but the same joy and laughter rings out each year when the brown pants are opened.

Life is short and the smallest joys can sometimes make the greatest memories. For our family, the brown pants have become a tradition, and each year the telling of the saga of the pants to the newest member seems to be a little embellished, but nothing changes the fact that something that once brought tears to a little face now brings warm laughter and Christmas cheer to a loving and growing family.

~Heather Rae Rodin

# 63

# The Battle of Perspectives

*Perhaps the best Yuletide decoration is being
wreathed in smiles.*
*~Author Unknown*

'll never forget the first time it occurred to me that some of life's battles are just a matter of perspective. It was Christmastime. I had only been married a few months and we did not have the first candle, blinking light or piece of tinsel to make the season bright. Our budget was small, and the enormity of the problem of a Christmas without decorations was causing my heart to palpitate to the theme from *Jaws*.

Suddenly, the angel of bargain shoppers appeared unto me (in the form of an ad in the newspaper) and said something to the effect of, "Fear not, for I bring you good tidings of great joy! There is a store going out of business, open twenty-four hours a day, with greater discounts each week. Tonight at midnight, everything will be an amazing seventy percent off! This includes the trim-a-tree department!"

"Ho, Ho, Ho and Merry Christmas to me!" I snarled and sneered. It was 1:30 a.m. when I grabbed that oversized shopping cart.

Have you ever been shopping at some strange hour and wondered why there were so many people shopping at such a weird hour? Talk about no room at the inn. This place was overflowing with customers. Obviously, the angel of bargain shoppers has a big mouth.

I battled my way through the masses and slowly made my way to the decking-your-halls area. And there it was… aisle upon aisle, packed floor to ceiling with every imaginable Christmas decoration. I had definitely hit the mother lode. But by the looks of things, everyone else in the greater Dayton area had discovered my jackpot too. This particular part of the store made a war zone look tidy. Stuff was thrown anywhere and everywhere, with each shelf ransacked into complete and utter chaos. I quickly decided that bargain shoppers are just a small step above looters and that last week's fifty percent off had been good enough for most folks.

I went into full-blown combat mode. I grumbled, fussed and manhandled my cart up and down each mistletoe row. I spoke only once to a two-female enemy unit that was trying to take the same aisle. I pointed to the debris-strewn floor and said, "I'd get out of your way, but I can't get my cart through these aisles." Let's just say my tone probably reflected a bit of tension.

Within minutes I heard these two women talking from the next row over. "I don't know why people come shopping at this hour if they're going to be grumpy," one of them said. The first thing that caught my attention was that she said it in a nice voice! How could anyone be nice under such conditions? I was shocked. Bargain shoppers didn't talk in nice voices. This looting stuff was hard work. Then something else started to dawn on me. Were they talking about me? They thought I was grumpy?

From my perspective, I thought I was being nice just by talking to them! The brief exchange was my way of establishing a superficial bond as comrades-in-arms. After all, they were the competition, potentially going to beat me out of some jingle-bell door hanger. So to my way of thinking I had just offered a ceasefire.

Besides, wasn't everybody grumpy at 2 a.m. while belly crawling through a virtual foxhole of merchandise to snag a really cute nativity set at seventy percent off? Don't we all get a little testy as we charge the next hill of discarded wreaths for that adorable inflatable snowman? Honestly, I was working so hard to find just the right decorations that I'm pretty sure I had stopped bothering to breathe for the last fifteen minutes! Then I heard these women laugh! Can you imagine? They were actually talking in nice voices and having a good time! How could it be so?

I stood puzzling and puzzling this dilemma until my puzzler was sore. Sure, it was easy for the two of them to have a good attitude. They probably already had a lawn full of dancing reindeer and a waving Santa. But I, on the other hand, felt just like Bob Cratchit, without so much as an extension cord to my name.

Then I thought of something I hadn't thought of before. Maybe those two women thought this was fun. Perhaps from their perspective, this was a chance to enjoy each other's company and welcome the holiday season. Maybe they came into this situation with an attitude that was happy and they thought of this shopping excursion as an adventure, not a battle to be won. Maybe there are some things in life that don't have to be quite so hard. Perhaps little adventures, like bargain shopping at 2 a.m., was one of those things. And just maybe it's up to me to make that choice. Then, just like the Grinch's heart, my small perspective grew three sizes that day!

~Jaycee Burgess

# That Darn Cat

*It is impossible to keep a straight face in the presence*
*of one or more kittens.*
~Cynthia E. Varnado

"Brace yourself," my brother warned as he hung up the phone. "Grandma is coming."

Don't get me wrong. We loved our grandma but when we heard that she and Gramps were coming for Christmas, we had mixed emotions. Gramps, a big, jovial fellow was always making us laugh. But Grandma, although tiny in stature, could be a grouch! She didn't mince words. "Nice girls don't wear tight dungarees." Now I wouldn't be able to wear my new jeans. "Only fools spend money on movies." There went our plans to see *A Magic Christmas*.

My brother and I quipped in unison: "When Grandma speaks, everyone cringes." Mom was not amused and warned us to be respectful.

Then we remembered Grandma's number one rule: "No pets in the house." Milot, our beloved cat would have to be banished to the basement. The basement wasn't heated. We glanced sadly at the gray and white Maine Coon, pregnant with her first litter. She was comfortably curled up on the counter in the kitchen — for now.

Mom had taken great pains to make everything perfect for the holidays. A bright, berry wreath hung on the front door. Live poinsettias adorned the windows. The vanilla fragrance and the soft light of scented candles created a calming effect. She smoothed out the festive red and green fabrics concealing the foldout tables and reminded us, "Mind your manners, don't talk with your mouth full, and use your napkin."

"What's a napkin?" half-joked my older brother, Dee.

The house was glowing. And so was Mom.

It was the first time all the relatives were coming to our new home. "Ooohs" and "ahhhs" were heard as each one entered. The grandparents were the last to arrive. We heard Gramps' old Chevy come to a screeching halt. I ran to the door as my brother removed the cat from the room. I gave Gramps a big kiss and turned to hug Grandma. She held me at arms' length, scrutinizing my face and blurted, "Too much rouge!" She meant "blush."

"Oh, Mama," Gramps jumped in protectively. "It's the cold that's making her cheeks so rosy."

My brother carried their overnight bag into the spare bedroom. They were staying a couple of days.

As Grandma's gaze took in the elaborate decorations, a "Humph!" escaped her lips. "Nothing better to do with your money, Mrs. Millionaire?" In the true essence of goodwill, Mom tactfully ignored the dig and welcomed her parents affectionately.

Everyone gathered in the tiny quarters. We spent a while catching up. Aunt Katherine got promoted. Adele announced her engagement. All good news except Grandma's arthritis was acting up.

Eventually, we took our places for the feast. Traditional American fare was tastefully arranged all around. There were even delicious side dishes from our grandparents' old country. The turkey took center stage. The parties at each table joined hands as the youngest, Cousin Mille, said her well-rehearsed grace. Things went without a hitch until she got to amen. Then an unexpected snicker arose from the kids' section, followed by increasingly louder chuckles and giggles. Soon boisterous laughter was in full swing. With a low moan coming from deep within, Milot, the cat was moving in slow motion, dragging Grandma's size 44 Double D bra behind her.

Mom's face was ashen. Grandma's mouth was open wide. Her complexion had taken on the color of the pickled beets on the platter in front of her. The laughter had come to an abrupt halt. An ominous silence ensued. My brother snatched the cat — which refused to let go of the brassiere — and whisked her out of sight. Mom threw us a harsh look and Grandma scolded, "An animal belongs in the yard; not in the house." Gramps grabbed a shot of Schnapps and practically shoved it under Grandma's nose: "Here, Mama. This will help your cold." Grandma slugged it down. And then another.

The Schnapps seemed to help because gradually the corners of Grandma's mouth turned up. She confessed, "That darn cat! She made me smile." Before long, we were all smiling and chatting, gladly putting the cat-and-bra incident out of our thoughts. The rest of the meal went smoothly. The supper was a huge success.

When all the dishes had been cleared, we gathered around the brightly lit tree and followed our custom of Christmas caroling. Aunts, uncles, cousins, brothers and sisters put aside any differences of the previous months. A feeling of contentment, gratitude and love enveloped us in a warmth not unlike a bear hug. For a few hours, harmony and accord prevailed; at least in spirit if not in our musical attempts.

Sometime later Mom noticed that Grandma was absent from this pleasurable and rare gathering. "Go find her," she urged.

I wandered toward the guest room. The door was slightly ajar. Without opening it further I peeked inside. Grandma was sitting in a recliner, her head bent over something. I looked closer. Milot, the cat was snuggled happily on her lap. Grandma's face wore a blissful expression. Her weathered hands gently stroked the cat's chin and behind her ears. "Pretty Milot. Whose kitty are you? Are you Granny's little darling? Yes, you are," Grandma purred. I don't know whose purr was louder.

Busted!

I sneaked away without being seen.

In February, when Milot had her litter, Grandma timidly asked for one of the kittens. She and Christmas spent the next seventeen years living together in peaceful contentment. And Grandma's disposition improved immensely.

~Eva Carter

# Merry Christmas!

## The Joy of Giving

# 65

# Charity

*Christmas is most truly Christmas when we celebrate*
*it by giving the light of love to those who need it most.*
*~Ruth Carter Stapleton*

I walked through the house looking for my twelve-year-old daughter, Jessica. Entering the family room, I found her sitting cross-legged in front of the Christmas tree. Her back was to me, her long blond hair nearly reaching the floor.

"Hey, what are you doing?" I asked.

She didn't answer, but I noticed her wiping her nose on the back of her hand.

"What's going on?" I persisted.

She paused. "Have you spent everything you were going to spend on me for Christmas yet?"

"No. Why?"

"How much is left?"

I thought about the budget and wondered where this was going. She was probably going to ask for something way too expensive.

"I'm not sure. Probably around ninety dollars." Again I asked, "Why?"

She turned to me, her gray sweatshirt streaked with tears.

"Honey, what's wrong?" I sat down beside her and cradled her in my arms. This was my baby, the youngest of my children. Jessica was the one who took my husband's death seven years earlier the hardest. At the tender age of five, she lost her daddy to a flash fire at the place where he worked and she still missed him terribly.

After her sobs subsided, she told me what was on her mind.

"There are so many people who don't even have food. They don't have a home or a place to sleep." She paused. "Can we give the rest of the money you were going to spend on my presents to the homeless?" Her request was pure and sincere. It was my turn for tears.

"Whatever you want, baby," was all I could muster. "Whatever you want."

The tiny bulbs on the tree sparkled, lighting the season with new hope... hope for my daughter's generation. Perhaps this would be the one to eradicate poverty and homelessness. At least I knew there would be one amongst them who would try.

On Christmas morning, the family gathered to exchange gifts. The pile of presents under the tree was considerably smaller that year. Yet somewhere close by, a family or two was enjoying an unexpected Christmas celebration. I glanced out the window at the gently falling snow and said a prayer for them. Looking up to the heavens, I had a heart full of gratitude. "Thank you," was all I could manage to say.

Jessica smiled as she watched her sisters opening their packages. And as she gave me my present, I looked at her precious face and knew there was nothing in that box that could be better than the gift she'd already given me.

~Hana Haatainen-Caye

# 66

# The Mitten Tree

*Winter must be cold for those with no warm memories.*
*~From the movie* An Affair to Remember

s a new teacher, I did not believe the myth that children's behavior could predict the weather. But after three years of teaching first graders, I no longer had to watch the weather on TV because I had twenty forecasters in my classroom! The way in which they were behaving one winter day led me to believe we were in for a major snowstorm.

I knew we had to get outside, even if it was just for a few minutes, to release some of their energy.

At our lockers, I made sure that the children put on their coats as well as their socks on their hands.

Socks on hands? You might think this a little strange, but since ninety percent of the students in this school were living in poverty, mittens were not a priority for their families.

Buying twenty pairs of mittens was something this new teacher wanted to do, but since I was still attending graduate school, and my husband was beginning graduate school too, I could not afford to do it. But I could always get my hands on some socks! Especially socks that had lost their mates.

After playing "Duck, Duck, GOOSE!" several times, it was time to go back inside. When we arrived back at our classroom, the children's rosy cheeks matched some ornaments that were now hanging on our classroom Christmas tree. There were twenty pairs of beautiful red mittens that had not been there before! How did they get there?

The children were so excited and all wanted to try on a pair. After they put them on, they did not want to take them off! So we did everything in them (math, reading, and going to the library) — except (after much insistence from me) eating lunch.

Before the children were dismissed for the day, we talked about who could have left these beautiful mittens on the tree. Most of the children thought that they must have been a gift from Santa. I had to agree, because I still had no idea who else would do such a wonderful thing.

After the bell rang to dismiss us, I walked my students outside and that is where I spotted Santa's helper.

Oohing and aahing at the children's beautiful mittens was Miss Johnnie, a senior citizen who volunteered at our school in the first grade classrooms. One of my students informed her that Santa gave them all mittens. She just smiled.

And just like Santa, her "eyes how they twinkled," as she replied, "Or maybe it was Mrs. Claus?"

Miss Johnnie's warm heart, as well as her warm mittens, chased away the chill, not only on that particular winter day, but still today.

After twenty-four years it still gives me a warm and cozy memory — thinking how precious the experience was. A special Santa's helper saw a need in my class and did something about it on her own without having to be asked.

I smile and think of her kind act every time I see a pair of red mittens.

~Stephanie Ray Brown

# The Magic in Giving

*Sometimes a small thing you do can mean everything*
*in another person's life.*
~Author Unknown

"I don't care about the other dresses, only the jumper," I snipped at my mother, who flashed me her warning look.

"You've got plenty of dresses you can wear. Besides, it was your sister's jumper and it barely fit her; I'm sure it would have been too snug on you," she replied. My mother was right. It was too tight, but I figured I could get away with wearing it once.

Considering there was the slightest chance that the jumper was still in our house, I continued to badger my mother. "But she promised I could borrow it for my Christmas program," I whined. "I've always loved that jumper! How could you give it away?"

"I'm sorry," she said, patting my back in a motherly fashion. "I didn't know about your plans. Now try to remember that Christmas is about the magic of giving. When you give, you receive." Luckily for me, I received the condensed version of Mom's lecture on giving. She turned to leave, then paused. "By the way, you know the rules," she reminded me. "If you see someone wearing your dresses, you're not to mention it. And you are not to discuss it with your friends. Is that clear?"

"Yes," I replied. "But who has it now?"

"Someone who needed it much more than you did," she answered. "Now, we're finished. I don't want to hear another word about it."

Back in my room, I fought back the tears. My mother routinely gave away our outgrown dresses, but this was different. I had coveted that black-velvet jumper ever since I first saw it. Not only that, but the dress was store-bought, not homemade like most of my clothing. She had even given away the silky-white blouse that went with it.

The evening of my Christmas program I remained sullen as my parents dropped me off at my classroom. Of course I couldn't help but envy the few girls — clothed like princesses — parading around in their velvet dresses. Unfortunately it put a damper on the whole evening and made me wish the night were over. When the teacher finally shouted, "Quiet class; it's time to line up," a feeling of relief swept over me.

As we shuffled into line, our chattering voices once again reached a deafening crescendo. The teacher attempted to quiet us, but to no avail. Moments later, the door opened and a sudden hush fell over the room as a beautiful girl entered.

Her long, blond hair swirled in gorgeous curls that shimmered against the rich, darkness of her black-velvet jumper. Against her naturally tanned complexion, her blouse appeared whiter and richer than when my sister had worn it. Her face glowed in ecstasy and I checked twice to make sure it was her. Honestly, the transformation was stunning. Even dressed in black velvet, she looked like an angel straight from heaven.

After a few minutes everyone finished gawking and we proceeded down the hall to the auditorium. As we walked, my mind drifted back to the first week of school. She was a newer student, bussed to our school from the overcrowded city schools. Unfortunately the popular girls had poked fun at her because she had worn the same plain clothing each week. However, the cutest boy in our class had confided in me that she could be the most beautiful girl in our grade if only she dressed better. As we waited to go on stage, I noticed whispers and eye rolling coming from a few girls. I left my place in line and walked over to her. "You look absolutely beautiful," I said to her and I meant it. "I love your velvet jumper! It's gorgeous!"

"Thank you," she meekly replied, obviously unaware that the

jumper had once belonged to my sister. "It's an early Christmas present. I've never had anything this beautiful before," she said, lovingly running her fingers over the rich fabric, affectionately stroking it as if it were a fluffy kitten or dog. As I studied her glowing face, I realized that I had seen her smile a million times before, but never like this. She positively beamed — particularly in a spiritual sense. As a result, the joy I felt as I watched her brought such a grand smile to my own face that my lips twitched and my cheeks ached, from using muscles I had never used before.

As I watched my beautiful classmate, I was completely unprepared for the sincere, warm, fuzzy emotions that I felt. I honestly felt as if a song had entered my heart. My mother's simple gift of giving had obviously transformed me, too.

In truth, my mother had been right. Not only had my beautiful classmate needed that dress more than I did, but there was a wonderful magic in giving. And even though I wasn't the one who had done the giving, I received the joy as I watched my mother's gift continue throughout the school year as one timid girl — dressed in our hand-me-down dresses — continued to grow and blossom into a graceful, confident person.

~Jill Burns

# 68

# Christmas Spirit in Aisle Three

*Set your heart on doing good. Do it over and over*
*again, and you will be filled with joy.*
*~Buddha*

The wind was howling and the snow swirling when I looked out my window. The worst winter in thirty years, and I was here for it, after twelve years away in Florida. It was a bitter cold night in the single digits; a perfect night to stay in and watch a Christmas movie after adding some finishing touches to the tree. I reached for the remote and my soft, fluffy new blanket. As I sat down, my cousin Joey called, "Get ready, we're going to Walmart." Before I was able to protest, he was in my driveway, honking impatiently.

"It's three days before Christmas. What's left for us to do?" I protested, with my teeth chattering, as I slid across his warm seats. He laughed, "You'll see." This better be good, I thought. A blast of cold arctic air stung our faces as we made our way across the frozen parking lot. About a dozen or more cars were parked close to the door. It was busier than I thought it would be; maybe everyone was looking for last-minute deals.

I love being in the stores at this time of year. Music playing, lights twinkling and the fun of watching people shop and share good cheer. Of course I headed directly to the toy department. This was exactly where I wanted to be. This was the fun stuff, seeing the shopping carts go by with noisy toddlers onboard who were mesmerized by plush, red fluffy animals and toys placed right within reach. Aisle after aisle of "ho-ho-ho" and "Merrrry Christmas," combined with children's laughter added to the excitement. This definitely was the action spot. So many choices, all tempting, yet many moms just passed by. Happy little faces began frowning and lips curled. Where were their toys?

That's when I noticed most carts were sparse, some were even empty. Maybe these people were shopping for needs... not wants. It was apparent looking into the carts that this wasn't about toys. I silently wished each child could pick a toy.

As I stood there, the joy I had felt a few minutes earlier slipped a little. Joey read my mind, whispering, "That's what we're here for. Let's go." Confused, I followed him to the back of the store. He said to the manager, "I'm here to pay off some kid item layaways."

"It's too late. That department closed yesterday," was the manager's reply. Disappointment swept over Joey's face. For a moment, he and the manager just stood there. But I could see Joey's mind was in motion. "We'll do something else instead."

"Come on," he said to me as he headed to the front of the store. When we reached the cashiers, he whispered to one, "I want to buy several gift cards of various amounts." She carefully picked out different happy cards; some with Santa's face, some with reindeers and sleighs and some with snow scenes.

Joey took off with the cards in hand and I followed him. He took his time walking around, and then spoke to a few moms and kids. He was getting a feel for each individual family, discussing how they spent Christmas. What were their traditions? His approach was intimate and personal. He chatted a few minutes, then simply said, "Merry Christmas" and handed them a gift card. Then he walked away as quickly as he had arrived. Moms were stunned, staring at the cards in their hands. The kids giggled, as if Santa had just paid them a personal visit. That's how the first few surprises went. Mixed emotions and expressions, all beautiful to see and experience.

One mom made a quick call, very excited, and then made a list.

Returning to the toy section, she placed one toy into the happy hands of her child. Another one pushed her cart as if in slow motion. Her son's little arms reached out for a stuffed animal, which she was happy to provide. This was much like a Christmas morning scene, where the kiddies sat by the tree, restless but excited, waiting impatiently for their special gifts. This and many more repeated moments of happy little faces brought the season back to life. Gone were the strained faces on the moms. Instead we saw waves of relief!

Soon Santa's helper was looking for more families to surprise. A boy who was with his grandma was looking at catcher's mitts. Joey gave her a gift card. She looked at it in disbelief. She rushed to the clerk, asking if it was real. Once she really, really knew it was, she handed her grandson the mitt he wanted, telling him, "Call your dad. Tell him we're bringing home a Christmas feast." And off she went into the food section. I loved watching this.

His final giveaway was to a young mom who was looking at the prices of space heaters. Joey approached and whispered to her. Instant joy came across her face as she accepted the gift card offered to her. She picked up the heater, placing it in the cart, and then went shopping for a doll for her daughter, all the while thanking him over and over. When she walked away, she looked back, seemingly to make sure this was real.

Joey's Christmas spirit warmed my heart and the hearts of others that cold blustery night. I am so happy I took that ride with him. Many people's wishes came true because of Joey's unexpected gifts. By sharing his blessings, Joey got so much back, too. That was a Christmas shopping trip I'll never forget.

~Paula Maugiri Tindall

# 69

# The Project

*There is nothing more essential to getting a project off*
*the ground than the underestimate.*
~Robert Brault, rbrault.blogspot.com

Many years ago, when our oldest two children were small, we tried to think of ways to save money at Christmas. We started early in the summer and decided that we would make all the Christmas gifts for the children.

It was easy for me to decide. I said, "I will make PJs and robes for the children. And I have time to make a dress for Tina and a shirt for Rob."

I loved to sew. So my project was simple — just get the material and patterns, and when the children were napping I would sew.

On the other hand, my husband's project was not so simple. That summer when we visited his family in Pennsylvania, he found that his grandmother had a pattern for a wooden beanbag-toss clown. It was cute.

"This is it!" my husband exclaimed. "I will make this for the children for Christmas and they will love it. Only we will enlarge the pattern so it will stand about four feet tall. That will seem huge to the kids."

We would make it in one room of our basement and the children would not be allowed to go into that room until Christmas. Simple — well, maybe!

We got a big piece of plywood and some paint and I helped enlarge and draw the clown. It had a big smiley hole for the mouth where you would toss the beanbags — very simple. We painted it bright orange with lots of other colorful colors on the face. I made buttons for eyes out of yellow yarn pompoms and hair out of red yarn.

My husband made a stand for it and I thought it looked very cute. But… my husband worked with electronics at that time and was not quite satisfied.

"I think that I can make the clown beep whenever a bean bag goes through the hole in his mouth. And I can make his eyes light up and flash at the same time."

He had been working on this idea for some time and now was ready to put his theory to the test. He began his project in earnest — welding in a box to hold all the wires and getting the electrical components he needed. Before we knew it, we had spent over eighty dollars on this one gift! So much for saving money. But my husband was having the time of his life fixing this clown so it would make noise and light up.

"We need some way to wrap the clown," my husband said one day. "But it would take a huge amount of paper." After some thought he continued, "What if we make a cardboard playhouse for the kids?"

"A playhouse?" I questioned.

"Yes," he responded, "we will get some big pieces of cardboard and a few 2x2s to make it sturdier and build the house over the clown so the children will be surprised when they open the door. There will be our big clown inside."

I thought it might be a fun idea so he went to the furniture store and asked for some big boxes, which they were glad to get rid of. Once again we worked on this project after the children were in bed at night. This one did not cost much because we used the leftover paint from the clown and the cardboard was free. It turned out to be a cute little house with windows and doors that could be opened and a roof that could be removed.

Christmas Eve finally came. We were anxious to get the kids into bed so we could get the clown out of the basement and set it up. We put the house up and over the top of the clown and put the roof on. We were excited to see what the kids' reactions would be in the morning.

Christmas morning arrived and the children opened their PJs

and robes and dress and shirt that I had made that were under the Christmas tree. They also had gifts from grandparents, so they were happy with what they got. But then the big moment arrived!

"Let's go downstairs." We all went together, and there, in the middle of the floor, sat the house. The children could not believe their eyes! They had a playhouse! They hurried over to go inside but much to their surprise the house was already occupied. They stepped back, not sure what to think.

My husband could wait no longer. "Let's get him out!" he exclaimed.

And immediately he dismantled the house. The children stood in shock as my husband removed the roof and had me help him lift the house up and over the clown. My husband quickly plugged in the clown and said, "Watch what happens when I throw this beanbag into his mouth."

The first beanbag he threw went straight into the clown's mouth and the clown began to beep and his eyes began to flash. Both children began to cry!

They were so confused! Here sat the playhouse they thought they were getting and then it was taken apart. And here was a clown bigger than they were, with eyes flashing and making a lot of noise. For one second I wanted to laugh. All our Christmas plans hinged on this clown and now it scared the children half to death.

When we finally calmed them down and put their playhouse back together, everything was okay. It took a little time for them to warm up to the clown, but once they did, he provided many hours of fun for the whole family.

More than forty years later we still have that clown at our house. His eyes no longer flash and he no longer makes noise when you throw a beanbag into his mouth, but we do occasionally get him out and have a beanbag contest or take him to some children's activity. And we fondly recall the Christmas we "saved money" by making our gifts.

~Shirley M. Oakes

# 70

# Real Christmas Joy

*We cannot live only for ourselves. A thousand fibers
connect us with our fellow man.*
~Herman Melville

Those new clothes I've been waiting for
I finally get to buy,
And I'm in such a festive mood
For Christmastime is nigh!

The store is crowded while I shop
But I don't mind a bit;
Arms full, I rush to try things on,
Wondering how they'll fit.

While walking past the twinkling lights
Hanging in the window,
Something there draws my attention
And my steps begin to slow…

A little face is pressed to the glass,
His eyes are shining and bright;
My glance falls to his ragged coat
And tears I have to fight.

He points to toys he cannot have,
His lips are moving fast;
His mom looks sad as she takes his hand
And tries to pull him past...

All the things she can't afford
But wishes that she could;
Her little boy deserves much more,
He's always been so good.

The clothes I hold now seem heavy,
They weigh upon my arm;
And suddenly my shopping spree
Has lost all of its charm.

Laying aside the things I chose
I hurry out the door,
Knowing Jesus wants me
To be generous to the poor.

I slip my gift into her hand
And feel my spirit soar!
For her eyes glisten as she leads
Her son into the store.

~Denise A. Dewald

71

# Chicken Soup
for the Soul

# The Goats
of Christmas Past

*What counts in life is not the mere fact that we have
lived. It is what difference we have made to the lives of
others that will determine the significance
of the life we lead.*
*~Nelson Mandela*

O ver the years, my three children have asked for and received plenty of "typical" Christmas presents. In younger years it was baby dolls and metal cars; now as teenagers they prefer an "alphabet soup" of technology: CDs, DVDs, Mp3s, iPods. But I know nothing will ever mean as much or be as well remembered as the goat that defined Christmas for us several years back. A simple barnyard critter embodied the true spirit of the season for us.

Our goat-centered holiday started at the mailbox on a gray afternoon in early November. Along with the usual junk mail, the postman delivered a very unusual catalog. Unlike the glossy brochures from the big toy stores and outlet malls, this little magazine came from a charitable organization dedicated to helping the poor in Haiti, and it offered page after page of items to give to the less fortunate. Selections ran the gamut from simple things like a week's worth of rice for ten dollars to an all-inclusive kit for building a two-bedroom house — complete with mini kitchen and bathroom — at just over $2,500. But the entry that caught our attention was a fuzzy little farm animal for the bargain price of only forty-five dollars. My children, ranging in age from eight to eleven, were mesmerized by the notion of purchasing a goat for Christmas.

"Your generous donation of a goat will provide a needy family with milk and cheese for years to come," the catalog blurb promised. "This life-giving gift could mean the difference between going hungry every night or having enough food for weary parents and growing children."

We were sold. That very day we cut out the goat's picture, taped it to an empty pickle jar and set it on the dining room table so everyone could drop in contributions. Our goal was to collect forty-five dollars by mid-December, making our Christmas goat dream come true.

The children immediately began referring to our sponsored goat as "Cheddar Bob." (Like most things my kids come up with, the logic of their thought process is foggy and elusive. The only thing I can figure is that "Cheddar" refers to the fact that goats' milk can be made into cheese, and "Bob" — who knows? Male goats don't give milk — let alone cheese — so that remains a mystery to me even now.) Whenever any of them were asked, "So, what do you want for Christmas?" they answered, "We want to send Cheddar Bob to Haiti."

The "Cheddar Bob Fund" grew at first by dimes and quarters; then paper dollars began showing up in the glass jar. My husband would forego his beloved Starbucks coffee and put the money toward the goat instead; the children took on extra chores to earn money toward meeting our goal. When Christmas cards arrived with cash inside from aunts and uncles and grandparents, the children gleefully stuffed the loot into the ever-filling jar, determined to purchase Cheddar Bob in time for the holidays.

Two weeks before Christmas, we dumped out the jar's contents and counted the money. To everyone's delight, our total was $91.25, more than double the amount of the required forty-five dollar donation! Ecstatic, my daughter immediately declared, "We can send the family two goats — a boy and a girl! Then they'll have goat babies!" Within seconds, the goat-bride was dubbed "Colby Jane" and plans for the furry couple's Haitian honeymoon were being made.

That was nine years ago, and I don't remember a single gift the kids got for Christmas that year, and I doubt they do either. I'm sure we received lots of lovely things, given from truly loving and generous hearts. But the lasting memory of that holiday will always be of two goats we never saw, who live on in our imaginations to this day. Every Christmas, we say a prayer for the Haitian family who taught us that it really is better to give than receive, and we speculate on Cheddar Bob and Colby Jane, and their happy adventures on a distant farm. By now, they surely must have quite a large family of goat children, whose names I won't offer, but you can probably surmise they would be cheesy!

~Miriam Van Scott

Reprinted by permission of www.CartoonStock.com.

# 72

# It's for Everyone

*There is no greater joy nor greater reward than to*
*make a fundamental difference in someone's life.*
*~Sister Mary Rose McGeady*

One would think a seasoned member of Santa's helpers, and Captain of the Golden, Colorado Elves, could
easily answer any Christmas-related question thrown
her way. However, that was not the case this time. My
inability to quickly formulate, let alone articulate, an answer was not
because it was a difficult question. It was due to the setting and what
appeared to be the reason behind the child's inquiry.

A few years ago, at Christmastime, my lieutenant elves and I were
helping Santa in a church-based homeless shelter. We were attempting
to keep the excited little ones in line while waiting for their one-on-one
time with St. Nick. I was distracted from my duties by someone pulling
on my elf shirt. The young fellow's head only reached the middle of
my five-foot frame.

I looked into his face and was greeted by twinkling brown eyes
and a wide grin showing some missing teeth. He motioned for me to
bring an elf ear closer to his mouth.

When I was within hearing distance, he asked, "Miss Elf, is Christmas
for me too this year?"

His hopeful expression broke my heart. I returned to a standing
position, hoping that moving slowly would buy me the time needed
to come up with an answer. Somehow, a simple "yes" just did not

seem to be enough.

"Yes. Yes, sweetest child," I said, "Christmas is for everyone. And it is especially for you this year."

His eyes sparkled as he received the answer, nodded his head and moved in the direction of the big guy in red. I was pretty sure there was a sparkle in my eyes as well, but it was due to tears. I wondered how many times he had asked that sad question, and what answers he had received, during his young life.

I watched as he and Santa engaged in conversation. I could not take my eyes off him until I heard a soft voice in my left ear: "Thank you. You made his Christmas. May I give you a hug?"

I turned to face a woman in her mid-twenties who looked like the boy's mother. She gave me that hug and then asked permission to tell me her story. I nodded again.

She related that for the past four years she and her two children had lived on the streets of Denver. She had fled an abusive marriage in the hope of keeping herself and her children safe. In summer months they slept under bridges. In winter they were housed overnight in shelters when there was room for them. She had not completed her high school education. So, at best, she was only able to find sporadic, temporary employment.

She had recently passed her G.E.D. and been accepted into a training program she believed would qualify her for permanent employment. In the past, she was unable to provide holiday celebrations for her children, and this was the first joyful Christmas her little family would know. She said she felt like there finally was light shining in their darkness, and that light was restoring her faith along with her hope.

At the conclusion of her tale, I more fully understood why her son asked the question. When mother and child reunited, they moved on to a table full of food. The aromas of roasted turkeys, hams and sweet potatoes, as well as a variety of fresh-baked pies filled the air. The little guy was literally pulling his mother toward the celebratory feast. Before they reached the table, he turned to look at me. I smiled and winked at him. He smiled back and attempted to wink by quickly blinking both eyes several times.

I left the church that night with elf bells jingling and pointed green shoes plodding along in a snow-covered parking lot. I thanked God for His mercies and for that little family. I felt gratitude for being allowed to be part of their celebration. As I considered what had just happened, I asked myself if I had ever really understood the true meaning of Christmas until that moment. Had I ever been such a close witness to hope offered to the hopeless? Had I previously, and intentionally, taken time from my busy schedule to observe others experiencing new life and another chance? Wasn't that really what Christmas was supposed to be about?

While sitting in my car and watching snowflakes fall on the windshield, I reflected on the numerous times I had celebrated in beautifully decorated churches, sang carols, opened presents and enjoyed delicious food. Yet, I could not remember ever before feeling the peace and joy I unwrapped that night as I answered the simple question of a young child made wise by life on the streets but refusing to relinquish his precious sense of expectant hopefulness.

I can honestly testify that in an old church, on a wintry Denver night, in the presence of a child angel who relied on a secular elf to answer a sacred question, I was a recipient of the true blessing of Christmas. And I understood that every year, in the busyness of the worldly holiday season, there is one question that must never go unanswered: "Is Christmas for me too this year?"

~Laura L. Padgett

**73**

# The Year We Got to Know Santa

*You can't live a perfect day without doing something for
someone who will never be able to repay you.*
~John Wooden

It was 1982 and we had two children, ages two and eight. We were both in graduate school and money was tight. I took a part-time job with House of Lloyd as a manager.

To know me is to wonder, "What the heck was she doing selling toys and other merchandise at home parties?" I hated it. I felt like I was taking people's hard earned cash. As a manager I only had to do three parties, but I had to find employees who were willing to earn cash, free gifts, plus their $300 kits, for selling people everything they thought they needed for Christmas. Fortunately, I had some great people. All but three earned their kits by selling more than $1,000 in merchandise. I was left with three kits to return, as well as the contents of my own sales kit.

Enter my social work brain. I called Congressman Kostmayer's office and asked if they could find a use for $1,200 worth of toys and gifts. They found a homeless shelter that had just opened. It was ten days before Christmas. I contacted House of Lloyd and they generously donated the three kits I had on hand. I then spoke with the caseworker at the shelter. I was in shock at how little they had on hand. Having just completed my social work internship, I knew she was in over her head. I asked for the ages and sizes of everyone in the shelter. Then the fun began.

I called a local children's clothing outlet, where I bought my kids' clothes, and the owner donated new coats for all the children. Boscov's department store donated items for men and women, and a local sock outlet donated new socks. Manufacturers donated baby food, diapers and formula. Food donations came from supermarkets. More new toys from friends and co-workers arrived. Every one of my friends knew they'd better donate items or cash to the cause — I can be very persuasive — and everyone came through.

The owner of the children's outlet was so moved that he added outfits for all the kids. When I was done arm-twisting, we had $10,000 in merchandise and cash for the residents of the shelter. Missing were Christmas stockings, a tree and Santa himself.

During the toy party season, my Great Aunt Jingo passed away and left us a little inheritance for a down payment on our first house. We moved into our new home on December first. At the time I was also busy finishing my practicum, so I couldn't have been busier. I paid for the stockings and enlisted my friend Joyce in the Christmas stocking project. We bought glitter and sat in my new living room, on the ugliest carpet ever, with no furniture, and wrote each child's name on the stockings with glitter. There were more than twenty-five, enough to wreck the ugly carpet and "force" us to replace it ASAP. We filled the stockings with candy and, courtesy of my dentist, toothbrushes, toothpaste and floss.

As for Santa, there was one problem. At this late date no one wanted to sub for the real Santa on Christmas Eve. Considering we were Jewish and had nothing else to do that night I decided my skinny, six-foot-two husband would be perfect as Santa's stand-in. We managed to scrounge up a Santa suit, stuffed a few pillows inside and, lo and behold, I was married to the jolly old elf! Even my daughter fell for it. My husband's personality was transformed in that magical suit. His usually laidback demeanor became animated. His eyes twinkled. He had quite the "Ho, Ho, Ho."

Not only was this the first Christmas season in our first house, it was also our first Hanukkah there. We always made a big fuss for Hanukkah so our children understood that this was our holiday. We never had a "Hanukkah bush," but we had blue-and-white lights and decorations all over our new split-level. Anyone walking in and seeing all of this Hanukkah and Christmas chaos would think it was a holiday-themed asylum.

We loaded our station wagon and Joyce's minivan, strapped the huge tree — a last minute donation — to the roof, and were off for our ride across the county. Santa was yelling Merry Christmas out the window at every red light. When we reached the shelter, the kids all ran to meet us. My husband, transformed, scooped up kids in his arms and carried them into the shelter's living room. The plan was not for him to have each child on his lap, but rather to help unload the gifts and food. Fortunately, all the caseworkers were available, as well as some of the dads. We were unloaded, stockings hidden, new coats tried on and the tree set up. Santa was still talking to the children, handing out candy canes and having more fun than anyone.

After passing around some Christmas cookies baked by the parents in the shelter, we hung all of the homemade tree decorations and placed wrapped gifts (Joyce had wrapped adults' gifts, too) under the tree. At the end of the day, we left the shelter full of holiday spirit. Our kids were with us, but I chose not to tell them this was a homeless shelter. As far as they were concerned, we were celebrating Christmas with new friends. I never wanted my kids to think of others as charity cases. Some people need a little help, that's all.

Santa remained jovial the entire ride home. Our kids went to bed right after hanging their own stockings, full of excitement to see what goodies Santa brought to good Jewish children. We left a snack for Santa and carrots for his reindeer. My husband took off his costume and changed back into himself. He was quite pleased that he had helped Santa by standing in for him on Christmas Eve. By the time we were able to sleep, the kids woke up, raced down to the family room and were thrilled Santa had their new address. The stockings were emptied. They played with their new toys, ate candy, watched TV, and then we did what Jewish families in America do for Christmas:

We went out for Chinese food.

In my sixty-two years there have been many great Hanukkahs, but this was a Christmas like no other. At the mall the following year my daughter told Santa that she was Jewish, so she wouldn't be sitting in his lap again. I still have that last Santa picture. My son wanted to kill his sister for ending the Christmas stockings, but Hanukkah was our holiday. From then on, Santa visited our friends and sometimes left a gift for my kids.

To this day we help those in need at the holidays, but Christmas 1982 is still most special. It was a year of transformation for our family and the beginning of new traditions. It was the year of the new house, the year I completed my degrees, and the last year Santa visited our home. It was also the year that Santa touched our hearts and souls. "Yes, Virginia, there is a Santa Claus." He even lives in the hearts of this old, observant Jewish couple.

~Judy Davidson

# 74

# Packages of Christmas Joy

*Blessed are they who see Christmas through the eyes of
a child. Let this be your gift at Christmas.*
~Author Unknown

Every first and third Thursday of the month, I barrel down Arrow Boulevard on my way to St. Catherine's where I meet with a dozen other women for a Bible study. We meet in the convent's chapel where the nuns once attended morning Mass and recited their daily hours of prayer. The nuns no longer live in this convent, but their beautiful spirits still linger in the rafters of this sacred space.

I like sitting at the table facing the magnificent stained-glass window that once was the backdrop for the altar. I feel at peace here where the morning light filters through the window in shafts of golden sunlight.

I have learned a lot from these women who have come together to study the Bible. I have seen them take pregnant women into their homes who had no place to lay their heads at night. They have baked dozens of casseroles in twilight's final moments for a stranger down the street in need of a decent meal. They have stayed with ailing people through their darkest hours, leaving their bedsides only when morning's light promised a new day. So I wasn't surprised this past Christmas when they decided to forego our regular gift exchange for something greater.

"Instead of exchanging gifts this year," Donna said, "let's bring a gift for a child in the parish who wouldn't have a Christmas otherwise." We all agreed that this was an excellent idea.

On the day of our Christmas gathering, our little Christmas tree in the chapel looked grand, and somewhat important, with all the brightly wrapped packages around it. Last year's CDs, scarves, clocks, and vases were replaced with yo-yos, stuffed toys, puzzles, and coloring books — gifts that either a girl or boy could enjoy.

After opening prayers and petitions were offered, we gathered the gifts in our arms as if they were precious cargo and headed across the street to the parish office. The secretary behind the counter was pleasantly surprised to see this caravan of Christmas joy come through the double-glass doors of the building.

"This will make a lot of children very happy this Christmas," she exclaimed. "We'll make sure each gift finds a home."

I couldn't help but feel that something very special had just taken place. My faith in all things wonderful blossomed a little more within me.

Returning to the chapel, we continued our celebration of the Christ Child's birth. Sharing Scripture, fellowship, and delicious food, the morning graciously slipped into the rafters of the chapel.

As our closing prayer, one of the members read a beautiful Christmas poem that she had recited every year since she was a child. We listened intently as memories of our own childhoods found their places between the lines of this special poem. She made a copy of the poem for each of us, rolling it in scroll fashion and wrapping it in red, satin ribbon — a wonderful souvenir for years to come.

Heading back down Arrow Boulevard toward my home, I thought of my now-grown children and how happy they used to be on Christmas morning when brightly wrapped packages magically appeared under the Christmas tree. And I thought of the children in my parish and how excited they would be this Christmas morning when brightly wrapped packages magically appeared under their trees.

I am reminded of a wonderful verse inside one of the Christmas cards I sent out a few years ago. Its message now takes on a special meaning all its own:

Blessed are they who see Christmas through the eyes of a child.
Let this be your gift at Christmas.

~Lola Di Giulio De Maci

**Chapter**
**8**

# Merry Christmas!

Traditions Worth Sharing

# 75

# Christmas Chimneys

*"Maybe Christmas," the Grinch thought, "doesn't come*
*from a store. Maybe Christmas... perhaps... means*
*a little bit more."*
~Dr. Seuss

"Ready for pumpkin pie?" I asked.

"Not yet," answered my sister Debra. "Thanksgiving dinner needs to settle a bit, but I am ready for Joseph to help me get something special out of my car."

Debra headed out the door with my five-year-old. Rachel and Rebecca, ages four and three, scampered onto the loveseat to spy on their aunt and brother through the front window.

Rachel yanked her thumb out of her mouth long enough to say, "They gotta box, Mama. Wonder what's in it?"

Debra settled cross-legged on the living room floor with three pairs of eyes fixed on her. Four pairs, if you count mine. The three pieces of cardboard my sister pulled from the box looked like miniature redbrick chimneys, only with drawers on them. Each stood about two feet high and four inches wide. My sister had printed the names of my children across the tops, one chimney per child, and numbered the drawers from top to bottom.

"We're going to celebrate the Twenty-five Days of Christmas," Debra told the children. "See the twenty-five drawers in the chimneys? One week from today is December first. On that day, you will each open drawer number one on your chimney." She slid open a drawer, revealing a small red package.

Rebecca leaned over her aunt's shoulder and whispered, "I wanna open it now."

"Nope. Not until December first and you each open one drawer each day."

Debra alternately opened several drawers of each chimney to display the little red, green, gold, and silver packages. I'd never seen such itty-bitty bows. Finally, the gift-giver exposed the contents of a bottom drawer, the one to open on Christmas Day.

"Aw," Joseph lamented. "There's nothin' in there, Aunt Debra."

My sister pulled him close. "That's because I'm bringing your last present when I come on the 25th. It's way too big to fit in that drawer."

"Oh, boy," exclaimed Rachel. Her hazel eyes sparkled with the possibilities.

While the children tugged at drawers and viewed their minuscule contents, I motioned for my sister to join me in the kitchen.

"Debra," I whispered, "you spent way too much money on this."

"No, I didn't," she insisted. "I got half of the stuff at the dollar store and the other half are free trinkets from fast food restaurants. Of course," she added with a laugh, "I did occasionally have to eat at the same place three times in one week."

"It must have taken forever to gather and wrap them all," I said.

"It did," she agreed. "I worked on this project all year and had a blast doing it. Don't let the kids tear up the chimneys because I want to do the Twenty-five Days of Christmas every year until they tire of it."

After breakfast each morning, the children marched into the living room and sat in front of their chimneys. Giddy with anticipation, they determined the appropriate drawers to open and unwrapped their gifts in unison.

Rings, necklaces, miniature candy bars, matchbox cars, packs of chewing gum. The presents were often identical except for the color. Other times, Debra had personalized them, like the white bead bracelets with the child's name spelled out.

Every time I talked with my sister on the phone, I rattled on and on about how much fun the children were having with their chimneys.

I told her they played and played with the little gifts, usually while discussing what might be in the next drawer.

Which gift turned out to be the favorite for each child? I don't remember. What large gifts did Debra bring on Christmas Day? I don't recall that either.

Well, then, what do I remember? A comment made by Rebecca. The children had just opened tiny packages of Christmas stickers and set about embellishing the packages under the tree.

Rebecca, kneeling beneath twinkling green branches, looked up at me. "Aunt Debra thinks about me all the time. Did you know that, Mama? She thinks about me all the time."

Rebecca was right. And that's the best gift ever.

~Arlene Ledbetter

# 76

# Keep Those Cards and Letters Coming

*True friendship is seen through the heart, not through the eyes.*
~Friedrich Nietzsche

When the first Christmas card arrives in the mail, I let out a groan. That's because my own cards, purchased in last year's clearance sales, are still stored in the "holiday" closet, a place overflowing with Easter pastel bunnies and assorted Halloween goblin masks. Receiving that first greeting card means I'm already behind in sending my own cards for the season.

With electronic correspondence so much easier than handwritten notes, cards in the mail seem to get scarcer every year. Instead of batches of Christmas cards arriving right after Thanksgiving, now there is only a dribble each day, if any arrive at all.

But that's okay, really. Signing cards and writing personal messages rings of chore more than cheer.

I have considered skipping this duty and simply phoning a few friends or e-mailing a holiday greeting to all. But then one day there was a special card in the mailbox. I knew it would be there; it has been every year since I was thirteen years old. It was a card from my pen pal.

For more than half a century I have been exchanging letters and cards with a stranger. At least she was a stranger when we began writing to each other as part of a school project. Thousands of miles separate our homes, and dozens of calendars have expired since that first letter from Texas arrived at a small junior high school in Wisconsin and was chosen by a young girl looking for diversion and an anonymous pal.

Throughout high school and college, Helen and I exchanged letters regularly, sharing new experiences as she studied nursing and as I became a teacher — typical occupations for our generation. We shared our hopes and dreams.

In those days before e-mail, our friendship grew steadily through written details of new adventures and increasing maturity, despite the different paths our lives followed. I married young; Helen married late. I wrote about my houseful of children; Helen wrote about nieces and nephews. I changed careers several times; Helen persevered in hers.

Because long distance phone calls then were reserved for emergencies, unthinkable for casual chats among friends, we maintained our relationship via the written word.

I used to think that we would certainly meet one day. We exchanged pictures and predicaments as perennial friends do, knowing that our lives would cross paths soon, and we would pick up in person what we began on paper. But that hasn't happened.

Although we have never met, Helen and I have been through college together, celebrated marriages and births, lamented over divorce and illness, and commiserated about our jobs. We grew into adulthood via old-fashioned pen and paper correspondence — and our relationship seems destined to remain that way.

We have grown up, branched out, and become complex adults. Yet we remain the same: two people separated by geography and lifestyles who still care about each other's lives. It's an experience in continuity, in grounding, in roots. I've depended on it through numerous address changes and for many holiday seasons.

Our letters are less frequent now than they were in the early years, the result of busy schedules and fewer changes in our circumstances. But the sentiments are just as strong. Neither of us would consider letting a Christmas slip by without a card and letter updating our lives.

Helen's annual card reminds me that I matter to someone out there, even if she has never met me in person. Our connection follows my life from adolescence to grandmother-hood. Hers is the longest friendship I have had.

Lately I find myself sending more cards to friends living in our new hometown than to those in the city where my husband and I spent virtually all our adult lives. After only a few years away, we maintain contact with just a handful of acquaintances. Relatives living in faraway places also grow distant.

But each year when Helen's card arrives in the mail I remember why I keep a list of names and addresses in a spiral notebook. Staying in touch, even if we saw our friends just last week, is worth the effort. It's even more important to maintain contact with those we seldom see.

So I leaf through my notebook as I sit at the table facing a stack of Santa prints and snow scenes lying open beside my pen. I'm ready to begin the ritual of writing heartfelt greetings. Through the annual exchange of Christmas cards, I touch the past and glimpse the future.

As I open the envelope from my longtime correspondent, I wonder what changes have taken place in the last year. I need to know: Is she healthy and happy? I send sincere wishes for peace and prosperity and realize that I care too much to skip the ritual. My cards will be in the mail tomorrow.

~Beverly Burmeier

# 77

# Love Notes on My Tree

*What cannot letters inspire? They have souls; they can
speak; they have in them all that force which expresses
the transports of the heart....*
*~Héloïse to Abelard*

"I wish I could find enough words to tell you how much I love you," said my tall, dark and handsome husband, holding me tight.

He worried about not being able to buy me a present. Emmitt had just finished his tenure in the Army and had enrolled in college on the GI Bill. We had been married only a few months, and he wanted our first Christmas to be special.

"You're my present and always will be," I answered. He smiled with relief. "Come on," I said. "Let's go shopping for a tree. Maybe we'll find one we can afford."

I think the salesman guessed our financial condition. "The trees have been picked over, but believe it or not, I have just the tree for you. I'll sell it for one dollar."

We thanked him and hurried home with the tree. We had nothing to decorate it with so we just sat and looked at it, listening to "White Christmas" playing on our little radio.

"Let's dance," Emmitt said, pulling me close. I thought I was in heaven.

Before he went to class the next day, he wrote me a love note. Telling me not to look at it until Christmas, he folded the paper carefully and tied it to the tree.

I decided to do the same thing. I would write a love note and hang it on the tree, too!

Emmitt noticed my creation and wrote another of his own the next day, and so did I. By the time Christmas Eve came, our "love note" ornaments "dressed" the tree in beauty.

Emmitt was still worried that I would be disappointed at not receiving a gift for Christmas.

Christmas Day arrived. Sitting together on the floor, we opened our love notes, and read them aloud to each other, moving ever closer.

Finally, I folded my last precious note and looked into his big brown eyes. "You are God's gift to me," I said, "and that's the greatest gift I could ever receive!"

He pulled me up, swept me off my feet, and twirled me around. We danced to the kitchen where we had a Christmas dinner of tuna sandwiches. To us, that tuna was a feast.

After Christmas, I took the notes off the tree and put them in a box. Little did we know we were starting a tradition. The next Christmas, we added new notes, and I carefully placed them in another box.

By the time our boys came along, we had a lot of Christmas notes. Each holiday, we wrote notes to them, too. They, of course, wanted to scribble on paper and hang their notes on the tree. We called it our "love tree."

As our sons grew, their notes became priceless. "Mommy, will you marry me when I grow up?" "Mommy, I love you because you pillow fight with me." "Mommy, do you want a dog that I saw outside for Christmas?"

"Daddy can we go rock hunting for Christmas?" "Daddy, I like the way you throw balls." "Daddy, you're the best daddy!"

All too soon, the boys grew up and had babies of their own. Yet, even today, every Christmas season, our grandchildren write love notes to hang on our special tree.

Our granddaughters never become tired of hearing stories about our first Christmas. "Mawmaw, could we read some of the notes Granddad wrote to you a long time ago on your first tree?"

"Of course," I say. I want them to know the extravagant love their grandparents have for each other.

We gather around in a circle, and each person gets a turn to pick a love note. Each one goes to the tree, picks a note on which his or her name is written, and pausing for effect, reads it aloud.

Jody starts. Pulling the first note from the tree, he unties the ribbon and unfolds the paper on which it is written. Smoothing the paper, he reads it to his granddad: "Granddad, I'm so thankful that you passed on a name to be proud of to my father, who in turn, passed it on to me!" I look at my tall, dark, and handsome grandson, and I see in him the tall, dark, and handsome man I married so long ago. In my mind, I hear the words "I'm Dreaming of a White Christmas," and in my heart, I dance with him again.

Love notes on our tree have become a legacy that has now soared with wings of love for four generations.

~Joan Clayton

# 78

# Christmas in July

*Christmas isn't a season. It's a feeling.*
*~Edna Ferber*

A few years ago a good friend of ours who was always "doing for others" was going through a really tough time both personally and professionally. As he was a self-proclaimed "Christmas person," a few of us decided to throw him a "Surprise Christmas" gathering in the middle of the summer to help boost his spirits.

As I love Christmas too, it was great fun simply preparing for the party. Of course there was some decorating to be done, a couple of presents to wrap, a tree to be put up and a few other items to add to the ambience.

Finally, the day arrived! The garland was hung; the little tree was decorated and the presents were under it; a video was playing on the TV with Christmas and winter scenes; the table was set for dinner with the holiday china; and the Christmas music was all set, simply waiting for the push of a button.

As it turned out to be the hottest day of the summer so far, up in the 90's, the curtains were all drawn and the air-conditioner was going at full blast so that it would actually feel cold when one entered the house.

All of the guests arrived. As we anxiously awaited the guest of honor, who had been told that it was a dinner party, it was really difficult to keep our excitement to a non-boisterous level.

Finally, one of the guests who had been keeping a "lookout" from behind a curtain said, "He's here!" So, we all took our places. One person was to open the door when our guest rang the doorbell, another was to begin the CD that played "We Need a Little Christmas" from the Broadway hit *Mame*, and the rest of us were to yell "Merry Christmas!"

Why no one thought to have a camera handy I'll never know, as the look on his face was priceless. Shock! Surprise! And a smile! He was speechless as he made every attempt to regain his composure. For one thing, he couldn't believe that we had pulled off the surprise. And as each minute passed, the smile on his face grew.

But, we weren't done yet. As we were eating dessert a group of carolers could be heard singing on the front porch. We, of course, invited these wonderful ladies inside where it was cooler, as they were all dressed in winter hats, scarves and mittens. We sang a few songs together.

After the carolers left, we had gift exchange — little mementoes of a wonderful evening together.

But the biggest surprise for all of us was yet to come. As we sat enjoying our coffee and each other's company we heard sleigh bells and a very hearty "Ho, Ho, Ho" coming from the front porch. As I opened the front door, there he stood — Santa Claus!

None of us could believe it! He not only had a gift for each of us but also had a list that told him if we had been "naughty or nice."

Then as quickly as he arrived, he was gone.

We spent the rest of the evening singing Christmas carols and enjoying the smile on our friend's face.

It had truly been one special and magical evening. So much so, that we all decided that what every July needed was "a little Christmas" for many years to come.

~Helen A. Scieszka

# 79

# Chicken Soup for the Soul

# Make Every Day a Holiday

*Celebrate the happiness that friends are always
giving; make every day a holiday and
celebrate just living!*
~Amanda Bradley

When Uncle Sam moved our family to Poulsbo, Washington, I was thrilled to call the Pacific Northwest my temporary home for another duty station. The ferryboat rides to Seattle offered breathtaking views of Puget Sound; the stately evergreens of ponderosa pines, Douglas firs, mountain hemlocks, and madrones towered on hillsides; and snow-capped Mount Rainier peeked its head out of the mist and clouds in a splendid display of beauty.

Yet, as the summer gave way to autumn, a slight depression settled around me. My husband, an outdoor enthusiast who had trouble adjusting to the constant rainfall and dreariness in our new home, blamed it on a solar deficiency. I, however, knew that it was the thought of spending our very first Christmas away from our large extended family.

Although we'd been married fifteen years, had four children, moved seven times, lived in six states, and survived separation during the Gulf War, David and I had consistently spent time over the Christmas holidays in our small and quaint hometown of Statesboro, Georgia. But not this year.

I decorated early to help dispel the gloom and add some cheeriness to our home. Even though I've always loved the festivities that Christmas brings, as well as other holidays and celebrations, I was surprised at how this act lifted my spirits.

I dreaded un-decorating, as I called it, when the season ended. Mostly because I feared it would bring back the sadness and longing for home that had been prevalent before the holidays.

I packed up the Santas and reindeer and gingerbread men, but decided to leave out the snowmen, and I turned the small, artificial tree we used in the den into a "winter" tree. I wrapped the plastic container that held the tree in a piece of fake snow, placed a stuffed snowman on top, and dangled snowy décor from the branches.

I hung a snowman wreath on the front door and left snowmen hand towels in the bathroom. For the next couple of weeks, my home-schooled offspring made snowy crafts and we added them to the dining room table and to my tree.

In January, we changed the theme to "all things penguins" to continue our winter celebration. Again, we made crafts, turned tootsie rolls into edible penguins, and found penguin plates on sale at a department store to decorate our table. Stuffed penguins from the toy box and crafty ones from our creative minds adorned my tree.

In February, I wrapped a red blanket around the bottom of the tree and filled the tree with red and pink hearts. We celebrated Valentine's Day for an entire month, with goodies, crafts, games, old movies, and lots and lots of love-notes.

March lent itself to St. Patrick's Day; April to Easter; May to a gardening theme; June to a beach theme; July, obviously, patriotic; August, back-to-school celebrations; September to all things apple; October to pumpkins and candy; and November to thanksgiving for a bountiful harvest. Our family had come full circle: we had feasted, and loved, and celebrated throughout an entire year.

During each season, I looked for bargain decorations to add to my collection. And I especially looked for clearance items after each season to place in my decoration box for the following year. St. Patrick's Day beads and Fourth of July flags at 75% off the original price make wonderful tree decorations a year later!

My family, at first, thought the idea of a "Christmas" tree staying out all year long was silly, but it didn't take long before it became as much of a treasure to them as it was to me. My holiday tree reminded us to celebrate each day as a precious gift. It brought a cheeriness to each day that I've not found in any other way.

That celebration began twelve years ago, and now, two houses later and back home in our little southeast corner of Georgia, my tree greets extended family and friends when they enter the foyer and reminds my own family to celebrate abundantly and to make each day a holiday.

~Julie Lavender

80

# Community Spirit

*This is the message of Christmas: We are never alone.*
*~Taylor Caldwell*

Our family of four missed the grandparents, aunts, uncles and cousins back home in Arizona when we relocated to Seattle, Washington. We missed the balmy weather of Phoenix. We missed strings of lights embraced in the arms of tall cacti in our neighborhood. I hoped the Northwestern holiday cheer would abate the chill in the weather and in our hearts.

Our son Nicholas listened to the local radio broadcasts and alerted our family when he heard about wonderful activities or yummy new restaurants. One day he said, "Mom! I just heard about The Great Figgy Pudding Christmas Caroling Contest on the radio. It's this Friday evening at Westlake Center. There is even a carousel that we can ride!"

Nick pleaded his case for a holiday outing in the crisp temperatures forecast for that weekend. "It will be fun to hear everyone sing Christmas carols. Radio station WARM, 106.9 FM is the sponsor." Nick, a gifted musician, is a huge fan of holiday music and this local Seattle station starts its holiday music broadcast on the day after Thanksgiving.

"Okay Nick, we'll check out the contest. That sounds like a great way to start our holiday." I searched our closets for long underwear, warm gloves and mufflers.

Nick, our younger son Dan and I met my husband Ray at the plaza. Nick is blind, so he couldn't see the dazzling lights, but his face lit up as the cacophony of carols greeted our ears. Even bundled in layers of warm winter wear, I felt goose bumps. My sense of awe, not the cold, caused me to shiver. "Wow guys, I am so glad we came!"

Contestants ranged from Starbucks baristas who belted out ballads, to attorneys and secretaries who sang their souls out. Anyone who carried a tune, read music and organized a group could participate.

We giggled at a group from a gourmet shop that sold garlic-themed products. The Garlic Gal and her Clovettes donned gunnysacks of garlic-shaped apparel and sang "Jingle Bells" in 1950's style.

Our favorite was the Beaconettes, a group of ladies who hailed from the Beacon Hill neighborhood. Tall beehive hairdos adorned with blinking lights accentuated their outrageous eyewear and brightly colored feather boas. They sang unique lyrics set to traditional holiday tunes. They lampooned major Seattle events set to the tune of "The Twelve Days of Christmas." Phrases like "a partridge in a pear tree" morphed into "one perfect game," a nod to Seattle's recent Super Bowl victory.

We wandered the area and listened to groups of singers. Our votes for the Beaconettes and the Garlic Gals were dropped, along with our donations, into the ballot box. We joined the crowds and sang along on a familiar chorus.

Warm libations from Starbucks and other vendors kept our vocal cords in tune. Grown-ups preferred hot coffee or lattes, but the kids' favorite was hot cocoa crowned with whipped cream.

Temptations tickled our noses. The savory aroma of chestnuts roasted on portable grills mingled with the festive fragrances of fresh pines. Piping hot nuts filled paper envelopes, perfect for hand warmers. Fresh doughnuts, hot from the kettle, bags of caramel popcorn, and waxed paper wrapped Turkish delights kept our tummies warm.

Nick maneuvered us toward the calliope music coming from the Holiday Carousel. As we stood in line, we sang an impromptu Christmas carol with our fellow passengers. Mounted side by side on festive steeds, we squealed like children. I waved to my husband and Daniel, who stood at the rail taking pictures to send to Grandma back in Phoenix.

When the ballots were collected and counted, the most popular contestants were summoned to the main stage next to the gigantic

Christmas tree. The finalists each performed an encore song. Thunderous applause, intended to sway the judges' decisions, almost drowned out the final notes of the ensembles on stage. The Beaconettes, our favorites, won second place. The Garlic Gals were not called on stage. "I guess the garlic repelled vampires and the voters too," I said.

After trophies were presented, officials on stage invited the audience to join in to sing "We Wish You a Merry Christmas." Tears welled in my eyes as we sang the notes of the familiar tune and declared our collective desire for "figgy pudding." My voice quavered on the chorus. I fished a tissue from my jacket pocket and I noticed I was not the only person in the crowd who dabbed at their eyes. No longer strangers, we were one big family and felt genuine warmth as we wished each other happiness in the coming holiday season.

In later years Nick joined carolers sponsored by a local law firm. The group, comprised of college students, sang avant-garde versions of Christmas carols. Nick, a quick study, was able to join in a hilarious song about a young couple's breakup and the events that ensued on the "Twelve Days after Christmas."

Our family was hooked. No other activities get planned on the first Friday of December.

Nick's little brother Dan is married now. His wife and her family join our group at Westlake Center each year. One day I hope to take some grandchildren of my own for a ride on the Christmas carousel ride!

Our holiday season begins each year, as we join over ten thousand Seattleites, who brave the cold, rain and occasional snow to stand shoulder to shoulder, in Westlake Center and sing, "We wish you a Merry Christmas and a Happy New Year."

~Kathy G. Passage

# 81

# In Service

*The ornaments of your house will be the guests*
*who frequent it.*
*~Author Unknown*

My father left the decision up to me, my mother cried when I told her, and I stood my ground. It was the 1960s, and the beginning of a new decade filled with hope and optimism. When President John F. Kennedy announced he intended to strengthen the military, I answered the call. Shortly after I turned eighteen, I enlisted in the United States Air Force.

I completed the aptitude tests, passed the physical and in September 1961, just months prior to Thanksgiving and Christmas, I was scheduled to begin training. When my departure date arrived, I took the oath of allegiance at the induction center, shook my father's hand, hugged my mother, who seemed to have adjusted well to my leaving, and shipped off to basic training in San Antonio, Texas, at Lackland Air Force Base, also known as the "Gateway to the Air Force." It was the same training center that all Air Force enlistees attend before they are sent to their first assignment. It was 1,500 miles from home and I was alone.

It wasn't until Christmas approached that I realized how much a holiday with family meant to me. It was my first time away from home and I missed my parents, relatives, friends and the celebrations and festivities that accompanied Christmas. My only solace was knowing I was not the only lonely airman. There were thousands of others around the world just like me.

Fortunately, the Base and Squadron Commanders understood how lonely single airmen felt being away from home for the first time, especially at Christmas, and took action to make the holidays as pleasant as possible. They encouraged military families to invite single airmen into their homes for a Christmas meal in a family setting. However, not everyone was able to get an invitation because of the large numbers of trainees compared to the number of families that could open their doors to us. I was one of the lucky ones, and the experience left me with profound memories.

The program soon became an Air Force tradition, with Commanders annually publicizing the "Christmas with a family" program and they posted signup sheets in the squadron or on office bulletin boards announcing the names of families that had agreed to host a holiday meal for single airmen. The only thing a single airman had to do was sign up, show up, and enjoy a holiday in a family atmosphere.

I never forgot the warmth and generosity of the family I visited during my first year in the military. They had turned their house into a perfect Christmas setting. It wasn't exactly home, of course, but it was the next best thing. It also gave me an insight into how military families lived outside of basic training and it turned out to be one of the many reasons I made the military a career.

After I was married with a family of my own, we decided to continue that Christmas tradition. Throughout the next twenty years, whether stateside or overseas, we offered an opportunity for single airmen to spend Christmas Day with us and share in our family meal and activities. Generally, we welcomed two or three young airmen, sometimes more. As it turned out, it wasn't difficult at all to set those additional plates at the dinner table. After the main meal, we opened presents, and there was always one for each guest as well. We also offered them an opportunity to place a call to a loved one. It was an exciting time for them and a rewarding time for us.

Throughout the years we heard from many of those young men and women. It was not long until our scrapbooks became filled with cards and letters from those who we befriended early in their military service.

One letter, written several years ago, especially touched home. I open it every year to reread it. It was from a young man we welcomed into our home more than fifteen years earlier. He was now married, had a family of his own and was carrying on the Air Force military Christmas meal tradition. He was a Sergeant, writing from his assignment in Alaska, reminiscing about the day he spent with us so many years before and the impact it had on his life. Aside from us treating him as one of our own, it also gave him an insight on what family life in the military was like, and he said it influenced his decision to make the Air Force a career. His words definitely brought back memories of my first Christmas away from home.

It was a heartwarming letter, one we keep pressed between the pages of our scrapbook along with many other military memories. It seemed to bring with it something special. It awoke feelings from within that we just couldn't explain. After reading his letter again, I carefully returned it to the scrapbook, smiling as I did so, wondering if someone, one day, would write him a letter that would bring him as much happiness as his letter did for us.

~Donald L. Dereadt

# 82

Chicken Soup for the Soul.

# When Should the Christmas Lights Come Down?

*Christmas is not about the lights — and it is.*
*~Author Unknown*

One of my favorite holiday season pastimes is driving around admiring Christmas lights. In other words, wasting lots of fuel in order to enjoy the creative ways my neighbors have chosen to waste lots of electricity.

But just how long should my neighbors leave their lights up? My friend Mark is of the opinion that Christmas lights are for Christmas. The moment Santa and his reindeer finish their rounds, he believes, you should be up on the ladder taking the lights down.

My friend Bill feels otherwise, which is why he just posted this notice on his Facebook page: "I hate the dark cold months of January and February. Therefore, I plan to leave my holiday lights up until March this year, and use them to ward off the winter gloom. Just consider them 'Winter Lights' and don't assume I'm lazy."

He quickly received a variety of responses:

*"I LOVE seeing lights through the winter. Thank you."*
*"Yes! Everyone should do this. Hate the short dark days. Love the lights!"*
*"Great idea! I may do the same."*

*"I always want everyone to keep their lights up to get us through the dreary months. Hope you'll become a trendsetter!"*

*"We're always the last house to take ours down. We'll take down the wreaths and bows, and retire our freestanding electronic Rudolph so that things look less Christmassy, but we keep the lights on to cheer everyone up. Glad you are joining us."*

*"We have two neighbors who compete every year as to who'll be the last to take their lights down. One made it to April last year, still burning brightly."*

*"We're not taking ours down for months either. Welcome to the dark side! (So to speak…)"*

Of course, Bill also received a touch of sarcasm along with his Christmas cheer:

*"So you're going to be 'that guy.' I'm sure your electric company applauds your decision."*

Inspired by Bill's example, I asked my own Facebook friends: When do you take your Christmas lights down? The day after Christmas? Two weeks after Christmas? Never? And when do you think your neighbors should take THEIRS down?

Some of my friends, as it turns out, are proud members of Team Bill:

*"I'd love to see lights up all through the winter. They make the cold and dark more palatable."*

*"When do our Christmas lights come down? The same day we get rid of the Christmas tree… on Valentine's Day!"*

*"For my family, Christmas Day means the end of the commercial frenzy and the true beginning of Christmas. We keep our lights up for all Twelve Days of Christmas, through January 6th."*

While I agree with the Twelve Days of Christmas concept, I'm already itching to take mine down. It's too cluttered around here, and all the extra glitter has me teetering on the edge.

Other Christmas light removal plans are more ad hoc:

*"They have to stay up until the Wise Men get there. Or they won't be able to find their way!"*

*"The sooner they come down, the better. Have to make room for the next holiday!"*

As for the question of when the neighbors should take down THEIR lights?

*"Whenever they feel like it. Their house, their call."*

*"If the neighbors are giving it the full Las Vegas treatment, that could be a problem. Otherwise, I trust them to use their intelligence guided by their experience."*

I also received a touch of bah humbug:

*"Christmas lights should never be installed in the first place. Waste of electricity."*

*"I don't need a light bulb to remind me that it's Christmas."*

*"When should the Christmas lights come down? Frankly, my dear, I don't give a damn."*

*"To me, Christmas lights are just light pollution. I'd rather see the stars."*

But the final word goes to the friend who has found a way to celebrate both Christmas and her companion animals:

*"When do our holiday decorations come down? Never! We keep the tree in the corner year round for the cats to play with. And light it on special occasions."*

So what do I do about holiday lights myself? I'm Jewish, which makes it simple. The menorah's candles glow in the window for the eight nights of Hanukkah, after which it goes back in the cupboard until next year. No Christmas tree, rooftop festooned with holiday lights, inflatable life-sized Santa or electric lawn elves for me.

But I still love a fabulous Christmas light show. Which is why I'm heading over to Bill's house. Maybe I'll see you there.

~Roz Warren

"That settles it. We're going shopping."

# 83

# Forty-Nine Perfect Hearts

*A hundred hearts would be too few to carry*
*all my love for you.*
*~Author Unknown*

I pulled back the dining room chair and saw a small, wrapped present sitting atop my seat. Dinner plate in hand, I stopped short, thinking of the unwrapped gift that lay hidden away in my dresser upstairs. "Oh," I said to my husband. "Are we doing this now? Yours isn't ready yet."

"Open it," he said.

I knew what lay inside, even though I didn't know the color, or the size, or even the material it was made of. I knew, however, that when I untied the bow, lifted the lid, and unwrapped the tissue I would find a perfect heart. An ornament for our Christmas tree.

My first heart arrived when we were newlyweds decorating a tree we had chopped down ourselves from a nearby farm. We had finished hanging the few ornaments from our blended households on its branches when Randy placed a small box in front of me.

"A present?" I squealed. "But it isn't even Christmas yet." He just smiled and nudged the box a little closer. I lifted the lid and gasped. A blown-glass, heart-shaped ornament with swirling colors lay inside.

"A heart for my sweetheart," said Randy. I kissed him and found a place on the tree where we could admire the heart all season long.

The next year I decided to surprise Randy with a heart bought especially for him. Weeks in advance I started looking for the perfect ornament to take its place beside the one he gave me. Finally I chose one made of wood, something pretty yet sturdy, to last through the years. We finished decorating our tree, and I pulled the package from my pocket.

"I got something for you," I said with a grin.

"I got something for you, too," he answered, pushing another package my way. And so a tradition was born. Much like our new marriage, in the beginning giving the hearts was easy. With no kids, few possessions, and time on our hands, we could shop until we found the perfect heart to add to our growing collection. Then our daughters came along.

Within a few years Christmas became a whirlwind of things we had to do with shrinking amounts of time to do them in. We hit the ground running the weekend after Thanksgiving and didn't stop until we sprawled exhausted beside a mountain of discarded wrapping paper on Christmas morning.

As our daughters grew, the rest of the year seemed to pass in a blur as well. We ferried the girls to art classes, soccer games, piano lessons, and set aside evenings to help with homework. There hardly seemed time for us as a couple; we were a family, a team of four, united in the purpose of raising girls who could take on the world.

Even so, every year Randy and I still gave each other a heart, despite feeling at times as though shopping for it was just another chore. Some years all the hearts we found looked like ones we had already given. Some years, heart-shaped ornaments were hard to find. Some years, we fought on tree-cutting day, hurling angry words at each other as we crammed one more event into our overbooked holiday schedule.

Those years, the hearts helped us put our anger aside. For how could we nurse a grudge when a tissue-wrapped heart lay waiting, a symbolic olive branch to put things in perspective?

Year after year, heart after heart, we filled our tree with ornaments of porcelain, glass, wire, raku, and wood, in colors of blue, red, green, purple, gold, silver, and swirling mixes. Each delicate piece is a reminder that though our relationship is fragile, it is also sturdy, and like the ornaments, with careful tending it will last.

Now, with our daughters in college, Randy and I once again decorate the tree on our own. We hang our favorite ornaments in prominent places, but every piece in our two-and-a-half decade collection is precious in some way, for they remind us that at the core, at the heart of things, we started out as two. And with any luck, we will face the world together as two once again long after our children go off to make lives of their own.

"You know," I say, as I unwrap this year's heart, a vibrant blue, blown-glass piece with a beauty separate from any that have come before it, "we're up to forty-nine hearts. At some point, we're going to have to quit this."

Randy looked at me as a quiet smile made its way from his eyes to his lips. "Never," he said. "Never."

~Cindy Hudson

# Chapter 9

# Merry Christmas!

## Around the Table

# 84

Chicken Soup for the Soul

# No Need for Carving

*One of the things that binds us as a family is a
shared sense of humor.*
~Ralph Fiennes

Soon after we married, I told my husband, "I'd like to host the family Christmas dinner."

Well aware of my limited cooking experience, he paused before he asked, "Seriously?"

"If I organize and plan it to a T, it'll be the perfect day."

To ensure success, I called my mother for her traditional holiday recipes. With pen and paper in hand, I dialed her number. Eager to end the initial chitchat, I blurted out my plan. "I'm cooking Christmas dinner for my in-laws." I thought the phone line had been disconnected.

Then I heard her chuckle. "Are you sure?"

When she realized I meant it, she suggested we compile a menu. After we made a list of what to serve, she dictated a detailed grocery list. Pumpkin spice? I had to ask where to find it. Extra cans of turkey broth? I thought it came from the turkey pan. She explained each item to me and after she hung up, I stared at the five pages in my hand. What had I gotten myself into?

When I braved the jam-packed grocery store, the items piled up. At the checkout, my cart looked like a dump truck — filled to the brim and ready to tip.

At home, I arranged ingredients according to each dish. Marshmallows, Karo syrup and brown sugar sat by the canned yams. Rosemary and sage lay by the package of cornbread dressing mix. Flour and cornstarch were ready for milk and turkey broth. Even the refrigerated items sat in groups.

I'm a detailed person — especially in uncharted territory. My method guaranteed there would be no chaos. And, I certainly needed a plan for this day.

I taped my mother's recipes to the kitchen cabinet doors and assessed what I could prepare ahead of time. I've never enjoyed dinners where the hostess serves the meat at room temperature, the veggies lukewarm and the rolls ten minutes later. Most assuredly, mine wouldn't be one of those. Everything would be ready at exactly the right time.

On Christmas Eve our house buzzed with activity. The smell of pumpkin pie hung in the air. My centerpiece complemented the red-berried holly leaves on the china; my festive mulberry candles waited to be lit, and my evergreen crystal goblets were shiny and bright. I placed the pristine sterling silverware on the just-bought linen napkins that matched the rich maroon tablecloth.

I instructed my husband, "No nibbling the appetizers on the lower refrigerator shelf. You can have the not-so-pretty ones on the top."

Eager for the perfect day, I slept little that night.

Christmas morning arrived with the sound of "Jingle Bells" from the radio alarm. I hit the off button and bounced out of bed... all ready to execute the plan.

"Need help?" My husband opened one eye.

"Nope. I've got it under control. Go back to sleep."

He rolled over and snored before I even shut the bedroom door.

In the hub of activity, I wrapped the seasoned turkey in foil and placed it on its assigned oven rack. A checkmark went on my to-do list. I added torn pieces of dried bread to the crumbled cornbread dressing. Check. Peeled and diced Idaho potatoes. Check. I scooped green and black olives into crystal serving bowls. Stuffed celery sticks lined a crystal dish. Check, check.

At the assigned times, I added the broth to the dressing and placed the pan below the already-cooked turkey. The yams had enough brown sugar to zap us into a sugar high. Every dish adhered to my schedule.

As guests arrived, I calculated where their food items fit into my plan. In the last thirty minutes before mealtime, I hummed as I finished the final tasks. Whipped potatoes steamed from their pan. Toasty brown marshmallows melted over the yams. I removed the foil from the roasting pan and slid the turkey back in the oven to turn it golden brown. My table would look like the delicious dinner pictured in the Poultry section of the *Betty Crocker Cookbook*.

I sighed and stepped away from the kitchen cabinet and then went to the living room to chat with guests while the turkey browned. From across the room, my husband winked at me. Everything was right with the world.

Then it happened.

A loud bang from the direction of the kitchen made everyone jump. My mother-in-law paled. Had she been shot? No, no, there was no blood.

"Sounded like a gunshot to me." My brother-in-law offered his two cents as he looked out of the street-side windows.

Nervous laughter and murmurs filled the room.

In the dining room, I surveyed the candles. Had a votive glass become too hot and burst? No, there was no evidence.

My husband took a few steps toward me. "I think it came from the kitchen."

We headed to the kitchen with a gaggle of relatives trailing behind.

Every dish looked exactly as I'd left it a few minutes earlier. I raised the lid on the stovetop items to take a peek. No one saw anything amiss.

"Who knows what it was." I shrugged my shoulders and erased my worry.

As we stood in front of the oven, I decided to baste the turkey once more. Ready for my in-laws to be awed, I reached for the hot pads and opened the oven door. Like synchronized swimmers, each of us leaned back as an extraordinary amount of steam rose.

And the source of explosion made itself known.

Pieces of turkey greeted me — on the inside of the door, on the sides of the oven, and… in the dressing. The marshmallow-topped yams were dotted with brown turkey pieces. The legs hung by thin sinews. More skin draped over the edge of the roasting pan. Parts unknown dripped from the oven ceiling and turkey skin sizzled on the bottom burner.

There was absolute silence — until I couldn't help myself. I laughed. Everyone joined in. Once the cackling subsided, I placed the roasting pan on a trivet. My mother-in-law peered at the bird's remains, patted my back and sighed.

My shoulders drooped as I bit my lip. Now they all knew my cooking skills were limited. My husband stopped laughing and wiped tears from his eyes. Then, he noticed the look on my face.

He kissed my cheek and returned the electric knife to its box. "Folks, let's head back to the living area and give my wife some space." As he herded the chuckling clan toward the living room, I mouthed a "thank you." Tears stung my eyes.

I surveyed the damage. Pieces of turkey were everywhere. I grabbed a fork and popped a piece in my mouth. Hmm… tasty. A strutting Tom turkey decorated a large platter, a gift from my mother-in-law. I smirked as I covered it with salvaged pieces from the exploded bird. The veggies were scooped to bowls, the gravy bowl filled to the brim, and rolls nestled in a basket.

When I announced "time to eat" wide eyes greeted me. Although hesitant, everyone gathered at the table and devoured the dinner. We all agreed exploded turkey tasted as good as well-carved slices.

The upside of the explosion? Whenever there's a family gathering, no one lets me near the oven.

~Gail Molsbee Morris

"Let's sit in front of the fire."

# 85

# Cookies for Christmas

*Cookies are made of butter and love.*
*~Norwegian Proverb*

There are so many sights, sounds and smells I associate with Christmas: the evergreen trees with their twinkling lights and colorful ornaments; the sounds of Christmas music on the radio, TV, and everyone's lips; and the smell of Christmas goodies baking in the oven. One of the memories I treasure is the smell of my mom's Christmas cookies as they grew golden brown in the oven. That smell said Christmas to me.

My mom made cookies year-round, and my brothers and sister and I loved to help her mix the dough and make the round, flat cookies that got popped into the oven and then into our mouths. Making cookies was a family affair, and we all had our chance at helping our mom and sharing in the rewards.

But making her golden Christmas cookies, which melted in your mouth and had just the slightest taste of vanilla, was a part of Christmas that brought our whole family joy. We would pour and mix and roll and bake the cookies, talking and laughing and singing Christmas songs throughout the morning of Christmas Eve. We looked over each cookie, picking out the best to leave for Santa. Knowing there would be a plateful of cookies waiting for us on Christmas morning made things even more special.

Remembering that feeling of joy, of sharing special moments of the Christmas season with my mom and my siblings, I decided after I got married and had kids I would do the same for my family. I would carry on the Christmas tradition and give my own children the chance to experience the joy I felt every time we slid a batch of freshly made Christmas cookies out of the oven.

My mom kept most of the recipes she used over the years in her head, and so I sat and wrote down the list of ingredients I'd need as she told them to me. Her instructions included such tidbits as "Make sure you use good genuine vanilla, and choose really tasty pecans if you're going to have nuts in your cookies. Keep them soft but make sure the edges are crisp, and give everyone something to do."

At the supermarket I felt my excitement and anticipation of my very first Christmas cookie bake with my family grow as I dropped each ingredient into my shopping basket. By the time I got to the checkout register I was nearly dancing with joy. I told the checkers and the customers behind me that this was going to be one of the best Christmases ever.

Back home I gathered up my wife and kids and led them to the kitchen. "We are about to create a Christmas tradition for our family," I told them. I handed each one either an ingredient of some sort, a bowl, or some utensil we'd need to create that golden perfection to come. "Get ready for a Christmas treat to beat all treats!"

At first the kids were confused about what they were doing in the kitchen. But after a while we all got into the swing of things, and after putting some Christmas music on the CD player we really felt the spirit. We laughed and sang and cracked eggs and whipped butter. By the time we popped the first batch of cookies into the oven the kitchen was a disaster but we didn't mind. All our thoughts were centered on the first taste of those wonderful Christmas cookies to come.

Twenty minutes later my wife slid the cookie tray out of the oven and we laid eyes on a dozen yellow, puffy, perfectly baked cookies. The smell that rose from those morsels took me back to my childhood, and I stood next to the kids, my mouth watering, barely able to contain my excitement. My wife took a spatula and laid a warm, soft cookie in each of our hands. Looking at each other, I nodded, and we bit into a little piece of heaven.

Well, not exactly heaven. The cookie was chewy, maybe more than chewy — elastic-like might be a better description. That tiniest taste of vanilla was more of a bitter aftertaste in the back of my mouth, and the cookie itself went from chewy to hard as a rock in a matter of seconds. I watched as my wife tapped her cookie against the counter.

"I think it's a little tough," she said.

"Maybe we over-baked them," I offered, but such was not the case. We left the next batch in the oven a little less time but the cookies were harder than steel. One sniff and my kids wouldn't even take a bite. My wife shook her head and patted me on the shoulder. I swallowed a hard, bitter-tasting bite of cookie.

"What went wrong?" I asked.

Just then, as if in answer to that very question, the doorbell rang. I went to answer it and there was my mom, with presents for the family and a plate of freshly baked Christmas cookies! The smell of those cookies hit the noses of my kids and they came running. When I bit into one of her cookies the taste, the smell, and the wonderful memories came flooding back. I realized then that I had left out one vital ingredient in making my mom's Christmas cookies: my mom! As we sat down to enjoy the Christmas ham that only my wife could possibly make, I came to understand that there's a secret ingredient you always need in life: the love that only those people most special to you can give.

~John P. Buentello

# 86

*Chicken Soup for the Soul*

# My First Hanukkah

*With all other foods, there's a right way and a wrong
way. With brisket, there's only "my way."*
*~Psychotherapist and top brisket maker Phyllis Cohen*

Michael and I dated for six years before we married,
so I had been to Hanukkah celebrations at his parents' house. I'd seen the beautiful table settings, the
traditional linens, the special platters and the beautiful family menorah. The celebrations were wonderful events and I
appreciated being a part of them. I was from a family of English and
Irish origin, raised a non-denominational Christian, and in my family
Christmas and St. Patrick's Day were the big celebrations. It was fun
to learn about other traditions.

One month after Michael and I were married, I decided to take
on the task of hosting the first night of the eight-night celebration at
our house. Just like my mother-in-law, Barbara, I love entertaining.
Hosting parties of any kind is right up my alley and I relished the
thought of planning and hosting this new kind of party.

I enjoyed all the planning. There were decorations, little gifts to
give my new family, candles, dreidels, chocolate coins and the food,
including the star of the show… the brisket! We all loved Barbara's
brisket and now it was my turn to make one. I was a good cook so I
wasn't worried.

Next came the shopping. I made my list and, to borrow from a
Christmas song, checked it twice, and decided I had all the fun stuff.

Now it was time to hit the market. Potatoes, lots of oil in which to fry the latkes, carrots, onions, horseradish, wine, applesauce and donuts. One more thing on the list... the brisket. With my shopping cart almost overflowing (our family never goes hungry), I headed to the meat aisle. I really wanted to impress my new family, so I picked out the biggest brisket I saw. It was funny how Barbara had never mentioned to me that brisket comes in a sealed bag and already has its own spices in with it. I called Michael to make sure I was getting the right thing, and he assured me there is only one type of brisket. Great. I threw it in the cart and headed for home.

The next morning, the first thing I did was put the brisket in. It needed to slow cook all day to be really tender and juicy. The spices that came with it smelled familiar, but I couldn't quite place them. No matter — I had this under control.

I busied myself for the rest of the day decorating, setting the table, wrapping the presents, placing the menorah, and even printing myself a phonetic reading of the Hanukkah prayer so I could say it with my new family as we lit the first candle. The brisket smelled delicious as it slow-cooked its way through the day. It was making me hungry. I hoped it was as good as Barbara's.

As I was frying the last of the latkes, the family arrived, ready to eat. Everyone commented on how beautiful everything looked. The table was set all in blue, white and silver, the traditional colors of Hanukkah. I even made a Hanukkah bush out of branches that I spray-painted silver, put into a vase and wrapped with blue and white twinkle lights. "It looks perfect," my mother-in-law said. Ah. I could relax. Everyone sat down at the table and I began to bring the food in, reserving a space in the center of the table for the brisket. Everyone was oohing and aahing at the dishes as I brought them in. It got a little quieter as I set the brisket down. I thought that everyone's mouth must have been watering too much to mention the brisket.

I sat, we said a prayer, made a toast and began passing the food. Everyone took a lot of everything. With the very first taste of my brisket, I recognized the flavor. This was not traditional Hanukkah brisket at all. It was a corned beef brisket like my family ate on St. Patrick's Day!

Everyone was watching and they all saw me realize what I had done, my English-Irish heritage trumping all my plans for a traditional Jewish brisket! There was complete silence. My face was turning red. Just then Barbara declared that this was the best brisket she'd ever had... even though it was corned beef. And, as with almost all of our family gatherings, we all started laughing hysterically.

The next year, when I was brave enough to host Hanukkah again, someone mysteriously put a little leprechaun at my place setting. I think it's safe to say that my first Hanukkah was anything but forgettable.

~Crescent LoMonaco

# 87

Chicken Soup for the Soul

# The Latke Legacy

*Food is our common ground, a universal experience.*
*~James Beard*

"This is not like Mom used to make," I had to confess. It was my first Hanukkah being the latke lady. My mother's potato pancakes were crisp, flat, and nicely rounded. The texture was smooth but not mushy and they shone with just a glint of leftover oil. I had been a latke apprentice for years, pressed into service by Mom. I was a key cog in the labor pool, peeling the potatoes, then wearing out my arm rubbing them against the stainless steel grater, using the side with the teardrop shaped holes. My mother must have known that enlisting my help would keep me from pestering her to make potato pancakes for other occasions. Only once a year did these delicious patties grace our table, when we lit the first candle of Hanukkah and began the eight-day Festival of Lights.

My debut latkes were pale and greasy, like something carelessly served in a late night diner. I myself was pale and greasy from the stress of trying to coax the patties into cohesion. First they had drifted apart—too little flour. Then they had turned cliquish, glomming into rebellious lumps. When I had finally worked through the potato/flour/egg ratio, I bumped into the complex dynamic between potatoes, onions, oil and heat. For three hours I had struggled to create what turned out to be a barely edible token of tradition.

Years passed. Every Hanukkah, I faced a different challenge. The oil was too cold, too hot, not enough, too much. The texture was too coarse or too fine. The grated onions were too strong or too weak. The latke mixture was too thin, then too thick. Every year, I hoped for pancakes that tasted like Mom's and got instead gray leaden latkes. My daughters, who peeled and grated potatoes with me, examined my finished product warily, smothering it in the traditional applesauce and often taking only a few bites. I worried that when they grew up, they would forego the holiday tradition and turn to something simpler and more delicious, like frozen hash browns. I felt a sense of failure as a mother and as the guardian of the tradition. My mother had shown me how to make the latkes: why couldn't I measure up and instill the potato pancake protocol in my progeny?

Then my daughter Sarah, fresh from college and a first job, moved back to town and offered to help me prepare the holiday meal. She was a food show devotee and had already orchestrated several dinner parties, creating the menus and cooking all the courses. She understood the relationship between vegetables, oil and heat.

"Mom, I think you need to squeeze more water out of the potato mixture," she advised. "Maybe you could use a food processor to grate the potatoes. What if you used two pans instead of trying to cram so many into one?"

I stepped back and she stepped forward, and under her guidance we prepared the latkes. As I watched my daughter mastermind the cooking, I realized that tradition could be kept alive in many ways. My daughter was starting the tradition of "doing what you're good at," giving me a chance to forget my own culinary challenges and applaud her self-taught abilities.

That Hanukkah night everyone at the table exclaimed at the sight of the latkes. Each one was golden brown and crisp, free of extra oil. I didn't even have to secretly search and pluck out a "good one," like I had been forced to do in previous years.

I looked around the table of friends and family and took a bite of my daughter's latke. My mouth filled with the crunch, flavor and intriguing texture of a well-fried potato pancake. This was the latke I had been waiting for; just like Mom used to make… only better.

~Deborah Shouse

# 88

# I Ruined Christmas Dinner

*At the end of the day, a loving family should find everything forgivable.*
*~Mark V. Olsen*

Nobody wants to be remembered as the jerk who ruined Christmas dinner. I certainly never thought that I could be a holiday saboteur, but the season can be full of surprises... good and bad.

For some families, Christmas is all about the presents, the carols, or going to church. For my clan, Christmas was all about eating. The feast was planned weeks ahead of time along with heated debates about whether there should be any deviation in stuffing ingredients. We licked our chops anticipating my dad's famous giblet gravy and shared collective fantasies about when the turkey would be revealed in all its delectable splendor. We were about substance and heartiness — the more, the better. As far as we were concerned, leaving cookies and milk for Santa was for amateurs.

"All that sugar?" my mother would exclaim. "We don't want Santa's teeth to fall out, do we?" as she'd assemble a cold cut platter by the stockings.

"Santa needs to keep his strength up after a long night of delivering presents," my dad would agree, as he'd contribute a few garlicky sausages and a bottle of beer.

It may not have been particularly charitable, but we judged those who could not keep up with our eating abilities, viewing small appetites as a sign of a repressed nature. We scoffed at carolers and Christmas shoppers. Who could possibly sing with a full belly? Why waste time shopping at a mall when you could be at the butcher's selecting the plumpest turkey? The dining room table was our altar and we were a devout and faithful flock.

In retrospect then, declaring that I was becoming a vegetarian a week before Christmas was probably not the best choice, timing wise. But declare I did.

You could have heard a pin drop.

"Where did we go wrong?" my mother lamented. "Why are you doing this to us?"

"I just don't want to eat anything cute anymore," I said.

"Have you ever *looked* at a turkey?" my mother cried, incredulous. "They're downright ugly!"

Actually, I considered turkeys to be in the category of ugly-cute. The hanging bit of flesh at their necks and their beady little eyes made them endearing. Their ridiculous gobble and off-kilter strut breaks my heart a little, kind of like seeing an old woman tottering in a pair of high heels. I just couldn't bear to eat them anymore, regardless of how delicious they were when basted to golden perfection.

"What do you expect to eat for Christmas?" my father asked quietly, unable to look at me.

"I don't like squash!" my mother yelled to no one in particular.

"What about soup?" my sister asked. "Are you still able to eat turkey broth? That's just the bones."

My father didn't say anything more as he glared into space.

My grandmother started playing with the paring knife she always carried in her pocket, narrowing her eyes at me menacingly.

"Well, you guys can still do the whole turkey thing and I can eat the vegetables," I suggested, forgetting for a moment that bacon is the secret ingredient in most of my parents' side dishes.

Silence.

"Or I can cook and we can expand our horizons," I chirped, trying to mask my mounting panic. "It's all about the sides anyway, isn't it? Nobody really likes turkey on its own."

Blasphemy. Maybe I was wrong and it was, in fact, all about the turkey. After all, meat was king in my family while vegetables served merely as window dressing: a hindrance, taking up valuable real estate on the plate. All eyes were fixed on me, my family members' expressions a mix of horror and disgust, as though I had grown a turkey head of my own and was gobbling at them.

"You'll never find a husband," my grandmother finally spat.

"You've chosen birds over your own family," my father muttered.

"I'll be damned if I'll touch a Tofurkey," my sister sneered.

"We could buy a small turkey," I stammered. "Or you'll just have extra leftovers for sandwiches. That's always fun."

My dad had already left the room. Somewhere I heard a door slam.

My untimely declaration of vegetarianism created a tragic chasm in my family. In the days leading up to Christmas there was a definite chill in the air that wasn't a result of the dropping temperatures outside. I had tampered with something that unified us and something that we all held dear. Regardless of our differences, we had always found common ground around the table. Food was love and meat was the glue that held our family together. Now I had dared to mess with it.

I started to worry that I had ruined Christmas. Instead of breaking bread with my family we would be breaking bonds and it would be all my fault. When it was time to gather around the table for Christmas dinner I was nervous. I tried to remove the bacon bits from the Brussels sprouts as discreetly as possible while the cauliflower gratin I had made sat untouched, a lone vegetable pariah among the dishes of giblet gravy and sausage stuffing. "Guess we know who's getting a lump of coal in her stocking this year," my sister whispered.

As the platters were passed, and I tried to swallow the anxiety in my throat, a strange thing happened. It began with my mom spooning heaps of mashed potatoes on my plate, piled high with mounds of butter. "Well, at least she's not a vegan," she said. My dad made his traditional joke about the turkey being the size of a sparrow when it was in fact the size of a small family camper. My sister took a modest spoonful of cauliflower and admitted that it was tasty. My grandmother put her paring knife back in her pocket. Soon we were smacking our lips and exclaiming over how delicious everything was and snickering at other families who declared themselves full after one helping. There was a definite thaw. I discreetly unbuttoned my pants, as I did every year, leaned back and basked in the joy that my family finds in sharing food.

These days I enjoy a Christmas Tofurkey while the rest of my family dines on a massive bird. My mother continues to insist that she hates squash to whoever will listen. We still know that Santa prefers beer and cold cuts rather than cookies and milk. The plates may look different, but the act of sharing and rhapsodizing about food remains. We will always love stuffing ourselves and mocking the lightweights who cannot keep up. I didn't ruin Christmas after all. In fact, I like to claim that my Christmas vegetarian announcement helped my family realize that our bonds are stronger than any turkey dinner and that it's not what's on the plates that matters but who is gathered around the table.

~Kristine Groskaufmanis

Reprinted by permission of www.CartoonStock.com.

# 89

Chicken Soup
for the Soul

# A Progressively Good Time

*If you really want to make a friend, go to someone's*
*house and eat with him… the people who give you*
*their food give you their heart.*
~Cesar Chavez

Christmas is my absolute favorite time of the year. But when I add decorating, baking, addressing cards, shopping, wrapping, and entertaining to my usual routine, even I can turn into the Grinch. "To Do" lists take over my life from Thanksgiving through New Year's. It's easy for me to forget to enjoy the holiday season with the precious friends in my life.

Two childhood friends, Janet and Mary, were especially dear to me. We attended junior high school together and remained close as adults. From January through November, we enjoyed Girls' Nights Out and family barbeques, and we celebrated birthdays, anniversaries, births, and graduations.

When December rolled around, we all wanted to open our homes to entertain the others. However, doing so would have meant setting aside three separate evenings in a month already bursting with commitments. We also did not want to add to the seasonal pressure by asking one person to host a complete sit-down dinner for all three couples.

I don't remember who first came up with the idea, but one year, someone suggested we try something different. I've heard it referred to in a variety of ways, including a round robin or progressive dinner. Whatever you call it, for us it meant one night, three homes, and three courses: appetizer, entrée, and dessert. We decided to give it a try, although our husbands were not nearly as enthusiastic. They could not understand why we did not simply pick one home for the evening.

But we knew what we wanted. We wanted to enjoy the pleasure of each other's company. We wanted to immerse ourselves in the spirit of the season. We wanted to delight in each other's beautifully decorated homes. We wanted to use the good china and treat ourselves as special guests. We wanted to relish each other's home cooking without having one person burdened with the responsibility of serving the entire meal. And we wanted to do it all in one night!

For appetizers in the first home, the men congregated in front of the TV watching sports bloopers. The women sat in the kitchen getting caught up on what was happening in our lives and in our families. At the next home, the six of us discussed everything from politics to religion over a formal dinner. Finally, at the third home, we ignored our tightening waistbands as we gave in to the temptation of a table full of decadent desserts. Our husbands reluctantly admitted that this wasn't such a crazy idea after all. The evening was pronounced a success and a new tradition was born.

We held our first progressive dinner during the Christmas season of 1987. We planned our final progressive meal more than ten years later, the Christmas before I moved from New York to Florida. We rotated assignments each year, so that over a three-year period each hostess would have served all three courses of the meal.

No matter whose home we were at, when it was time to move on for the next course, one couple would surreptitiously glance at their watches, then grab their coats and slip out the door to prepare for the next round. The other two couples would give them a ten-minute head start and then follow in their own cars.

We would pull up to each house and take a moment to admire the brightly lit outdoor Christmas decorations. The warm lights of a Christmas tree usually glowed through the window. The front door was always unlocked, and as we entered, the sights and smells of the season beckoned us in. Christmas carols would be playing softly in the background. We'd admire the new and old decorations, and examine the Christmas tree to identify recently added ornaments.

The progressive nature of our evenings did not end with the meal. Even our gift exchanges were progressive. Instead of opening our gifts all at once, the hostess at each home would pull the packages from beneath the tree and present us with our gifts. We adults were as excited as children when we opened presents while sitting in the soft light of each home's Christmas tree.

Recollections from these evenings range from frightening to humorous. One year an ice storm caused us to move all three courses to one house rather than give up our celebration. We selected the home where the entrée was prepared, since that course would be the most difficult to move. Unfortunately, though, that house was located at the top of a steep hill. Trying to drive up the hill was bad enough. Skidding down was terrifying.

Another time it was my turn to make dessert. I tried a new recipe, but we all declared it an unmitigated disaster. A word of advice: Grasshopper Bars taste as bad as they sound!

Yet another year, Janet wrapped all her packages in plain brown craft paper, and then used her artistic talent to decorate each package. The wrapping was beautiful and unique, and so special that we were reluctant to tear the paper to get to the gifts!

Some years our schedules were so busy that one of us would cheat, serving a store-bought appetizer, entree, or dessert. Even so, the most important thing was that we refused to give up our evening together.

It didn't matter what we talked about or what we ate. It didn't matter whether we were in a three-room apartment or a four-bedroom house. What mattered was that we enjoyed the holiday season together, and our friendship continued to grow... progressively.

~Ava Pennington

# 90

# Momma's Christmas Cookies

*What was silent in the father speaks in the son, and*
*often I found in the son the unveiled secret of the father.*
*~Friedrich Nietzsche*

Because I am the smartest man alive, I lived in my parents' basement until I was twenty-six years old. While I was still in school, my father and I would spend several hours each night hanging out in the basement spending time with one another. I was usually studying or reading something while he was on the computer playing games or checking e-mails.

One day during the holiday season my mother informed us that she was making a batch of cookies for work. She wanted to know if we would be her test-dummies. Yeah! Who would pass that up? However, my father, Tim, and I were quickly disappointed when she came downstairs with only one cookie for the both of us. After we begged and earnestly explained that half a cookie was not the appropriate size to adequately determine whether or not a cookie should enter a competition, my mother informed us that she only made twelve. This cookie meant she was going to work with eleven. Okay! We would share one.

To say that the spicy-gumball-gingerbread-cookie was the worst thing I had ever eaten would be an understatement. It was terrible. After forcing myself to swallow, I saw my dad equally devastated by how terrible the cookie had turned out.

"We have to tell her." Timbo informed me.

"Heck, no! I'm not tellin' her."

"Son, we have to. She will be so upset if she hears it at work."

"She is your wife; you tell her."

"She's your mother; you tell her."

"Not by choice!"

Ha! This was my go-to move. I always resorted to that — I didn't choose my mother, but my father chose his wife. And I won!

If only the dog could tell her. She never got mad at the dog.

Later that night my lovely parents went out for dinner without me. This was normal, as my father believed that putting a roof over my head was more than enough to fulfill his fatherly duties. While they were at dinner, I decided to take a break from studying in order to play some video games.

During my game, I heard a loud thud from upstairs that sounded very similar to a cooking stone slamming against a kitchen floor. I didn't think too much of it — at least not until I was at a good stopping point in my game. Then I proceeded upstairs to investigate.

At that time, we only had one dog. Her name is Laci, and she is a Border Collie and Lab mix that we rescued in 2004. Laci is a great dog! But like all dogs, she won't turn down an opportunity to eat people-food. At least, that's what I thought.

I looked down at the kitchen floor to see the cooking stone just as I expected. But what I also saw were ten little spicy-gumball-gingerbread-cookies. Mind you, this was at least fifteen minutes from the time I heard the thud, so Laci had more than enough time to stuff her little face.

"Man," I said aloud. "Even the dog won't eat them."

My mother's potential humiliation factor went from a batch of bad cookies that some people might not like, to a batch of bad cookies that even a dog would not eat. But the fact that a dog wouldn't eat her cookies puts her in an elite group. I mean — how many people do you know who have made something that even a dog will refuse to eat? I know one — my mother — and I couldn't wait to tell her.

~Kevin J. Kraemer

# 91

# Fruitcake by Committee

*There is only one fruitcake in the entire world, and
people keep sending it to each other.*
*~Johnny Carson*

I knew you're not supposed to lie at Christmas, but I was desperate. I was in the fifth grade when my teacher decided the class should share their family Christmas traditions. The project required a poster, written report and an example — a picture, or, if it was food, a sample.

The overachievers' hands filled the air when the teacher asked for volunteers to share their family traditions. Going to midnight church services, baking cookies, decorating the tree and house with lights and treasured ornaments were mentioned quickly. Next came riding around town, looking at lights and even caroling. Marybeth and her family served Christmas dinner to the homeless. I didn't want my family to appear weird by admitting we had no exciting traditions, so I blurted out, "We make fruitcakes and give them to friends and relatives."

Who wanted to hear the reality? At Christmas all my crazy relatives came over for dinner and spent the evening arguing about who would take the leftovers home. So when my turn came, all I could come up with was the fruitcake story. The problem was that my family hated fruitcake.

The report and poster came easy. We had *Encyclopedia Britannica*. The main thing about fruitcake is that it isn't cake. There is no chocolate icing and it tastes awful with ice cream. But it's been around since

Egyptian times. It's been found in tombs. Roman soldiers carried it to battle because it lasted so long. Even the crusaders took bricks of fruitcake to Jerusalem. Victorians made it palatable by adding alcohol to it. There are probably a lot of people who like it, but no one I know.

Like everything in our home, my problem was discussed around the kitchen table. Mom got out the only cookbook we owned and looked up fruitcake. "When did you say this was due?"

"Next Monday."

"Well, this says you need nine different candied fruits, spices, nuts and brandy. And you have to soak cheesecloth with brandy, whiskey or your favorite liquor and once a week brush the cakes with more liquor for a month or two or even three."

"Hey Mom, what is our favorite liquor?" Trust my little brother to zero in on the liquor.

"We are a God-fearing family and there is no liquor of any kind in this house," Granny said as she entered the kitchen to see what was going on. "What else do we need?" she asked my mom.

"Dried figs, candied pineapple, dried currants, candied citron, cherries, orange peel, dates, raisins, cinnamon, allspice, cloves, flour, molasses and a bunch of other stuff," Mom read from the cookbook. "None of which we have."

"Sounds disgusting," my sister said. "What are currants and citron?"

"I don't know," I replied, "but I've seen that candied fruit and it all looks like little pieces of neon green, yellow and red plastic."

"Currants are black things, a type of raisin, only with a tart, tangy taste. Citron is some sort of citrus, a lumpy yellow-greenish looking fruit. I think it tastes sort of lemony," Mom said.

"Way to go, Mom." I was impressed. My mother wasn't much of a cook, much less a baker.

"Here's an unbaked fruitcake recipe," Granny announced as she flipped through the cookbook. "It takes marshmallows, candied cherries, coconut, pecans and walnuts, vanilla wafers, raisins and sweetened condensed milk. You mix it all together and chill it overnight in the refrigerator or you can freeze it. No liquor. It makes nineteen rolled logs. This we can do. You can take some to school Monday and we can eat some and give away some."

"Sounds good." I was thrilled. My family had come through. We now had a family Christmas tradition. Problem solved.

"I don't like coconut and I hate candied cherries."

"I don't want vanilla wafers and I absolutely don't want walnuts."

"It doesn't matter what you want," I objected as my brother and sister made their dislikes known. "It's my school project."

"But we have to eat it, too," my sister replied.

"I'll tell you what," Granny intervened. "We'll leave out the coconut, add dates, and replace the vanilla wafers with graham crackers. Then double the pecans and skip the walnuts, and finally replace the candied cherries with maraschino cherries." And we did.

It was the best-tasting unbaked fruitcake in the world. I got an A! Even the teacher, who hated fruitcake, liked it.

Marybeth, one of those overachievers, got an A+ because nothing tops serving Christmas dinner to the homeless.

**My Family's Unbaked Christmas Fruitcake**

6 or 7 cups chopped pecans
16 oz. dates
2 cups raisins
2 one-pound boxes of graham crackers
1 large jar (28 oz.) of maraschino cherries
2 pounds of marshmallows
1 can sweetened condensed milk
½ cup sugar

Drain cherries and keep juice. Crush graham crackers very fine; chop nuts, dates, raisins and cherries. Mix together in a very large bowl or roasting pan. Melt marshmallows with one tablespoon of the cherry juice, condensed milk and sugar over low heat; add to mixture. Mix all together with clean hands. (If dry, pour more juice from the cherries a little at a time. If too wet or gooey, add more crushed graham crackers.) Shape into rolls. Cover with plastic wrap then foil. Chill overnight.

Keep in the refrigerator or freeze. (Lasts a long time in freezer, can make well ahead of Christmas.) ENJOY.

~Jeri McBryde

Chapter
**10**

# Merry
# Christmas!

Honoring Memories

# 92

Chicken Soup
for the Soul

# Counting Down to Christmas

*Smile... heaven is watching.*
*~African Proverb*

We gathered around the Christmas tree, six of us instead of seven, trying to grab onto something familiar. Mom had only been gone eight days.

I had just turned seventeen, but the long journey to that Christmas began when I was fifteen. Before then, I didn't even know what breast cancer was, let alone the devastation it would cause my family. It wasn't caught in time, and after a mastectomy and months of radiation they let us know it was too late. We would lose her; it was just a matter of when.

Still, I chose not to believe it. I was, after all, a teenager. This was my time to rebel against my mother, not mourn her. I needed to spend time with her, but there wasn't any. I wouldn't know until later just how much I needed that. By then, she was gone.

How do you celebrate Christmas one week after your mom has passed away? We sang "The Twelve Days of Christmas," and I think we opened presents. It's so hard to remember. Most of my memories of that day revolve around a single, grainy Polaroid photo my brother took. Sitting among unwrapped gifts, we're smiling but it doesn't quite reach our eyes.

Everything reminded me of Mom; nothing reminded me of Christmas.

For five, ten, fifteen years, I wandered. I tried to fit my life into eight states and thirty-six towns and struggled to make a career out of an untold number of jobs. From Iowa to Michigan to New York to Vermont to Indiana to Missouri to Colorado, I fled, running from loss, searching for peace or joy or some kind of contentment.

Looking for family.

Then, a miracle happened. My youngest sister married her college sweetheart and they introduced a chubby little spitfire we call KatyKat into the world. Four years later, LuLu joined the family. And, just like that, everything changed.

I found what I was missing when I visited them in Ohio. So I left my home in the Rocky Mountains to be closer. A few years later, Ollie-pop entered the world… my first nephew. A couple of years ago, I had the amazing opportunity to move within four miles of these three kids. I can drive to their farm in six minutes for dinner or a campfire or snuggle-time on the couch while we watch Disney movies. I can babysit when my sister needs me or pick up my nieces from school.

It's good to live close to your heart.

One day, I hoisted Oliver into my arms to take him up to his room for a nap. He melted into me and fell asleep almost immediately. When I laid him down on the bed, I brushed his thick, wavy hair from his forehead and it hit me just how much my mom would have adored him and his sisters. For the first time, I realized what she had missed out on. My heart broke for a second, then a voice whispered, "Enjoy this. Enjoy this for me."

I have a new responsibility this Christmas, to embrace the enchantment of each moment with my family, not only for me, but for her. I've always loved this time of year despite that early heartache. How everything smells like evergreen trees and peppermints taste so much sweeter. I count the months, then the weeks, then the days. And I believe something magical can happen.

Now I see it has.

Merry Christmas, Mom. You can count on me.

~Sharyn Kopf

# 93

# Scarlet Ribbons

*A mother's treasure is her daughter.*
*~Catherine Pulsifer,* Inspirational Words of Wisdom

It was Christmas Eve, decades ago, when I first heard the song "Scarlett Ribbons" sung by Harry Belafonte. I was a young mother surrounded by the people I loved: my husband, my children, my parents, my husband's parents, his brother, and his beloved grandmother. My Christmas that year was filled with joy as our families spent Christmas Eve at our home. When my brother-in-law arrived a little later he brought a gust of cold air and a sprinkling of snow in on his hat and coat. As he brushed it off he said, "It is really coming down." I opened the curtains so we could see the large flakes begin to cover the ground.

We had a wonderful, companionable evening. We breathed in the smell of the freshly baked cookies and the scent of pine as we munched on cookies, drank eggnog, opened our presents and enjoyed seeing the children play with the toys they'd gotten from their grandparents. My gift from my mother-in-law was a Harry Belafonte album. She and I were fans and coaxed my husband into playing it for us on the stereo.

The song "Scarlet Ribbons" told the story of a father who hears his little girl fervently praying for scarlet ribbons for her hair. It was Christmas Eve and all the stores were closed, so though he searched into the night, he was unable to find any ribbons for her hair. However, in the morning, when he looked into his little girl's room, she was still asleep but her bed was covered with scarlet ribbons. He never knew where the ribbons came from, but secretly he wondered if it had been a miracle. It is a beautiful song and the memory of it plays an unexpected part in my life on another Christmas.

As the years passed our Christmases changed. We added new people to our family as our children grew up, married, and had children of their own. Sadly, as we added some, we lost others. My parents, my husband's parents, his brother, and his grandmother all passed away. Though our family changed, my husband and I had started a tradition of spending our Christmas mornings together. We'd have our coffee and then open our gifts from each other. I treasured that time together.

Then the time came when it was just me. It had been three months since my husband died and I dreaded that first Christmas without him. My children were doing everything they could to make it easier for me. My older daughter invited me to her house for Christmas Eve. I spent the evening with her family and then returned home Christmas morning. When I walked into the empty house I could tell that someone had been there. If it was a burglar or ghost, it was a friendly one. The house was warm and cozy. There was the smell of freshly made coffee, a freshly baked coffeecake was on the table ready to be sliced, and the lights were aglow on the Christmas tree.

Then when I went into the bedroom I was amazed at what I saw. Like the little girl in the song, my bed was covered not only with scarlet ribbons, but with ribbons of every color in an artist's pallet! Each ribbon was tied around a gaily-wrapped gift. Like the father in the song, I wondered, "How? What? Who? When?" For a second, I even wondered if this was a miracle. As I unwrapped the first gift I saw that it was from a close friend; the next was from my niece. There were gifts from more and more friends and family. I was beginning to see my younger daughter, Janice's, fine hand in this. My suspicions were confirmed when she wandered in.

After all the gifts were opened, we went into the kitchen. Then, over tea for her and coffee for me and a coffeecake for both of us, she explained, "I knew that you would have gifts later today from the rest of the family but I talked to some people and none of us wanted you to be alone this morning." Tears welled in her eyes when she added,

"And I just wanted you to have gifts to open… just as if Dad was here."

I told her, "Your dad was always proud of you and would be especially proud of you for understanding and making it easier for me today."

Four Christmases have passed since that one. I have found that missing my husband, my soul mate, hasn't lessened. However, the joy I get from my memories, my wonderful children, grandchildren, and friends has truly been a blessing.

Unlike the father of the little girl who wondered if the ribbons he saw on her bed could have been a miracle, I know mine were, and her name is Janice.

~June Harman Betts

94

# Chicken Soup
## for the Soul

# Gifts to Keep

*Grandma's heart is a Patchwork of Love.*
*~Author Unknown*

nly three Christmas gifts were under the artificial fir tree. All the other presents had been opened. These three big packages were wrapped identically, green ribbon tied around red-and-white striped foil. Inside were gifts that my mom had planned to give her three grandchildren — my son, daughter, and niece. Gifts she had begun making, but didn't finish. A heart attack had ended her life in April.

Six months later, Dad sold the family home and moved into a one-bedroom apartment. The first Christmas without Mom was made even sadder as our family sat cramped in a small living room — so different from Mom and Dad's home where we'd always celebrated past Christmases.

Dad looked at his three teenage grandchildren. "Those presents are for you from your grannie," he said as my brother and I and our spouses sat nearby. Alicia and Sarah, age seventeen, and Eric, age fifteen, all frowned. "She was making something special for you to have this Christmas," Dad said. He looked at me as tears flooded his eyes and then he lowered his head.

Taking a deep breath, I said, "It's three almost identical gifts."

"Is it something we asked for?" Alicia asked.

"No," Dad said. "It's something you can use now. Your grannie hoped you'd each keep it and maybe even pass it on to your kids." The teenagers sat up straight, pulled their shoulders back, raised their eyebrows, and looked at each other.

"Is it something that we've seen her working on?" Sarah asked.

"No, she kept it a secret from all of you. But your parents and I knew," Dad said.

"So, how do we know which box is ours?" asked Eric.

"By numbers. The same way Grannie always let you choose. Take one of those folded papers in the basket. They're numbered 1, 2, 3, and the presents have numbers on the bottom of them," Dad explained.

As Alicia, Sarah, and Eric held the unopened gifts, silence filled the small living room. They had quickly ripped into the other packages, but now they sat cross-legged on the floor beside Dad's chair. Silent and still. "Go ahead, open them," Dad said.

The teenagers paced themselves so that they saw their gifts at the same time. "A quilt!" Sarah and Alicia said, almost in unison. Eric stood and wrapped his quilt around his shoulders. It fell to the floor. The girls did the same, holding their quilts close around their bodies.

"I love it!" Sarah said, "But Grannie always said that she'd never make a quilt." She pulled her white and navy blue patchwork quilt tighter around herself.

"This is beautiful! My quilt is just like yours. Same colors. Same everything," Alicia said to Sarah. Then she turned to her brother. "Yours is the same, except it's dark red. Almost maroon." They held their quilts up and compared. The quilt pattern, with triangles and rectangles, was exactly the same. All three quilts had solid white pieces and some calico printed fabric; only the solid blue and maroon pieces were different.

"Grannie made so many things but this is the best." Eric lifted his quilt over his head and sat down on the floor. None of us adults said anything. We wiped tears, coughed, and took deep breaths.

"Yeah, this is the best. But don't forget all the matching outfits she made when we were little," said Alicia.

"Remember the stuffed Raggedy Ann and Andy dolls?" Eric said. "Wonder why she decided to make us quilts now?" Alicia and Sarah held their quilts in their laps as they, too, sat on the floor.

Dad blew his nose, wiped his eyes with his wet handkerchief and said, "Your grannie wanted you to have something that you'd keep. You girls will be going off to college next year; maybe you can take your quilts with you. She began cutting and putting the pieces together about two years ago. She was determined to finish them for this Christmas, but…" Dad's voice faltered and he looked at me.

I continue the story. "She'd finished one, was quilting the second, and had pieced the third, but hadn't started quilting it.

"So who finished the quilts that Grannie didn't?" Sarah asked.

"Dad and I found a lady named Mrs. Horst who finished the last two. We really wanted you to all have your quilts for Christmas. Mrs. Horst is an excellent quilter and normally makes tiny stitches. When Grannie quilted, her stitches were much longer. Mrs. Horst wanted her quilting stitches to be exactly like Grannie's so the quilts would be the same," I said.

"She even wanted to do the binding exactly like the one your grannie did," Dad added. "She said quilters did bindings and corners differently and she did them the same way as the one that was finished." Alicia, Eric, and Sarah held the corners of their quilts close together.

"They look the same to me, " Eric said. All of us were silent — each in our own thoughts, as the lights on the tree twinkled in Dad's tiny apartment.

"Aunt Susan, do you know which one Grannie really made?" asked my niece Sarah. I shook my head and smiled.

"I'll answer that," said Dad. He blew his nose one more time. "She made them all. That wonderful lady stitched for your grannie. When we picked up the finished quilts, she told me that she'd said prayers of blessings as she quilted and she hoped that someday she could make such beautiful quilts for each of her five children."

The three quilts have been used and loved. They covered twin beds in college dormitory rooms and were moved to apartments when each of Mom's grandchildren married. And now, more than twenty years later, those quilts cover Mom's great-grandsons' beds. Mom's quilts were gifts to keep.

~Susan R. Ray

# 95

# My Christmas Fantasy

*For the two of us, home isn't a place. It is a person.*
*And we are finally home.*
~Stephanie Perkins, Anna and the French Kiss

After living four months in a cramped apartment, my new husband and I found a nice little cottage to rent. It was perfect lodging for us with its hardwood floors, a massive stone fireplace, and a great room that served well for dining and socializing.

I especially liked the fireplace, and even though it was summer, I envisioned how our Christmas stockings would look hanging from the mantel. I also knew immediately where to place the tree. "Right over there in that corner," I announced decisively. After three plus years of dating, Steve already knew how much I loved Christmas and decorating for the season, so any early decisions weren't a surprise.

In October, my excitement for the upcoming season waned considerably when my father unexpectedly passed away. We knew it would be a particularly difficult year, and somehow, a joyful celebration seemed impossible.

As the holidays approached, Steve and I decided it might be less sad for everyone to invite both sides of our family over for Christmas Eve. Since both mothers were now widowed, it seemed the best way to continue the feeling of family, and we could include our siblings' families as well. "Maybe a Christmas Open House could become a new tradition," Steve suggested, "and we can easily schedule it around the later Christmas Eve services."

With "how" to celebrate Christmas decided, we put up our tree, and I confessed to my husband my secret childhood fantasy. "I've always wanted to sleep under the Christmas tree, but my parents wouldn't let me — they thought it was too dangerous to leave the Christmas lights on." Of course, the tiny new lights were safer now, but I really thought nothing more about it since it seemed a bit impractical with all of the presents neatly piled beneath it. But my wonderful, new husband didn't forget.

After our Christmas Eve open house and late service at church, we arrived home and I went into the bathroom to get ready for bed. During this time, Steve was silently at work. When I finally emerged from the bathroom, I noticed that our bed was stripped of the heavy blanket, bedspread and pillows, and Steve was nowhere in sight.

"What's going on?" I yelled as I searched for him.

"I'm in here," he replied.

Walking quickly to the great room, I was surprised to see all of the gifts piled to one side and sleeping quarters arranged neatly beneath the tree. Suddenly, all the happiness and excitement of childhood came rushing back to me.

As we lay there together, snuggled close and with only the mini lights on the tree illuminating the room, my fantasy was fulfilled and slumber came easily. But hardwood floors are unforgiving, even with the padding of several layers of bedding. Around 3 a.m., we turned off the Christmas tree lights and contentedly scampered to rest on own soft bed.

Steve and I had many wonderful Christmases together before he left this world, but the memory of our first will last forever. It was the beginning of forging our own traditions along with the promise that he would always know how to make things better. Even in the midst of sadness such as losing my father, he proved that happiness can still occur. He taught me life is simply richer when celebrated with a child's heart full of wonder.

~Vicki L. Julian

# 96

# A Different Kind of Hanukkah Blessing

*The darkness of the whole world cannot swallow
the glowing of a candle.*
*~Robert Altinger*

"So tell me, can I light the first candle soon?" asked May, the branch manager of my local bank. She pointed to an electric menorah on a table beside a Christmas tree. All the "candles" were in place, but none were lit. Yet.

May and I have known each other for years, ever since our now grown-up kids played baseball together. Season after season, she and I sat together on the sidelines, dispensing snacks, water and praise to the entire team, cheering their victories and lamenting their losses. May's a very kind, as well as a competent person, with a sunny disposition and a big heart. She also is Catholic. And I am one of her Jewish customers.

It was a Friday morning in mid-December. The holiday of Hanukkah would begin at sundown, when the first candle would be lit. Which is why I told May, no, she couldn't flip the switch on the bank's menorah today because they closed at 3:00 in the afternoon. Two more candles would be lit in Jewish homes over the weekend, so during banking hours on Monday, she should light...

"Three candles? Am I right?" she asked. Clearly, she wanted to do it correctly.

I nodded yes, and explained that usually candles are placed in the menorah from right to left, and lit from left to right, although it isn't mandatory. But I didn't say that Hanukkah candles don't burn in Jewish homes during the day, and that lighting them when she came to work in the morning, which is what she — and countless other well-intentioned managers and merchants — wanted to do, was basically incorrect. Silently, I thought about the difficulties we all face at times, when we want to do the right thing for other people, but don't know how to do it. Here was May, a Christian, trying to honor my religion in a respectful way. Although I deeply appreciated her efforts, silently, I thought if secular businesses insist on lighting menorahs, maybe they should just ignite all eight candles at once, and let it go at that. But the whole thing reminded me of the childhood puzzle game: What's wrong with this picture?

Also, because I knew that May's concerns were heartfelt and sincere, I didn't say that personally I don't like seeing religious objects or symbols displayed in public places. In the same way that many Christians think that the commercialization of Christmas profanes it, I agree with Jews who believe that lighting menorahs in non-Jewish settings is inappropriate. The menorah is a key religious symbol of Judaism; it's not the Jewish equivalent of a Christmas tree.

Christmas trees are part of the Christmas holiday, but they are not essential to it. Kindling the lights of the menorah, however, is a sacred act, central to the celebration of Hanukkah. Jews, in fact, are required to do so, and we say: "We praise you, Eternal One, Source of the Universe, who teaches us holiness with your Mitzvot, and commands us to kindle the Hanukkah lights."

May and I talked briefly about the story of Hanukkah, which commemorates the victory of the Maccabees, who crushed the mighty armies of King Antiochus Epiphanes, in 165 B.C.E. Led by Judah Maccabee, the Jews revolted against Antiochus' campaign to destroy their faith by banning the study of Torah, demanding that Jews worship idols, and deliberately desecrating their Temple by sacrificing pigs on the altar.

After the Temple was cleansed and repaired, oil was collected and lit in candelabras. Part of the story of Hanukkah describes the "miracle of the oil which lasted eight days instead of one," but the primary message focuses on resisting assimilation into the mainstream, no matter how attractive and tantalizing it may be. The word, "Hanukkah," means rededication. Lighting the oil first occurred on the eve of the 25th day of the Hebrew month of Kislev, and it has been observed at that time ever since.

"Celebrate and rejoice with mirth and gladness," said Judah Maccabee.

But there was something else.

"By the way, we don't just light candles," I told May. She looked at me quizzically.

"We recite a blessing in Hebrew," I explained. "It's fundamental in Judaism to do an act, and say a blessing. In that order."

Her shoulders slumped. Was she sorry she had started this discussion? "But I can't recite a Hebrew blessing," she replied.

I agreed. But we both knew that saying nothing was not the answer.

"Maybe you can recite something, May," I said. "Some sort of universal prayer — for peace, good health, and love."

She smiled. "Of course, I can," she said.

I smiled back and thought, that sounds good to me.

~Susan J. Gordon

# 97

# Grandmother's Skirt

*Grandmas hold our tiny hands for just a little while,*
*but our hearts forever.*
*~Author Unknown*

My heart broke a little when I hung my grandmother's skirt in my closet this Christmas. It's a red and green plaid skirt that sits perfectly on my hips and floats at my knees, a "traveling pants" sort of miracle being that I'm six feet tall and my grandmother was five feet tall on her tallest days.

The skirt is one of two items I took from her closet when she passed away. The other was a bland oatmeal sweater that smelled like her. I kept that sweater on for days after she died, breathing in her smell even as I lay in bed nights, listening to the sounds that felt all wrong in her house.

But the skirt went unworn.

The first Christmas season after she died, I couldn't put it on without crying and so it hung at the back of my closet, its red and green merriment lost in a dark corner. The second Christmas season after she died, I was able to wear the skirt with only the slightest quiver in my bottom lip when I looked in the mirror.

I paired my grandmother's skirt with a black jacket zigzagged with zippers and tall, black boots with the skinniest of heels. For good measure I added my favorite leather studded bracelet. I remembered my grandmother wearing the skirt, so proper in her heels and pantyhose and a red sweater on top. She would've laughed and shaken her head at her modest skirt paired with my hints of edginess.

A thousand times I wanted to send her a photo. I wanted our pictures to stand next to each other, each of us wearing this magical skirt, her red lipsticked mouth smiling next to my own pale grin.

I'm not fashionable or trendy in any sense of those words. I'm gangly and awkward and when I can find pants that don't look like I'm readying for a flood, that's a fashion win in my book.

When I stepped out in my grandmother's skirt, it was a whole new experience. Compliments were showered upon me.

"I love that skirt."

"That is a fantastic skirt!"

"You look radiant in that skirt. It really brings out the color in your cheeks."

Needless to say, I felt great in that skirt, so great that I carefully put it in my clothing rotation as often as possible. I wore the skirt when I went to see *It's a Wonderful Life*. I wore it to three Christmas parties. I wore it to the Christmas sing-a-long on the last day of school.

So, as I carefully put away my grandmother's skirt that Christmas Day, I smiled, because somehow, in spite of her passing, my grandmother still manages to give incredible gifts.

In her skirt I felt vibrant. I felt confident. I felt beautiful. The most magical gift of my grandmother's skirt is that long after I took it off and put it back in the closet, those feelings remained.

~Alicia McCauley

# 98

# The Pages of Our Lives

*A book is a gift you can open again and again.*
*~Garrison Keillor*

Thirty-two years ago when I was pregnant with my firstborn child, my husband placed a book under the tree in our tiny apartment. *'Twas the Night Before Christmas*, by Clement C. Moore, was the first gift for our little boy who would still not be joining us for six more months. On that Christmas Eve I lay on the sofa while Daddy read to his baby boy growing safely inside my tummy. It was such a sweet and intimate moment for us and one that was the beginning of a tradition that would see many Kodak moments over the years.

Every Christmas Eve since then, my husband sits in front of the tree and reads that story aloud to all of us. First it was just the three of us sharing a moment in our new home; then before long we welcomed three more little boys. Mommy (me), Jason, Brian, Christopher and Kevin would sit quietly listening to Daddy read. We had heard the story many times, but each time Al read the story it was as though we were hearing it for the first time.

One year I remember Al reading to my cousin's baby, her one and only Christmas as she passed away a few months later. Not only did he get to share that special moment with this sweet angel, but he also gave her parents a cherished memory of their baby girl. I recall my aging parents sitting on the sofa with their grandchildren around them, loving every moment of this quiet "peace" with only the lights from the tree illuminating the room as they listened quietly.

As the boys grew so did the audience. Their friends, big and small, would lie on the living room floor and listen as my husband read to them as if they were little boys. Even the teenagers would sit still, taking in every word, and then grab the car keys and head out the door.

The year that my father lay in a hospital bed on life-support, his nurse held the phone to his ear so he too could listen in. The boys were too young to bring the story to Pop Pop, so instead, they sat in their pajamas, all ready for bed, snuggled up next to Nanny. She was surrounded by the love of four little boys. She knew in her heart that this would be her husband's last Christmas but I think it gave her comfort knowing that he was with us, listening to his son-in-law read him a bedtime story. He passed away two weeks later.

Years later, when Jason was in the Army, we sat patiently waiting for the phone to ring on Christmas Eve. "We can't start without him," his brothers said. So in the freezing cold, dressed in uniform, Jason called us from a phone booth outside his barracks at Fort Riley, Kansas. I imagined him standing at attention as his father read to him. I missed having my "baby" home for Christmas, but I was so happy he was "here" to share that tradition, as he was the one for whom it started nineteen years before. His father read to him before he was born and on this night he read to him as he was preparing to head off to war in the Middle East. It was a bittersweet moment and I longed for that time when he was an infant, safe in my arms.

Our family has multiplied over the years. Every chair is taken and the sofa and love seat are packed with bodies when Al takes his place in front of our tree. Our little boys are all grown up. We have "daughters" now, as three of our sons have married. Extended family, in-laws and numerous friends now join us on the 24th of December to celebrate the festivities. We have three precious grandsons — Luke, Beckett and Nathan — who help us continue the tradition of story time on Christmas Eve. They sit with Al, or Pop Pop as they call him, as he turns each page carefully. The cover is held in place with thick tape and the corners of many of the pages are worn. There are sticky fingerprints on the faded cover but I cannot bring myself to wipe it clean. Each fingerprint or tear represents a moment in time when my boys were babies, when my father was alive, when my mother was here on our sofa.

I can't help but look around the room as Al begins: "'Twas the Night Before Christmas and all through the house…" Adults and children are quiet, staring and listening as if they had never heard this story before. Occasionally the sound of a sweet babble or coo will echo in the room and everyone smiles at the baby who broke the sounds of silence. Some of us look stoic, some of us have eyes filled with tears, but all of us marvel as we witness a simple tradition that has nothing to do with fancy packages or big red bows.

When the last page is read and the book is closed for another year, the babies get ready to head off to bed. Santa will be arriving soon. The lights are slowly turned up again and the party continues for the adults. I look around the room and think back to how so much has changed, yet how so much has remained the same.

For thirty-two years this husband, father and, now, grandfather has read to those he loves the most in this world and I have been blessed to be witness to it all. He reads the words and we all listen. All in all, he is reading a story of simple words, a story of make believe, a tale of a sleigh that can fly through the night and deliver presents all over the world. But it really is so much more.

There will come a day when the book that was placed so lovingly under our tree many years before will be passed on to a new generation. Someone else will be sitting in front of the tree. Someone else will have the attention. But those faded and sticky pages will carry on a tradition that belongs to our family and those we love. Someone else will read the words, but the echo of Al's voice will be in the room, and the love that we all share today will remain forever in the hearts of those we left behind.

~Trish Bonsall

# Making Woochies

*Life is better with fresh baked cookies.*
*~Author Unknown*

I'm not Italian but I play one in my kitchen. Every year, Christmas at my in-laws' house was celebrated with a feast of food, followed by the obligatory overflowing homemade cookie tray. The centerpiece of the tray was fig-filled cookies in assorted crescent and roll shapes with sugar icing and colored ball sprinkles.

The family called them "woochies," short for "woochie-dadas." No one made these better than my mother-in-law Nina, with invaluable help from my father-in-law. Nina made hundreds of these cookies, shared them with her family, and even mailed them to her six brothers and sisters. One brother loved the woochies so much she mailed tins of them to him overseas when he was in the Army. After he died, we went to his wake and we brought some woochies with us for the family. I'm not sure if it's legal, but his children put one in his casket.

Traditionally, these Sicilian Christmas cookies are *"cucidati"* — Sicilian for "little bracelets," but Nina's mother-in-law called them "woochie-dadas" and so does the Panzica household at Nina's insistence.

My husband jokes he knows where the misnomer "woochie" came from. He'd say, "Since there's wine in the fig mixture and wine in the pastry batter, when my grandmother had finished mixing, my grandfather would disappear with the wine. About an hour later, he would come back slurring, waving the wine bottle, and say, 'Hey, where's the woochies?'"

The original recipe, handwritten by Nina's mother-in-law on the back of a tattered sheet of a paper from the town's department of sanitation where old Uncle Gus worked, had the list of ingredients, the cooking time and temperature, but no other information. It's assumed that if you make the cookies, you know the process.

The procedure to make these gems takes two days, one to make the filling — a ground mixture of figs, raisins, nuts, and wine. No one trimmed the tips off the figs better than my father-in-law, who looked like Gepetto and worked just as faithfully. A second day entailed the making of the pastry dough.

When my dear father-in-law passed away, it was too big a task for Nina to do on her own. Though I'm not much of a cookie baker, I love the tradition attached to these cookies. So I began a new tradition. My kitchen is now the annual hub of woochie production.

In early November, my e-mail goes out to an expanding group of cousins to set a date for woochie-making. On the Thursday before the gathering, my husband Tony and I spend hours preparing the filling — grinding together figs, raisins, nuts, orange peel, wine, and a touch of pepper, using a food processor rather than the traditional hand grinder used by my in-laws.

Then on Saturday or Sunday, the troops arrive. Everyone brings an appetizer and/or dessert, as Italians cannot survive without their snacks. Four generations surround my kitchen table, from ninety-year-old Nina to my nine-year-old niece.

Two huge bowls filled with flour, shortening, sugar and more wine are needed for the dough-making process. It takes many hands to mix the dough to proper form. Once the pastry is ready, the assembling of the woochies begins.

The kitchen table, covered end to end with wax paper, is Woochie Central.

Armed with large and small rolling pins, scoops of dough are flattened, stuffed, shaped and cut. The shapes take on myriad forms. My son, the master cookie sculptor, creates such unique designs we can't eat them, but only admire them. One year, he sculpted an image of Nina herself.

I stand at the ready, putting cookie sheet after cookie sheet into the oven for exactly thirty-seven minutes apiece. As the cookie sheets come out of the oven, I place the woochies on cooling racks covering every square inch of counter space.

During the cooldown, the snacks are devoured in the dining room amid much joyful and poignant reminiscing.

Then step 3, the icing process, commences. Just the right consistency must be attained. An extra drop of water in the massive bowl of confectioners' sugar will make the icing drip right off the cookies. Too little liquid makes the icing hard and unmanageable. And the sprinkles must be sprinkled immediately after applying the icing or they won't adhere.

Before the icing is dry and the woochies are packed into their containers for the bakers to take home, a few must be sampled just to make sure they are up to Nina's standards.

My mother-in-law passed away last year, but the legacy she left carries on with side-splitting laughter, delectable cookies, family gatherings, and new memories being made each year. As my son said, "This symbolizes the connections in our family — something as simple as a cookie."

~Susan Panzica

# Mom's Christmas Stocking

*Open your heart — open it wide; someone*
*is standing outside.*
*~Quoted in* Believe: A Christmas Treasury
*by Mary Engelbreit*

O ur mother, June Parker, was a spiritual researcher, historian, student of life, journalist and writer. She did none of these as a profession, but as her passion. After she died, I found myself in her sunny, well-organized office looking through the files of her many newspaper articles, letters to the editor and genealogy notes, each neatly typed on her IBM Selectric typewriter.

One sheet of paper caught my eye. It was entitled "Mom's Christmas Stocking" and here's what it said: "Every Christmas you have always filled a stocking for Mom. I want you to continue doing so. Choose the very things I would love. Find someone to give this filled stocking to — a woman in prison, or in a rehab, or a homeless center. This is the most precious Christmas gift I could receive or you could give — sharing the love we know with someone who really needs a shot of love. And, in this way I will continue to share your Christmases and continue to be a part of my wonderful family."

I gave copies to my sisters and brother and tucked a copy away for myself.

As our first Christmas season without Mom approached, I purchased some fun and useful items for her Christmas stocking. I bought a beautiful white stocking and wrapped each item, filling that stocking with care. I found an organization in New York City, where I live, called Women In Need (WIN) — this would be the perfect place to donate Mom's stocking! I felt the presence of my mother with me as I walked to the center on my lunch hour. I told her how happy I was to be sharing our love in this way, knowing she was right there with me.

The women at the office of WIN were grateful and touched by my mom's request and promised to find a special woman to receive the stocking.

The loving feeling carried me through the day and when I saw my friends that evening at my gym I shared with them what I had experienced. The following Christmas season we had a Girls' Night and played board games, had refreshments and filled eight stockings for Women In Need.

Their enthusiasm helped me create our annual Mom's Stocking event where we collect donations of needed items and fill upwards of 150 Christmas stockings for women living in homeless shelters in New York City. The event has grown to include filling stockings for babies and young children and gift cards for teens. Friends and their children are invited to our open house Christmas event to fill stockings, enjoy refreshments and participate in giving and sharing shots of love.

My sisters and brother live in other states, and they and their families fill Christmas stockings and deliver them to their places of choice. Our mother's extended family also donates to our Mom's Stocking event in various ways. All donations are welcome and all are used for this loving cause.

Each year I thank my mother for giving me the most precious Christmas gift, the opportunity to share love where truly needed.

~Daryl Wendy Strauss

# The Wink

*We light candles in testament that faith makes
miracles possible.*
~Nachum Braverman

very year at Hanukkah Grandma Sally lit her menorah
from the wrong end. Every year my dad (her son) blew
out the incorrect candle and lit the right one before the
blessings and the dinner began.

And every time he did that Grandma Sally chastised him affectionately for not leaving well enough alone.

That was the signal for me to begin reciting a scaled-down version of the Hanukkah Story, making sure to include an explanation as to why the holiday began with the lighting of the candle on the far right.

As I recited, Grandma Sally would wave her hand dismissively from side-to-side always with an accompanying "tsk-tsk" to show her disapproval for the exactness of this candle-lighting tradition.

Sometimes I was convinced that Grandma Sally had gone slightly senile and that accounted for her confusion, but when I brought that up to my dad in her defense, he countered by telling me she was sharper than our finest holiday cutlery.

I knew Grandma Sally adored my dad so I could not imagine her intentionally trying to upset him by knowingly lighting the wrong candle.

I also knew that she knew Jewish customs and law as well as any rabbi. So what accounted for this aberrational Hanukkah behavior?

After many years of candle-lighting chaos I finally asked Grandma Sally (out of earshot of my dad) what was behind her apparent rebellion.

"When Grandpa Joe passed away I wanted to stop celebrating Hanukkah. To me, the world had grown dim. But your father was adamant that we celebrate the holiday for your benefit, and because you were my first-born grandchild I honored his wishes. That first Hanukkah I unpacked the menorah Grandpa Joe had used ever since he was a little boy. He would always cup my hand in his and we would light the menorah together as a perfect team. I couldn't light it without his hand around mine so I bought a new menorah, the kind with orange bulbs rather than candles.

"That first year, right before you came over for the first night of Hanukkah, I tested all the lights to be sure they worked. Every bulb lit up except the one farthest to the left. I tightened it, then loosened it, then re-tightened it and then tried all the other bulbs on the menorah in its place. It stubbornly would not light so I figured the socket was bad and I would return it to the store in the morning.

"After you left that evening I switched off the menorah and went to bed. I had trouble sleeping so I curled up in my favorite cozy corner by the fireplace and started looking through one of our photo albums. I came to a beautiful picture of Grandpa Joe and me lighting the menorah many years before you were even born. As I went to turn the page I noticed a light flickering by the window. When I moved the curtain aside, the little orange menorah bulb farthest to the left was blinking on and off. It only blinked long enough for me to notice it and long enough for me to smile. When I turned the menorah back on and tightened all the bulbs in place every one lit up brightly except the one farthest to the left. Each year since then when I light the candles on our menorah I honor Grandpa Joe by starting on the left. It's my special wink to him. I know that God would understand and I hope that every rabbi would find it in his heart to do the same."

Grandma Sally has not celebrated with us for a very long time (at least in the traditional way that is). But, I certainly feel her hand cupped around mine every Hanukkah when I light the first night's candle (the one farthest from the left).

~Lisa Leshaw

# Meet Our Contributors

This is **Val Fletcher Adolph's** third story published in the *Chicken Soup for the Soul* series. She writes historical fiction based on the lives of women in gold rush times. Her first novel, *Bride Ship Three*, is about three women arriving on a bride ship. Val worked in a large institution for many years, appreciating vastly different realities.

**Joan Bailey** is a Wisconsin writer and farmer currently living in Japan where her work focuses on food, farming and farmers markets, with a bit of travel thrown in for good measure. When she's not getting her hands dirty in the garden, she and her husband Richard are off hiking, biking, or just plotting their next trip.

**Rosemary Barkes** began her writing career at age sixty-four, after winning the 2000 Erma Bombeck Writing Competition. She has been published since in newspapers and magazines, and has written *The Dementia Dance* to honor her mom. She holds B.S. and B.A. degrees from OSU and an M.S. degree from the University of Dayton.

**Mary Kay Bassier** lives on a farm in southeastern Michigan. She is a mother of three, proud grandma of four, and a retired teacher. When she is not helping edit her daughter's stories, Mary Kay is writing her own memoir detailing the misadventures of being the only Christian teacher in an Islamic school.

**Andrea Bates** is a native New Yorker living in North Carolina and has become accustomed to wearing flip-flops year-round. An LCSW, she spends her free time volunteering to support women in various stages of motherhood. She blogs at *Good Girl Gone Redneck*, where she shares the ins and outs of parenting, family and relationships.

**June Harman Betts** is the author of the trilogy *Father Was A Caveman*, *We Were Vagabonds*, and *Along Came a Soldier*. June's stories have been in *Chicken Soup for the Soul: Thanks Dad*, *Chicken Soup for the Soul: Food and Love*, and *Chicken Soup for the Soul: Thanks to My Mom*. Learn more at www.authorsden.com/junehbetts.

**Lil Blosfield** is Chief Financial Officer for Child & Adolescent Behavioral Health. She loves writing and sharing her stories. Lil also enjoys reading, going for long walks and pretty much anything else that is fun! E-mail her at LBlosfield40@msn.com.

**Trish Bonsall** has been married to Al for thirty-three years and still refers to him as her "boyfriend." She is the proud mother to four sons and three daughters-in-law. Her heart has been hijacked by her three precious grandsons, Luke, Beckett and Nathan, and being their Nanny is the highlight of her life. Life is full and fabulous.

**Stephanie Ray Brown** is thrilled and tickled each time a story so near and dear to her heart touches another person's heart. She dedicates her story to Aunt Myrna Stone. She loved children and wanted them to be warm in the winter, just like a good pair of red mittens.

**John P. Buentello** has published fiction, nonfiction, poetry and essays in many publications. He is the coauthor of the novel *Reproduction Rights* and the short story collections *Binary Tales* and *The Night Rose of the Mountain*. E-mail him at jakkhakk@yahoo.com.

**Jaycee Burgess** has a Bachelor of Arts degree in Humanities and a master's degree in Personal Development and Communication. She has two daughters, four stepchildren, and a supportive husband that are a constant inspiration for her hobby of writing humorous anecdotes about the joys and challenges of daily life.

**Beverly Burmeier** is a former public school teacher, now a freelance writer for numerous national and regional publications. She blogs about travel and also writes about family, health, gardening, and life. She lives in Central Texas and loves sharing stories about her children and grandchildren.

**Jill Burns** lives in the mountains of West Virginia with her wonderful family. She's a retired piano teacher and performer. She enjoys writing, music, gardening, nature, and spending time with her grandchildren.

**Allison Barrett Carter** is a freelance writer who lives on the coast of North Carolina with her husband and two young boys. She is on a journey to keep learning and finding the best life amid the chaos, documenting it all on her website allisonbarrettcarter.com. Every year her New Year's Resolution is to take yoga classes.

**Eva Carter** is originally from Czechoslovakia. She was raised in New York and resides in Texas with her husband Larry. In her past life she was a dancer in New York and Las Vegas. She enjoys photography, yoga and writing. She is a stay-at-home mom to a kitten named Ollie. E-mail her at evacarter@sbcglobal.net.

Founded in the UK, but representing artists all over the world, **CartoonStock** is a searchable database of over 500,000 humorous and political cartoons, cartoon pictures and illustrations by more than 1000 of the world's top cartoonists, all available for instant licensing and download.

**Joan Clayton** retired in 1992 after thirty-one years as a teacher. She then began her second career as an inspirational author. Joan has been published in over 300 articles and has six books to her credit. She also served as the long-time Religion Columnist for the *Portales News-Tribune*, Portales, NM.

**Rose Couse** is a Registered Early Childhood Educator with a Bachelor of Arts degree in Psychology. She lives in Cambridge, ON. Rose is passionate about time with family and friends, writing and photography. E-mail her at rose.46@hotmail.com.

**Judy Davidson** received a BSEd degree, *summa cum laude*, from Temple University. She has been helping people in need since she was a teenager. Judaism teaches that helping others is a commandment. This was the first time she undertook the task of assisting an entire family shelter. She continues to help people in spite of her disabilities.

**Lola Di Giulio De Maci** is a retired teacher whose stories appear in numerous anthologies, newspapers, and children's books. She enjoys crossword puzzles, books, her children, and new beginnings. Christmas traditions brought to America from Italy by her parents still grace her holiday table today.

**Donald L. Dereadt** is a retired Air Force Officer, currently residing in Shelby Township, MI. His works have been published in *Reader's Digest*, *Michigan History* magazine, *Reunions Magazine*, *Good Old Days*, *Reminisce*, and *The Storyteller Magazine*.

**Victoria DeRosa** is a writer and editor living in New York City. She received her Master of Arts in Literature from New York University in 2012. She previously has been published in *Mental Floss* magazine and spends her free time reading and baking.

**Denise A. Dewald** is an inspirational writer whose work has been read on Family Life Radio and printed in many publications. She has two grown sons and has been married to her husband for thirty-four years. Denise enjoys the outdoors and travel. Her first book, *Book of Carmichael*, was released in August 2015.

**Laurie Carnright Edwards** is a writer and a paraeducator, as well as ministry partner with her pastor husband, Dale. She has previously been published in the *Chicken Soup for the Soul* series and on Leadership Journal's website. Laurie is a proud mother and mother-in-law, and a graduate of Berkshire Christian College and Gordon-Conwell Theological Seminary.

**Cindy L. Ely** is a previous contributor to the *Chicken Soup for the Soul* series. As a retired educator she has opened the door to new adventures in her writing. She is currently working on a children's book and her twelve grandchildren are her best critics. Cindy spends time traveling to schools as a storyteller and a mystery reader.

**Nancie Erhard** received her Ph.D. from Union Theological Seminary in New York City in 2002. After teaching Religious Studies for ten years at Saint Mary's University in Halifax, NS, she retired to Windsor, ON, where she lives with her husband, writes, and gardens.

**Joanne Faries**, originally from the Philadelphia area, lives in Texas with her husband Ray. She was published in *Doorknobs & Bodypaint*, and also has poems in Silver Boomer Books anthologies and *Old Broads Waxing Poetic*. Joanne is the film critic for the *Little Paper of San Saba*. Look for her books on Amazon. E-mail her at jlf58@tx.rr.com.

**John Forrest** has placed seventeen stories in ten *Chicken Soup for the Soul* books. He writes about the exceptional events and wonderful people that have enriched his life. He lives in Orillia, ON with his wife Carol. E-mail him at johnforrest@rogers.com.

**Shari Cohen Forsythe** received a B.A. degree in Teaching from the University of Illinois and a J.D. from Suffolk University Law School. She is the mom of two sons, one of whom she wrote about in *Chicken Soup for the Soul: Raising Kids on the Spectrum*. She is married to the love of her life and enjoys writing, singing and tennis.

**Cindy Willimon Fricks** received a master's degree in Reading from Furman University in South Carolina in 1984, and became a NBCT in 2001. She's taught for thirty-six-plus years. Cindy has always told amusing stories and is now planning to publish them. Cindy's husband Pug is her inspiration! E-mail her at Furmanfans@gmail.com.

**Beck Gambill** lives in the foothills of north Georgia with her husband Chris and children, Max and Maggie. She enjoys the beautiful things of life like hiking, laughing with friends, traveling, exploring art museums, and time with family. Her novel *Sisters* is available on Amazon.

**Donna Goering** is a Registered Dental Hygienist. She volunteers in the Awana program at her church. She enjoys spending time with husband Marvin, daughter Rachel and Charlotte the puppy. She enjoys reading, watching sci-fi, drinking hot tea and eating chocolate.

**Susan J. Gordon** writes essays, articles and short stories for magazines and newspapers. She and her husband have three wonderful sons, two amazing daughters-in-law, and six spectacular grandchildren. Susan's book, *Because of Eva: A Jewish Genealogical Journey,* will be published spring 2016. Learn more at www.susanjgordon.com.

**Kristine Groskaufmanis** has been scribbling in a journal since she was eleven years old and spent too much time writing poems about squirrels. She lives in Toronto with her two favourite playmates, her husband Andrew and their dog Bella. She writes about battling her hoarder tendencies on her blog, *Minimalist Wannabe*, which can be found at minimalistwannabe.com.

**Sharon Grumbein** graduated from Craven Community College in 1986 with an A.A. degree. She plays flute at Two Rivers Healthcare for the elderly. She lives in Havelock, NC with her four youngest children, and her cat Dusty. Sharon has been writing for the *Chicken Soup for the Soul* series since 2011.

**Hana Haatainen-Caye** is a professional voice-over talent, writer and editor living in Pittsburgh, PA. Hana has been published in previous

*Chicken Soup for the Soul* books, numerous magazines, and over eighty children's books. She teaches writing and is available for speaking engagements. Learn more at www.wordsinyourmouth.com.

**Janet Hartman** sailed away from New Jersey in 2000 to follow the sun along the East Coast for six years. While afloat, she left software consulting to pursue her never-forgotten dream of writing. Since then, her work has appeared in a variety of anthologies, magazines, newspapers, and e-zines.

**Beth Braccio Hering** graduated from Northwestern University in 1990 with honors in Sociology. She has been a freelance writer for more than twenty years, specializing in career and workplace issues, education, and trivia. E-mail her at BBHering@att.net.

**Eileen Melia Hession** is a former teacher and publisher's representative whose writing has appeared in various publications. She has one daughter and enjoys running, yoga and ceramics. She believes there is a need for more levity in life and her writing reflects that belief.

**Cindy Hudson** is the author of *Book by Book: The Complete Guide to Creating Mother-Daughter Book Clubs*. She lives in Portland, OR with her husband and two daughters and enjoys writing about things that inspire her: family life, her community, reading, and family literacy. Learn more at CindyHudson.com.

Author of *Do-Overs* and *Murder Goes to Church*, **Christine Jarmola** started life as a small-town Oklahoma girl, but followed her adventurous side living in Europe and various other states. In her heart she was always an Okie, where she now resides working as a theatrical director at OKWU when not writing her next book.

**Vicki L. Julian,** a University of Kansas alumna, is the author of four inspirational books, various newspaper and magazine articles, and a contributor to four anthologies. She also writes a faith-based blog as well as a column for the *Topeka Humanitarian Examiner* on the make-a-difference theme. Visit her at www.vickijulian.com.

Published in four *Chicken Soup for the Soul* books, eight anthologies, *Angels on Earth* and *WordSmith Journal*, **Alice Klies** hopes her essays produce a smile. President of Northern Arizona's Word Weavers, she can be reached at alice.klies@gmail.com.

Award-winning author **Sharyn Kopf** longs to offer hope to single women over forty through her novel and nonfiction book, both titled *Spinstered*, and through her speaking ministry. Besides writing and editing, she spent seven years in radio production at Focus on the Family. And she adores living near her nieces and nephews.

**Joyce Laird** is a freelance writer living in Southern California with her menagerie of animal companions. Her features have been published in many magazines including, *Cat Fancy*, *Grit*, *Mature Living*, *I Love Cats* and *Vibrant Life*. She contributes regularly to *Woman's World* and the *Chicken Soup for the Soul* series.

**Julie Lavender** is married to her high school sweetheart David, and the two are proud parents of Jeremy, Jenifer (married to Adam), Jeb Daniel and Jessica. Julie loves an excuse to celebrate and enjoys writing for *Guideposts* and her local newspaper.

**Arlene Ledbetter** earned her Bachelor of Arts degree in English from Dalton State College. She has written adult Sunday school curriculum and been published in numerous magazines. She relishes the time she spends with her children and grandchildren at her home in Chickamauga, GA.

**Lisa Leshaw** is now dreaming of her midlife career as a writer. Until the dream pans out she is quite content to spend her days watching Mush and Gab on the lacrosse fields of Long Island. When she has free time, Lisa suns herself and plays with her husband Stu.

**Crescent LoMonaco** used her knowledge from years of working behind the chair and owning a hair salon to write the "Ask a Stylist" column for the *Santa Barbara Independent*. She is a frequent contributor to the *Chicken Soup for the Soul* series. She lives on the Southern California coast with her husband and son.

**Cynthia A. Lovely** is a freelance writer and musician from upstate New York. Published in various periodicals and anthologies, she is a member of American Christian Fiction Writers. She has completed a contemporary woman's novel and a Christmas novella. Visit her at www.cynthialovely.com.

**Maighread MacKay** is an author from Toronto, ON. She has published three books for children: *Bedtime Treasures*, *The Mysterious Door* and *The Crystal Grove* under the name Margaret Hefferman. Her novel *Stone Cottage* is her first foray into adult literature, to be published in 2015 by Solstice Shadows Publishing.

**James C. Magruder** is an award-winning advertising copywriter and executive speechwriter. He has had articles published in *Writer's Digest*, *Marriage Partnership*, *HomeLife*, *Christian Communicator*, the *Chicken Soup for the Soul* series, and other publications. He blogs about the writing life at www.thewritersrefuge.wordpress.com.

**Carole Marshall** was a newspaper columnist and has written numerous features and health articles for *American Profile* magazine. Two of her stories were selected for the American Profile/HarperCollins book *Hometown Heroes*. She has written three books, poetry, and blogs at www.spiritexplored.com.

A day in **Katie Martin's** life begins with a vigilant eye, and an open mind to the many stories that lay behind the daily events of people, places and things. A well-published writer, with an appetite for life, Katie brings a warm glow to ordinary things… making them extraordinary!

**Terri Martin** has a B.A. degree from Norwich University. She has led self-esteem groups for women at recovery clinics and worked as a counselor at summer camps for underprivileged kids for over ten years. She has published three children's books and many articles on women's issues. Her new book, *The Whirlpool*, will be available in spring 2016.

**Debra Mayhew** is a pastor's wife, mom to seven (usually) wonderful children, and writer. She loves small town living, long walks, good books and family time. Visit her at www.debramayhew.com.

**Jeri McBryde** loves sharing her life experiences in *Chicken Soup for the Soul* books in the hope of helping others. Jeri lives in a small southern delta town. She is retired and spends her days reading and working on her dream of publishing a novel. A doting grandmother, her world revolves around her faith, family, friends and chocolate.

**Shannon McCarty** is a freelance writer and personal trainer from Austin, TX. Her hobbies include soccer, fitness competitions, and one season of women's professional football. Her teenaged children, Riley, Tess, and Tabitha, are underwhelmed with it all and just want to go to the mall.

**Alicia McCauley** is a first grade teacher and a teacher consultant for the Writing Project. She's happily married to her high school sweetheart. Alicia is President of Vigilante Kindness, a non-profit organization dedicated to bringing sustainable education opportunities to students in developing countries.

**Jen McConnel** writes YA and NA fiction, in addition to poetry and nonfiction. When she isn't writing, she can be found on her yoga mat or teaching composition. Once upon a time, she was a middle school teacher, a librarian, and a bookseller, but those are stories for another time. Visit www.JenMcConnel.com to learn more.

**Erica McGee** grew up in Knoxville, TN, and is a University of Tennessee graduate. She is a playwright and currently performs and tours in her production, *Girls Raised in the South–GRITS: The Musical* throughout the U.S. She now calls Charlotte, NC home, where she is proud to be Tara's mom and Ryan's wife!

**Carolyn McLean** started her life on a farm in Ontario. She married her childhood sweetheart and together they have raised three children. In 2001 a fork in the road took her life's journey to Canada's Arctic (Nunavut and the Northwest Territories) for twelve years. She enjoys travelling, gardening and genealogy.

**Danielle Soucy Mills** is the award-winning author of the children's book *Tina Tumbles* and novel *Illusion of an Ending*. She studied creative writing at Rhode Island College before earning her MFA degree at Chapman University. She enjoys nature, gymnastics, reading, and writing, and resides in San Diego, CA with her husband and daughter.

**Vince Monical** is an entrepreneur and former Googler who lives in Piedmont, CA. He is the father of three wonderful children: Erica, David, and Max, the inspiration for "The Sinister Snowman" story. Vince's mission is to enjoy life, spread the word that life is good, and leave the world a little better than he found it.

When **Gail Molsbee Morris** isn't chasing after God's heart, she chases rare birds across America. She can be reached through her nature blog, godgirlgail.com, or Twitter @godgirlgail.

**Ann Morrow** is a storyteller, photographer and frequent contributor to the *Chicken Soup for the Soul* series. She and her family live in the beautiful Black Hills of South Dakota. You can contact Ann through blackhillsblogger.com.

**S.K. Naus** has enjoyed writing since grade school and likes to enter contests on a lark. Words are important and arranging them in the right order can create wonderful stories, which is her favourite part of writing.

**Judy O'Kelley's** work appears in magazines, newspapers, greeting cards and musicals from the Midwest to Beijing. A passionate tutor, Judy finds inspiration in her insightful students. She enjoys sunrises, storm chasing, midnight board games and any time she spends with her adult kids. E-mail her at judyokelleycards@gmail.com.

**Shirley M. Oakes** is a wife, mother of four, grandmother of thirteen, and great-grandmother of two. Her greatest joy is her family. She and her husband live on a mini-farm where she enjoys all that the country life has to offer. Her hobbies include family history, writing, painting, gardening, sewing, and knitting.

**Lynn Obermoeller** is an author of articles and essays and lives in St. Louis, MO, where you can find her hand-writing letters to family and friends. Lynn blogs at lynnobermoeller.blogspot.com.

**Laura Padgett** is an award-winning author who received her M.A. degree in Storytelling, with honors, from Regis University in 2009. She loves writing, dancing, and traveling with her husband, Keith. Her first book, *Dolores, Like the River*, about beauty and purpose in aging, was published in 2013 by WestBow Press.

**Susan Allen Panzica** works with her rock-star chiropractor husband, is a mom of two, a speaker for women's groups, Bible teacher, writer of the devotional blog *Eternity Café*, and co-founder of Justice Network, which educates and advocates about human trafficking. Learn more at www.susanpanzica.com and www.justice-network.org.

**Mark Parisi's** "Off the Mark" comic panel appears in over 100 newspapers worldwide and is distributed by Universal Press Syndicate. Visit www.offthemark.com to view over 8,000 cartoons. Mark's cartoon feature has won best newspaper cartoon twice and best greeting card once by the National Cartoonist Society. Lynn, his wife/business partner, and their daughter, Jen, contribute with inspiration, (as do four cats and a dog).

**Kathy Passage** calls Edmonds, WA home. Life with her handyman hubby, two Elkhound pups and her autistic adult son provides fodder for her pen. After eighteen years as a specialty food broker, she changed course. She swam laps, gained two puppies, lost fifty pounds, and started writing again.

**Lisa Pawlak** is a San Diego, CA-based freelance writer and regular contributor to the *Chicken Soup for the Soul* series. Additionally, you can find her work in *San Diego Family*, *Hawaii Parent*, *Coping with Cancer*, *The Christian Science Monitor*, *Mothers Always Write*, *Sweatpants & Coffee*, *The Imperfect Parent* and *Working Mother*.

**Ava Pennington** is a writer, speaker, and Bible teacher. She authored *Daily Reflections on the Names of God*, endorsed by Kay Arthur. Ava has written for magazines such as *Today's Christian Woman* and Focus on the Family's *Clubhouse*, and contributed to twenty *Chicken Soup for the Soul* books. Visit her at www.AvaWrites.com.

**Saralee Perel**, an award-winning columnist, is honored to be a multiple contributor to the *Chicken Soup for the Soul* series. E-mail her at sperel@saraleeperel.com.

**Casie Petersen**, a wife for thirty-three years and a mother of four children, is passionate about her faith, family, fitness and food! She is using her personal experiences to inspire others to be healthy and successful in all areas of life. Learn more about her devotion to living a healthy lifestyle at www.healthydevotion.com.

**Susan R. Ray** writes a weekly newspaper column entitled "Where We Are" available at susanrray.com. A retired teacher, she volunteers in a second grade classroom, and she writes, reads, and takes field trips with her eight grandchildren. Susan likes to travel, bake bread, and quilt. E-mail her at srray@charter.net.

Known as the Wandering Writer, **Karen Robbins** and her husband have visited all seven continents and circumnavigated the globe. Karen is the author of five novels. The most recent, a historical romance, *Ruby*, is set in the Cleveland area where she grew up and still resides.

**Heather Rodin** currently serves as Executive Director of the mission Hope Grows Haiti and from these experiences wrote the book, *Prince of Vodou: Breaking the Chains*, released in 2014. Heather also has a passion for story and humor and as a freelance writer and author she loves when they come together.

**Loretta Schoen** grew up in Brazil and Italy, and now resides in Florida with her husband, a cat and two dogs, all of which are of retirement age. She enjoys traveling, and spending time with her grandson. She conducts workshops on how to survive medical adversity, and is writing a devotional of medical parables.

**Helen Scieszka** is a retired advertising executive, psychologist, college professor, parish pastoral associate, diocesan married and family life director, and a published author. She is an avid reader, loves travel, music, photography, art, sports, collecting books autographed by the author and working on her family genealogy.

Is there anything more wonderful than daughters who can cook? **Deborah Shouse** is a writer, speaker, caregiver's advocate, editor and creativity catalyst. Her writing has appeared in a variety of periodicals and books. She is the author of *Love in the Land of Dementia*. Visit her blog at DementiaJourney.org.

**David Michael Smith** of Georgetown, DE, loves Christmas and writing, so his story's appearance in this volume is the completion of a "bucket list" item he is most proud of… almost as proud as he is of his wife Geri and children, Rebekah and Matthew. E-mail David at davidandgeri@hotmail.com.

**Jackie Smith-Thrasher** is a baby boomer who returned to school and completed two master's degrees. She is a native of Atlanta, GA, mother to three adult daughters and grandmother to six (five boys, one girl). She is an avid reader who enjoys writing, creating inspirational plaques, and traveling. She has three children's books finished.

**Bonaventure Stefun** was pastor at a parish in Ohio when the incident reported took place. He has published many articles, especially in theological magazines. He now sends poems to friends as a substitute for the homilies he is no longer physically able to preach. The Christmas story is another way to share beauty and love.

**Sandra Diane Stout** received her associate's degree in Business Studies from Indiana University and is a graduate of the Institute of Children's Literature. Diane is a retired secretary from Indiana University, an accomplished pianist and loves to sing. She writes children's non-fiction. E-mail her at dstout@iuk.edu.

**Daryl Wendy Strauss** is a Certified Angel Card Reader, Reiki practitioner, trained actress, and heart lover. She self-published a photo book of heart rocks and enjoys creating calendars of her other heart find collections. A firm believer in angels and the spirit of the Universe, she seeks to continue following her heart.

**Mary Vigliante Szydlowski** has published seven novels, one novella, and four children's books under various pseudonyms. Her articles, essays, short stories, poetry, and children's stories appear in anthologies, magazines, newspapers, and on the Internet. She lives in Albany, NY.

**B.J. Taylor** fondly recalls that special Christmas twig tree. She's an award-winning author whose work has appeared in *Guideposts*, *Chicken*

*Soup for the Soul* books, and numerous magazines and newspapers. You can reach B.J. through her website at www.bjtaylor.com, and check out her Charlie Bear dog blog at www.bjtaylor.com/blog.

**Jayne Thurber-Smith** is an award-winning freelance writer for various outlets including *Faith & Friends* magazine, ofhorse.com and cbnsports. com. Her favorite activity, along with her husband Peter's, is being included in whatever their four adult children have going on.

**Paula Maugiri Tindall**, **RN,** finds inspiration through personal life experiences and nature overlooking Lake Emerald in South Florida. She was previously published in *Chicken Soup for the Grandma's Soul*, *Chicken Soup for the Soul: Count Your Blessings* and *Chicken Soup for the Soul: The Gift of Christmas*. E-mail her at lucylu54@aol.com.

**Jana Tritto** lives in rural North Idaho with her husband and family. She is retired from a career in medicine, and now loves all things outdoors, woodworking, and travel. Jenna has always enjoyed writing to record personal experiences and thoughts.

**Miriam Van Scott** is an award-winning freelance writer and photographer whose works include books, magazine articles and television projects. She's a graduate of George Mason University and resides in Northern Virginia. Please visit miriamvanscott.com for more information or to see Van Scott's photos, reviews and excerpts.

**Aaron Vlek** is a storyteller whose work focuses primarily on the trickster mythos in its role as transformer, bringer of delight and wonder, and proponent of strange and disquieting humors. Her short stories, poetry, and novels center on the jinn, and the Native American trickster Coyote. She lives in Berkeley, CA.

**Roz Warren,** the author of *Our Bodies, Our Shelves: A Collection of Library Humor*, writes for *The New York Times*, *The Funny Times*,

*The Huffington Post*, *The Christian Science Monitor* and *Forward*. And she's been featured on the *Today* show.

**Ernie Witham** writes the syndicated humor column "Ernie's World" for the *Montecito Journal* in Santa Barbara, CA. He is the author of two humor books and his work has appeared in many anthologies, including twenty *Chicken Soup for the Soul* books. He is on the faculty of the Santa Barbara Writers Conference.

**Ferida Wolff** is the author of seventeen books for children and three essay books for children. She writes a blog at feridasbackyard.blogspot. com that looks at the nature/human connection. She has a passion for traveling and observing the world's birds, plants, and animals. E-mail her at feridawolff@msn.com.

# Meet Amy Newmark

Amy Newmark was a writer, speaker, Wall Street analyst and business executive in the worlds of finance and telecommunications for thirty years. Today she is publisher, editor-in-chief and coauthor of the *Chicken Soup for the Soul* book series. By curating and editing inspirational true stories from ordinary people who have had extraordinary experiences, Amy has kept the twenty-two-year-old Chicken Soup for the Soul brand fresh and relevant, and still part of the social zeitgeist.

Amy graduated *magna cum laude* from Harvard University where she majored in Portuguese and minored in French. She wrote her thesis about popular, spoken-word poetry in Brazil, which involved traveling throughout Brazil and meeting with poets and writers to collect their stories. She is delighted to have come full circle in her writing career — from collecting poetry "from the people" in Brazil as a twenty-year-old to, three decades later, collecting stories and poems "from the people" for Chicken Soup for the Soul.

Amy has a national syndicated newspaper column and is a frequent radio and TV guest, passing along the real-life lessons and useful tips she has picked up from reading and editing thousands of Chicken Soup for the Soul stories.

She and her husband are the proud parents of four grown children and in her limited spare time, Amy enjoys visiting them, hiking, and reading books that she did not have to edit.

Follow her on Twitter @amynewmark and @chickensoupsoul.

# Thank You

We owe huge thanks to all of our contributors and fans. We loved your stories about Christmas and Hanukkah and how you and your family spend the holidays. We could only publish a small percentage of the stories that were submitted, but we read every single one and even the ones that do not appear in the book had an influence on what went into the final manuscript.

We owe special thanks to Senior Editor Barbara LoMonaco, who read the thousands of stories submitted for this book, with the assistance of Managing Editor Kristiana Pastir, Executive Assistant Mary Fisher, and our fabulous freelance editor Susan Heim. Barbara also selected the finalists for the book and did the first round of editing. Chicken Soup for the Soul's VP and Assistant Publisher D'ette Corona created the initial manuscript, complete with fabulous quotations on many of the stories, and worked with the contributors to perfect their stories. The whole publishing team deserves a hand, including our editor, Ronelle Frankel, our Director of Production, Victor Cataldo, and our graphic designer, Daniel Zaccari, who turned our manuscript into this beautiful book.

# Sharing Happiness, Inspiration, and Wellness

R eal people sharing real stories, every day, all over the world. In 2007, *USA Today* named *Chicken Soup for the Soul* one of the five most memorable books in the last quarter-century. With over 100 million books sold to date in the U.S. and Canada alone, more than 200 titles in print, and translations into more than forty languages, "chicken soup for the soul" is one of the world's best-known phrases.

Today, twenty-two years after we first began sharing happiness, inspiration and wellness through our books, we continue to delight our readers with new titles, but have also evolved beyond the bookstore, with super premium pet food, a line of high quality soups, and a variety of licensed products and digital offerings, all inspired by stories. Chicken Soup for the Soul has recently expanded into visual storytelling through movies and television. Chicken Soup for the Soul is "changing the world one story at a time®." Thanks for reading!

# Share with Us

We all have had Chicken Soup for the Soul moments in our lives. If you would like to share your story or poem with millions of people around the world, go to chickensoup.com and click on "Submit Your Story." You may be able to help another reader, and become a published author at the same time. Some of our past contributors have launched writing and speaking careers from the publication of their stories in our books!

We only accept story submissions via our website. They are no longer accepted via mail or fax.

To contact us regarding other matters, please send us an e-mail through webmaster@chickensoupforthesoul.com, or fax or write us at:

Chicken Soup for the Soul
P.O. Box 700
Cos Cob, CT 06807-0700
Fax: 203-861-7194

One more note from your friends at Chicken Soup for the Soul: Occasionally, we receive an unsolicited book manuscript from one of our readers, and we would like to respectfully inform you that we do not accept unsolicited manuscripts and we must discard the ones that appear.

Christmas is an exciting and joyous time of year, a time of family, friends, and traditions. You will delight in reading these 101 festive stories about the joy, wonder, and blessings of the season. This collection is filled with merry and heartwarming stories about holiday traditions, family, and goodwill. Remember, all of our stories are "Santa safe" so they can be enjoyed by the whole family. A fantastic holiday gift and a great way to start the holiday season every year!

978-1-61159-925-1

# More holiday spirit

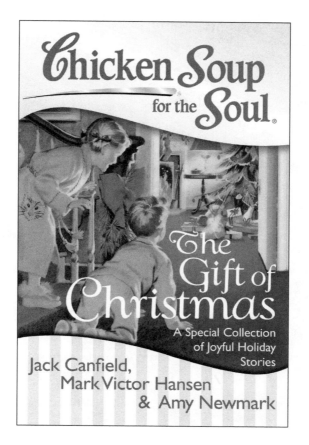

Share in the magic and joy of Christmas! This special, extra long collection of 121 Christmas stories will warm your heart and spread the wonder of the holiday season with its tales of love, joy, and awe. You'll delight in reading these inspirational and merry stories of Christmas miracles, family reunions, charity, the wonder of children, the joy of giving, and family and religious traditions. All of our stories are "Santa safe", making it the perfect book to share with the whole family. A wonderful holiday gift and fun way to start every holiday season!

978-1-61159-901-5

and great entertainment

# Chicken Soup for the Soul

Changing your world one story at a time®

www.chickensoup.com